COUNSELLING IN DIFFERENT SETTINGS

Counselling in Different Settings

The Reality of Practice

Edited by

Maggie Reid

First published 2004 by
PALGRAVE MACMILLAN
Houndmills, Basingstoke, Hampshire RG21 6XS and
175 Fifth Avenue, New York, N.Y. 10010
Companies and representatives throughout the world

PALGRAVE MACMILLAN is the global academic imprint of the Palgrave
Macmillan division of St. Martin's Press, LLC and of Palgrave Macmillan Ltd.
Macmillan® is a registered trademark in the United States, United Kingdom
and other countries. Palgrave is a registered trademark in the European
Union and other countries.

ISBN 1–4039–1628–4

This book is printed on paper suitable for recycling and made from fully
managed and sustained forest sources.

A catalogue record for this book is available from the British Library.

A catalog record for this book is available from the Library of Congress.

10	9	8	7	6	5	4	3	2	1
13	13	11	10	09	08	07	06	05	04

Printed and bound in China

To Euan, David, Katrina and Hilda

Contents

Illustrations

Acknowledgements

I want to thank all those without whose ongoing support, encouragement and help this book would never have happened. This includes my family, especially Euan and David, solid rocks to counter many a moment of doubt; Dorothea Ross Simpson, Irene Hall and other friends and colleagues at Hope; each and every one of the book contributors; Ian Taylor who truly engaged with my writing and Margie Coles whose creative spirit is always a treasure and inspiration; and editors and reviewers for Palgrave. I am grateful to the British Association for Counselling and Psychotherapy, Hope University College and Palgrave for financial help and premises for crucial meetings of contributors. I am also indebted to John Rowan who took the time to read an initial outline for this book, judged it as 'good', if 'overambitious', and helped set the challenge to encourage me!

Note: the British Association for Counselling (BAC) was founded in 1977. The association changed its name to the British Association for Counselling and Psychotherapy (BACP) in September 2000, in recognition of the fact it no longer represented just the counselling profession.

Foreword

This book will be useful to counsellors at every stage in their professional development, from the newest trainee to the experienced practitioner.

It is timely, because it is published as counselling is 'coming of age' as a profession. When I began as a voluntary counsellor in the mid-1970s none of us expected to be able to make a career of counselling. Now counsellors are to be found in a growing variety of settings, many of which are covered in the pages that follow.

During the past 20 years there has been a parallel development of professional expertise. This has been disseminated mainly by training courses and the publication of books and journals. It is easy to forget just how remarkable and rapid this development has been. This book testifies to a wealth of accumulated specialized knowledge on the possibilities and some pitfalls of applying counselling expertise in different settings.

Trainees embarking on the first step of their counselling career today will usually be faced with a variety of choices about their future career path. This situation is both exciting and confusing. The opportunity to learn from experienced practitioners who have been this way before helps enormously to make appropriate and satisfying career choices without having to try everything first. We all know the importance of detail, and the 'day in the working life' sections provide the kind of detailed picture that enables us to walk in the steps of a working practitioner in a way that is seldom possible.

Following a path when you already have a map helps enormously in avoiding dead ends and the kind of 'culture shock' that may otherwise be faced, for example by counsellors when they embark on private practice for the first time. It is an onerous responsibility to take on initially all the supporting functions – statistical records, psychiatric cover, risk assessment, to name but a few – most counselling agencies provide.

Surveys of British Association for Counselling and Psychotherapy (BACP) membership show that many counsellors work in several settings in the course of each week. Every setting offers particular challenges and satisfactions. It is of vital importance, for example, to consider how confidentiality is best maintained in private practice and in an agency setting: boundaries that work in one may be counterproductive in a setting where interdisciplinary teamwork is crucial for the overall well-being of the client. In all agency work, relationships within what has been called the 'clinical rhombus' of counsellor, client, supervisor and organization need careful and sensitive negotiation. All this is to be found within these pages, together with practical exercises to help you apply your learning, in the best tradition of counselling training.

Counselling is, at its best, a vocation to which we have a deep commitment and which affords us profound satisfaction and a career in which we can progress and develop our expertise. Work in the field offers a range of working relationships, with employers, referrers and colleagues. With each of them we need to negotiate effective and efficient working relationships. This book provides a guide to all these aspects of the work. It is something to keep by you, a 'pilgrim's progress' for your life's work as a counsellor. I wish you a satisfying and fruitful journey.

Val Potter
Fellow (BACP), Chair (BACP)
and Director of WPF

Notes on contributors

Jill Brennan is a counsellor and supervisor with the Clinical Psychology department at North Manchester General Hospital. She was accredited as a counsellor by the British Association for Counselling and Psychotherapy (BACP) in 1999 and is currently studying for her doctorate in counselling at Manchester University. Her sanity is preserved by her Nichiren Buddhist practice and her love of music and literature. Jill contributes regularly to the BACP research conferences and strongly supports practitioner research in counselling.

Basia Davey is a psychodynamic counsellor, a staff member at Highgate Counselling Centre, and has her own client practice. For several years she has been retained as a student counsellor by an organization managing students from a range of US universities doing semesters in London. Basia has studied and taught English literature and has undertaken occasional journalism. She also works on projects that combine her experience and interest in therapy with literary research. She is married with two children and lives in north London.

Joyce Evans is married with two grown-up sons. For many years she worked with the families of pre-school special needs children and also counselled on a voluntary basis. Seven years ago she took early retirement and became a freelance counsellor. Since then her particular interest has been in her work at a residential rehabilitation centre. It is with very mixed feelings that she is now reducing the amount of counselling hours.

Caroline Jones is a UK registered counsellor and a senior registered counsellor and fellow of BACP. She is an experienced counsellor in workplace settings and is now working independently. Caroline is an associate editor of BACP's *Counselling and Psychotherapy Journal*, (Rugby) challenge column, co-author of *Questions of Ethics in Counselling and Therapy* (Open University Press, Buckingham,

2000) and co-editor of *Forms of Ethical Thinking in Therapeutic Practice* (Open University Press, Maidenhead, McGraw-Hill, 2003).

Julia Layton is a BACP registered practitioner, who works as a counsellor, supervisor, operations manager and social work practice teacher at the Counselling and Social Work in South East London (CASSEL) Centre, in the London borough of Lewisham. Julia is also an advocate for children and young people in care with Voice for the Child in Care (VCC), contributes to the advisory group for the Candle Project (a bereavement service for children and young people) at St Christopher's Hospice, and is a parenting group facilitator with Parentline Plus.

Elisabeth Long joined Relate as a voluntary counsellor in 1991 to provide her with what she thought of at the time as an interesting part-time hobby. After a career in the media, Elisabeth became increasingly fascinated by working in an environment staffed by people whose only reward was to learn more about themselves and others; and to be able to use this knowledge beneficially. The part-time hobby has evolved into a full-time career. Apart from her voluntary counselling work with Relate, Elisabeth works as an external trainer with the agency and teaches to professional diploma level at Bolton Community College.

Louise Mackinney is a BACP registered counsellor working in the south-east of England. She is particularly interested in working with women and with issues around trauma. She has a small private practice as a counsellor and supervisor, and is senior tutor in counselling at a college of further education. She also works in her local refuge and hospice.

Lindsey Neville is currently a lecturer in the Institute of Health and Social Care at University College Worcester. She began her professional life as a schoolteacher, teaching in a variety of settings in West Sussex and Gloucestershire. She gained counselling experience, training and qualifications with Relate later leading to accreditation with the BACP. Until recently she was the College Counsellor at Evesham and Malvern Hills College.

Maggie Reid is a registered practitioner with BACP, having been accredited as a counsellor, and is currently working independently.

She remains an associate lecturer at Hope University College having recently taken early retirement from her college counselling job, where she had been in the post since 1992. She has also counselled in a freelance capacity and in medical settings. For a period she ran an independent training agency, Opal Training, with a colleague. She has spent the bulk of her working life in education as a teacher, lecturer, trainer and counsellor. Alongside this for six years she wrote a monthly column for a family magazine on healthy living issues.

Kevin Rodgers has been Head of the Counselling Service at Liverpool Hope University College since 1998. He is a BACP accredited counsellor and a member of two committees of AUCC: the Service Recognition Sub-Committee and also HOCCHE (Heads of Counselling in Colleges of Higher Education). He taught for 12 years in various secondary schools, his most recent position being head of a sixth form in Liverpool. He obtained a Master's in psychodynamic counselling in New York and has been a member of Liverpool Hope's counselling team since 1992.

Alistair Ross is a lecturer in counselling at Birmingham University. He is a BACP accredited counsellor and also works in private practice as a counsellor, supervisor, trainer and consultant. He is a founding partner of the Institute of Pastoral Counselling, Nottingham and is also a personal tutor and honorary research fellow at the Queen's Foundation for Ecumenical Theological Education, Birmingham. He is also a Baptist minister.

Sue Santi Ireson is an accredited counsellor and psychotherapist with the BACP, which invited her to become a fellow in 2002. She works part-time managing a counselling service for an NHS doctors' practice. She is a guest lecturer and consultant for India's first counselling and psychotherapy course in Bangalore. Sue has her own private counselling/psychotherapy practice; she also offers training and supervision. In 2002 Sue contributed a chapter on somatised presentation of sexual abuse to *Counsellors in Health Settings*, edited by Kim Etherington, published by Jessica Kingsley, London.

Elspeth May Schwenk has trained in three continents, and together with her husband and children has made Wiltshire her home. Establishing a private practice in counselling, supervision and training alongside a systemic workplace counselling consultancy, she specializes in reintegration to work after long-term absence. Having taught in further education for many years, she has now released this time for doctoral research exploring the systemic role of the workplace counsellor. As an executive member of the Association for Counselling at Work (ACW), Elspeth believes in the exciting developments in workplace counselling and the creative opportunities that lie ahead.

Pat Seber is a BACP accredited counsellor and a fellow of BACP. She started her counselling career with Relate but moved from working with couples into medical settings where she set up and ran a counselling service for women in the obstetrics and gynaecological department of a large hospital. Currently she is lead counsellor and service manager of a primary care counselling service in Liverpool and Trainer and Supervisor for Bradford Cancer Support Centre. She is Deputy Chair of the Faculty of Healthcare Counsellors and Psychotherapists (FHCP) with special responsibility for employment issues and an editor of the *Healthcare Counsellors and Psychotherapists Journal*.

Linda Sheffrin (Chevin) has recently been appointed Assistant Special Needs Coordinator at Carisbrooke High School. She taught for over 20 years in mainstream education prior to training as a counsellor and to working with children who have socio-emotional difficulties. She worked peripatetically in a multi-agency setting for four years with Kent County Council's Behaviour Support Service before taking up a post as Behaviour Support Teacher at Carisbrooke. Here, with the help of colleagues, she has set up a centre for students with emotional and behavioural difficulties. The centre is now in its fourth successful year, catering for the students needs through counselling, part-time off-site educational provision and a firm, structured, nurturing environment.

Sally Wilson is a UK registered independent counsellor and a BACP senior practitioner. She was a teacher for some years before moving to Hong Kong on her marriage. She also lived in Singapore, publishing two books about her experiences and contributing to the *Guardian* newspaper. On her return to England, she qualified as a counsellor, working in a comprehensive school, a teenage drop-in centre and the Royal College of Nursing, before taking up private practice. She lives with her husband in south London, and has a son and a daughter.

1

Overall Introduction

Maggie Reid

When I got the idea for this book I was about to start a new academic year as a counsellor at Liverpool Hope, a higher education institution. Going into my 11th year seemed to be a watershed. I needed a change. But where to go? Searching for a book that gave me the real picture of counselling in different settings, I felt frustrated. Nothing seemed to be there in one handy format, with the inside story. So here is the answer. Each of the following chapters represents one counselling practitioner's voice telling you what it's really like, warts and all. It has been an adventure putting it together and fun finding and working with the people involved. Chosen for their experience, knowledge and respect attained within their settings, they will give you pearls of wisdom not easily gained elsewhere. For many of the contributors it is their first publishing experience. I want to thank them all for their wholehearted participation and excellent work. Portraying the reality of their day-to-day work life succinctly and accessibly is a challenging and potentially exposing task. In their willingness to be vulnerable lies their strength, and what a great role model and exciting reading this provides.

The book sets out to show the scope and reality of counselling in the UK today and the directions in which it is moving. It provides an overview, in snapshot form, of a complex situation. It illustrates what professional therapeutic counselling involves in the various settings in which it occurs. This includes current practices and concerns as well as future directions. You will be able, within one book, to compare and contrast different work settings for counselling. You can then see where your particular background and interests might fit you best to pursue such a career. Presented with details of a variety of successful role models, you will be inspired to develop your chosen path, based upon suitable choices for initial training, as well as continuing professional development.

The book also demystifies the counselling world, making the job a more transparent activity. You will be able to see what a typical counselling environment is really like and also to appreciate the highs and lows of the 'hands-on' work. You will be alerted to particularities of different settings, which demand certain practices, abilities, aptitudes, interests and traits. You will discover whether the special opportunities, as well as possible limitations, appeal to you. You will also hear of any special ethical dilemmas peculiar to the settings.

It's a multifaceted mirrorball of a world – counselling: hard to represent as a whole. What you find here is a reflection of some of those facets illustrated through five sections:

- Not-for-profit.
- Health.
- Education.
- Workplace.
- Freelance and independent.

Each section contains a number of chapters, the format being roughly the same for all, for ease of comparison. Individual chapters can also be read as a discrete entity allowing you to pick and choose what grabs your attention and interest at any one time. You will hear about a typical day. Examples will show you how everyday demands are met, including record keeping; multidisciplinary teamwork, such as work with other mental health professionals in some cases; relationships and communication with other colleagues – counselling and non-counselling; and any boundary conflicts or issues.

The counsellors share their route into their particular setting and explain how they got the job. They briefly state their theoretical approach and training plus any adaptations or extra experience called for within the setting or by the employer. They share how they resolved any dilemmas over adaptations of theoretical frame.

A clinical vignette is chosen to highlight the work context and identify any particular responsibilities to the client as well as demands on, or shape of, the therapeutic work. It highlights ethical considerations and how the setting affects what constitutes good practice. Confidentiality issues have been carefully considered. Either ethical consent has been sought from the client or the story is a composite picture of several clients, and in most cases various disguises have been inserted.

The chapters discuss the tools used and ways of evaluating service and counselling effectiveness. This might include service feedback required by employers or resource providers. You will find out how counsellors demonstrate they are worth employing.

Initial professional counselling training is vital but just the beginning. Continuing professional development (CPD) is an important promoter of the requirements for continued occupational status, efficacy and personal potency of any counsellor and is now engrained within the annual re-accreditation process of the British Association for Counselling and Psychotherapy (BACP). Practitioners in these chapters write about their CPD planning, opportunities and experiences particularly of value for work in their setting and how these get funded. Many also detail the importance to them of BACP and its activities.

The chapters finish with discussion of forthcoming relevant developments in each setting along with the realities of current and future prospects for counsellor employment.

An extra chapter introduces the Health section. This is included because it is difficult for the two following chapters exemplifying counselling practice in primary and secondary healthcare settings to represent the complex and changing picture of the health sector as a whole. As the biggest employer of counsellors in the UK it deserves some special attention.

You will read of the issues that unite us as a profession and keep the mirrorball operating as a relatively cohesive whole, despite differences of orientation and style. You will also see how certain skills, abilities, aptitudes and knowledge seem to be generically required while others are more specific to the setting or context. This is discussed further in the 'Final reflections' chapter.

This is ultimately not an academic but a practical book. So where do you go next? The 'personal fit' box has been included in the appendix to help you look more closely at the settings you may wish to enter, and assess yourself in relation to what you have read. Make as many copies of this box as you need. Then use it as the basis for reflection with another or on your own. Are you the kind of person who could work in this setting? Is your experience useful here? Do you have relevant qualifications and knowledge? If not, how could you gain these? What attracts you? Could you live with those aspects that put you off? How? Cut out examples of current advertised jobs, in this setting, from local and national newspapers or on websites. List anyone you know who has worked in this area or knows anyone currently working in this setting. It is important to build your network. I've found it incredibly useful to arrange to meet people and simply talk about what they do. In editing this book, I arranged for contributors to meet, on two occasions: at the beginning and at the end of the writing period. We discussed our work together and I felt we gained important insights as a result of this personal contact.

Eventually work your way towards a strategic plan. Where do you ideally want to be in five years' time? Is this pie in the sky or really possible? Just as in chess, start to plan your moves. In my view, experience is vitally important in counselling. Maybe some voluntary work will supply the initial step. As a trainee your placement is an important starting point. What local opportunities are there which would fit your plan? How, specifically, will a particular one help? You are now launched on a process. Of course many things happen by happy accident but going through the thinking helps you appreciate this more. Keeping an open attitude combined with some planning means you are better placed to 'seize the day'. It is not only exciting and rewarding but hopefully self-fulfilling too.

I sense a change in the counselling world. Now we are entering an era where it may become a more acknowledged profession in its own right. At this moment, whatever your view of it, statutory registration and regulation is on the horizon. We need to prepare for a world where career structures exist, where we ensure that our traditional grassroots humanity, as well as our measurable professional knowledge and performance, is treasured and rewarded, not least by ourselves as a starting point. So in this book be prepared to hear the practitioner's voice proudly acclaiming the work as it occurs in the current reality. We practitioners open the doors of our counselling rooms and invite you in.

Section I

NOT-FOR-PROFIT SECTOR

2

Counselling in a Not-For-Profit Setting

Basia Davey

I am a psychodynamic counsellor and a member of staff in a voluntary capacity at Highgate Counselling Centre (HCC). I also carry out initial interviews with prospective clients, and am on the panel of readers for students' diploma papers. Here I describe the life and work of the centre and give an idea of my work with clients.

A typical day

Up the stairs, familiar now after 12 years, to the first floor, through two doors, and I am in 'the office'. A client would be shown through the swing doors and into the waiting room beyond. The office room is the administrative and meeting heart of HCC, a

British Association for Counselling and Psychotherapy (BACP) accredited counselling and teaching body. I exchange greetings with the receptionist, coordinators and counselling colleagues. There may only be one or two people here, but 35 part-time counsellors, 15 trainees and 15 external trainees will be doing this at their chosen times in the week. The director takes up residence on Mondays. The office varies in its 'congestion component' according to more or less popular client times.

I check 'my' room for seating arrangements, tissues and airing. Today I am seeing Richard, a middle-aged client halfway through our two-year contract. He has been feeling considerably less depressed and frustrated with work lately, but for the third time, his wife has accompanied him here. He expresses some ambivalence about this. She leafs through magazines in the waiting room during our session. I try to address this new development without contributing to unnecessary conflict between them. Afterwards, I have a few minutes between clients. My short-term (12 week) client Cathy arrives on time for her fourth session. Her second child will be born within a month. She smiles but looks weary. She is anxious about the possibility of another bout of post-natal depression which brought with it guilt about its effects on her son. She has now begun to express long-held feelings of fear and anger from her own disrupted childhood. My supervisor has said that it will be fine for her to bring her new baby to our sessions after the birth. I am intrigued as to how that will work out.

I have an hour's break before seeing a client for an initial interview. After writing a short resume of each session for the file, and some more for the purposes of supervision, I chat with colleagues. In the office the atmosphere is quietly supportive though a lot is going on today. A counsellor has just finished with his long-term client, a trainee is drawing breath before her very first session, another's client has not turned up, and someone else is asking: 'How many for tea or coffee?'

Occasionally there may be anxiety that the counsellor using 'your' room is out in good time, or some small oversight in the centre's communication channels has caused puzzlement. We are subject to the same challenges as the clients who come for help. In this world of boundaries, allocated space, transitory organizational upheavals and occasional changes which not everybody likes, a succinct quote from Iris Murdoch, as delivered by Christopher

Mackenna during the last HCC annual lecture comes to mind; 'Love is the extremely difficult realisation that something other than oneself is real.'

Before meeting my initial interview client, I read the application form and the accompanying letter from his general practitioner (GP). I take the receipt book and go and shake hands with a young man with spiked hair. This first session is a time of information gathering, which I emphasize, to make a distinction from a more typical counselling session. I am also aware of the fact that after weeks of anticipation during the administrative business of form filling, telephone enquiries and awaiting the first interview, this is at last a face-to-face encounter. Today Brendan, a resting actor, is wary at first but becomes more animated while we draw up his family genogram (systematic representation of family relationships in terms of generations, gender, ages, whether deceased, divorced, and so on, in a pictorial diagram). How much relevant family history surfaces during this process! At the end, he wishes to know when his counselling will begin, and I give him a letter that describes the next stage.

As I leave the centre, my head is buzzing with the assimilation of people's stories. I take my initial interview notes home to write a report of several pages, with recommendations to the allocation committee. Some like to do this immediately. I tend to leave it to 'settle', and put it together a day or two later.

There have been many generations of counsellors and clients through these doors, experiencing the centre's distinct ethos of fully professional counselling provided to those who need it, irrespective of their ability to pay. We have four counselling rooms named after pioneering and significant figures in the history of the centre – William Kyle, Henrietta Meyer, Dennis Duncan and Peggy Thornborough. The Reverend William Kyle founded the Highgate Counselling Centre in 1960, before going on to found the Westminister Pastoral Foundation (WPF). Benita Kyle, his widow, continues to preside at graduation celebrations. The body of the organization includes joint presidents, chairman, vice-chairman, council of management, 12 psychotherapist supervisors, and medical psychiatric consultants.

A variety of issues necessarily arise. A few years ago at a staff meeting one counsellor was heard to say; 'Could we do something about those half-alive plants on the window sills? I don't want to feel more depressed than my clients.' In fact the rooms were given a fresh coat of paint and a budget was found for some new prints to go on the walls.

At the centre of my work is a relationship with another person. Each is a unique and unpredictable piece of work, with its own particular dynamics, struggles, oscillations between aliveness and impasse, frustrations and rewards. In some ways the counselling setting provides a microcosm of life 'out there', and in the words of my first training supervisor 'a mutually creative process'.

My route in

In 1990 I found a series of weekend courses at the WPF focusing and helpful. These included 'Is counsellor training for you?' I took their advice, and chose a well-structured course, which offered supervised work with clients for six of the seven terms. I was in my mid-thirties, with two small children, having some teaching and academic supervision of students in my background. My intention was to train and gradually take on more work as my children needed me less, but it was important not to be in a great hurry over this. I found the HCC course in psychodynamic counselling a stimulating time, and bonds made during this formative experience have proved strong and vital. Twelve years later many of us keep in touch. Several meet monthly in a reading group, a splendid opportunity to catch up, read and discuss new ideas. Latterly, we have been perusing some old classics, with Karen Horney's intricate map of the underlying currents of our psychic convolutions in *Neurosis and Human Growth* (1991) as this month's reading matter.

After graduating, some of us applied and were accepted via an interview with three senior staff, to be members of staff at HCC, which meant a regular commitment to a minimum of three clients, with encouragement to participate in training days, staff meetings, representing the staff 'voice' at council of management meetings and so on.

One of the factors I have enjoyed is that trainers and supervisors do not all work in the same way. My first supervisor was a Jungian and so I thought that everyone had their clients drawing, writing and recounting their dreams. Each supervisor, whether Freudian, Kleinian or integrative, brings their own distinct emphasis to the work, which has evolved from their training, life and experience until now. There was much to learn, but it was ultimately freeing not to expect anyone to have the 'answer to all things', and it sharpens up one's own evolution of a therapeutic way of working.

Using the experience of working with a number of clients with a variety of presenting problems, I felt able to contemplate working privately at home. The model of the work at HCC was invaluable in clarifying issues of boundaries and ethics in my private practice. The contacts and friendships I have been fortunate to make there have resulted in mutual client referrals and occasional offers of other paid work, such as training at other centres and educational establishments. Continuing work at HCC has enabled me to find proved and tested supervision for my private practice. Later I joined the panel of readers, which examines papers for our diploma course.

Client stories

We see a very wide variety of clients, in terms of age, profession and presenting problems. HCC offers couples counselling, family therapy and group work, though my niche is with individual clients. Trainees are allocated clients by the allocation committee. More disturbed cases are generally forwarded to more senior staff. We use the generic psychodynamic model, but the counsellor needs skills to adapt it to the very different needs of specific clients.

Sometimes short-term counselling can be effective in getting under even a long-term problem. However, long-term counselling allows gradual establishment of a trusting therapeutic relationship which has time to name, explore and work through some of the conflicts underlying relationship breakdown, depression, and all the losses and traumas that afflict us. If there is a common denominator in our client stories, it is one common to the human condition: the difficulty of accepting ourselves as fallible beings in a fallible world.

I have worked with clients from north London, and those who at some time have joined London's melting pot of cultures from different parts of the British Isles, and many other countries including Brazil, Canada, Australia, Russia, Jamaica, Finland, Croatia and the United States. Some have been the adult children of immigrants, or of one English and one immigrant parent from India, Mauritius, France or Armenia. A relatively new aspect of our work is with refugees, and multilingual counselling.

As early as 431 BC Euripedes (*Medea*, p. 36) has the Chorus lamenting Medea's predicament;

> Oh my country, my home! May the gods save me from becoming a stateless refugee.
> Of all pains and hardships none is worse than to be deprived of your native land.

Irena

A Polish-speaking social worker has come, as arranged, accompanying a Roma refugee, and I meet them both in our waiting room:

'Dziendobry Pani.'

'Dziendobry.'

Already the strangeness of articulating and hearing a once familiar but now foreign-sounding language within these walls puts me in touch with that sense of displacement that comes with leaving your home, and having to live in-between worlds, and in-between languages. The social worker leaves, having ascertained that her (and now my) client will find her way to the relevant bus stop, after our session ends. Despite encouraging words to each other, they both look a little doubtful. I am witnessing some separation anxiety as I usher this lady, wrapped in a long deep green gown and looking like a lost child, into the consulting room. And so we start, tentatively, exploring the reasons for counselling, with the added complication of this woman coming from a community where it is shameful to seek help from the outside, and so the husband mustn't know.

Margaritte

I am sitting with a lady in her forties who came to England from Brazil at the age of 18. Margaritte felt happy to leave a household fragmented by violence, neglect, divorce and poverty, where she looked after younger siblings from the age of five, with special responsibility for a handicapped sister. These days she has a position of considerable responsibility in the medical profession. By all accounts she has done well in her new country, language and career. She came presenting mild depression over a disruptive relationship with one of her daughters, ambivalent feelings about her ex-husband who wants to get together again, and also something she finds difficult to talk about; growing feelings of panic and dislocation at work, which she identifies as a fear of responsibility. She fears letting this unconsciously show to staff who look to her for guidance. If she looks at it too closely, it might become uncontainable, take her back to some place when life felt perpetually discordant and unmanageable. She fears breakdown and disintegration.

In this session we have been looking at the paradox of home being a stifling, difficult place she desired to get away from, and at her long-suppressed feelings of terrible homesickness for the familiar climate, sounds, tastes, colours, music and festivals of her childhood. In a moment of insight she says, 'You know, I never had asthma until I came to England. I always thought it was the change of climate, but do you think it might have been the difficulty of, literally, having to breathe my own air?'

'A fear of freedom, the very thing you desired?'

'Yes, and I still fear it. I never felt I had any choice about anything back home.'

We then think of babies whose lungs have not yet fully developed independent action, and she sees her inhaler and nebulizer as a support system to her walking in adult air.

After this session she is able to identify some good things she had to sever herself from: a loving, though rarely seen grandfather, siblings she loved and hated, a school friend's family she was sometimes able to visit. The sense of having been a victim of abandonment as well as guilt at having abandoned her sister, and the wave of longing which she allows herself to experience over the coming weeks, leads us to identify other, often uncomfortably strong, feelings and contradictory impulses which belong to her true self. These were feelings she had sometimes unconsciously, sometimes knowingly, acted out in her relationships, but she was generally alienated from them as her 'own'.

Many of Margaritte's conflicts and her suffering would have been present had she never left her homeland. However, sometimes a feeling of body dislocation, confusion, as well as a sense of the loss of meaning and inner resources afflicts people who have migrated. As with other forms of trauma, a disruption of the sense of going-on being is experienced. Sebastian Kraemer (1995) describes a secure attachment as 'an invisible elastic which can stretch and contract depending on the need for protection'. What happens if the elastic snaps? Often, life before the rupture becomes crystal clear in memory, and sometimes it is idealized when the necessity to hold onto something good is of vital importance in an alien or disorientating environment. In *Invisible Cities* by Italo Calvino, the author has Marco Polo explaining to the emperor that to leave behind one's native city is to return to it repeatedly in one's imagination. 'Elsewhere is a negative mirror. The traveller recognizes the little that is his, discovering the much he has not had and will never have' (Calvino, 1997, p. 29).

Much creativity has resulted from experiences of grief and dislocation. However, Freud differentiates between loss, 'mourning' and the more pathological state of 'melancholia', in which the sufferer displays 'an extraordinary diminution in his self-regard, an impoverishment of his ego on a grand scale. In mourning it is the world which has become poor and empty; in melancholia it is the ego itself' (Freud, 1991, p. 254).

The journey towards catching up with oneself takes time, facing pain, giving up magic solutions, and then knowing we can never go back to the same place as before. This struggle for integration, wholeness and growth is frequently witnessed in my therapeutic encounters, during which my role as counsellor can be variously experienced in the transference (for example, the idealized or abandoning parent, or an enabling witness). The ultimate goal is to help travellers/clients find themselves. In her autobiographical book, *Lost in Translation*, Eva Hoffman divides her story of loss of home and of having to find herself in a new language into paradise, exile and the new world. These terms could apply to anyone who feels at some stage dislocated in the world, in themselves, or both.

Michael

Since the early 1990s with the introduction of 'care in the community', and the shutting down of various facilities such as local day centres for psychiatric patients, HCC has had an increase of client referrals from psychiatrists and their staff. This has been a learning curve, where adaptability and an open mind have been important, as the strict psychodynamic model may not always be the most appropriate.

When seeing a client on medication for a psychotic illness, with a long-term history of intermittent hospitalisation and two attempts at suicide, I was grateful for advice from our consultant psychiatrist, who also, with the client's permission, put me in touch with the patient's own consultant. Was the rocking or falling asleep in sessions a side-effect of the medication, or due to our work together? Could I contribute to a psychotic episode by challenging Michael's apparent passivity, compulsive cycle of idealization and disillusionment, and insistence that all anger is 'out there?' Conversations with a doctor or psychiatric nurse can be of great benefit to me, but I have also been telephoned by a GP or a psychiatric social worker eager to discuss some matter of their concern. These interventions are not a frequent feature of the work, but provide a network of safety for client and counsellor, as well as the sense that we are not working in a vacuum.

Alice and Simon

Boundaries, boundaries …

I have come to the end of a session with a young man. Each week he tries to draw out the time, by coming up with an urgent new topic as the session ends. This in itself is a topic. He infringes boundaries with his friends, his workplace, the legal system, and seeks to relieve his anxiety by frequently sought sexual relationships with women. 'Boundaries, boundaries …' echo the words of my supervisor, as I end the session on time, but have to leave the room first in order to find change for my client's contribution. When I start my next session with another long-term client, an attractive young woman with an eating disorder, she is agitated and tells me that in my absence, the previous client asked her to have coffee with him in a local cafe. She said 'yes' but actually felt angry because she didn't really want to. Startled at the turn of events, I wonder if I had missed something in 'protecting' my clients. I also ask why she said 'yes' when she meant 'no'? What follows is an extremely useful session on this, as it turns out, recurring theme in Alice's life. The immediacy of her feelings of anger makes this topic alive, and lead to her decision to behave less passively and take responsibility for what she actually means. The infringement of boundary, here, in this apparently safe setting, leads fortunately in the end to a moment of clarity. The following week Simon and I discuss the issue of boundaries and privacy and infringement in a focused way. This continues to be a pertinent issue for our future work together.

Some clients do not stay the full course, and this needs evaluating. Some return for another phase of counselling after a year or more. Some write, or send a symbolic wedding invitation from New Zealand or East Finchley. It is good to hear that a client is thriving and living his or her life more fully.

Continuing professional development

HCC provides three training days a year (Saturday mornings) for its staff and trainees free of charge. The topic of the next one is usually suggested at the staff meeting that follows the training morning, and we are always on the lookout for what would be popular and useful. A multitude of topics have been covered such as post-traumatic stress disorder, the use of fantasy, training counsellors in Bosnia, 'masks'. Recently Val Potter, Chair of BACP, took us through the new 'Changes in ethics' literature. 'Adolescence' was presented by Robin Anderson (Tavistock Clinic), Dr Elphis Christopher presented 'Counselling adults who were abused as children', 'Perverse states of mind' was given by Stanley Ruszczynski (Portman Clinic), and 'The role of neuro-sciences in counselling' by Dale Mathers. He invited us to look at the brain as an ecosystem which, like a forest, tends to preserve stability at all costs. This gave a different emphasis to our views of innate resistance to change. Whether by helping to make 'changes' through counselling we are also remodelling cerebral architecture is a question that has had the circuits in my brain occupied since.

There are also opportunities for developing skills and experience by applying to train with the family counselling team, or by training to become an initial interview counsellor. This requires being a member of staff for at least a year. Continual assessment of the initial interview procedures is followed in regular meetings organized by the initial interview coordinator and the director.

Over the years, I have invested in shorter-term post-diploma courses which HCC has offered, either as a refresher, or because the subjects were particularly relevant to my work with clients at the time, for example, 'Addiction', 'Time-limited counselling' and 'Working with dreams'. The noticeboard in the office highlights further training, lectures and seminars all over London. I once asked at a staff meeting, 'Why don't we run an "Is counsellor training for you?" day course?' I was told to go and organize it!

Evaluation and conditions of work

In 1984, the Highgate Counselling Trust was converted into a company limited by guarantee, and the former trustees became members of the company's governing body, the council of management. So far, the centre has survived financially by its own efforts. It depends on the sliding-scale contributions made by clients, any donations, and on the support of its friends. The centre provides guidelines for the determination of contribution levels, which is a basis for discussion of this between counsellor and client. These levels are reviewed annually and may be varied if circumstances alter. Looking for other sources of possible funding is kept under review.

The centre complies with the BACP's *Ethical Framework* and its work includes self-evaluation. One criterion is the counsellor's ability to hold clients. Each trainee counsellor is required to complete 30 sessions with two clients, and 12 sessions with two short-term clients. The judgement of supervisors is important here. Repeated referrals from other professionals and indeed from past or present clients are also an indicator of 'effectiveness'. Frequently at an initial interview, I find that new clients have come at the recommendation of a friend of theirs, who had had a good counselling experience in the past. At the end of a period of counselling, the counsellor fills in a 'closure sheet', giving an outline of the work and any plans the client may have for future help, if necessary. This is overseen and signed by the supervisor.

Counsellors need to be open, adaptable and predisposed to continual learning to meet the challenges of a wide variety of clients and presenting problems. Client and counsellor are matched for suitability and availability, but the counsellor may accept or turn down client work, usually after discussion with a supervisor.

Trainee counsellors receive professional supervision as part of their training. All counsellors work under supervision, which is funded by the centre. All supervisors are qualified psychotherapists and supervision comprises a once-weekly group session of three to five participants, lasting one and a half hours. Counsellors are able to choose their supervisor. There is a formal reappraisal of supervisor availability and an opportunity for change every two years, near the end of each training course. However, changes in supervision can also be made at other times, if necessary.

The centre, as a predominantly voluntary body, offers limited scope for salaried work but there is room for development. Our last two assistant coordinators have been ex-trainees who applied and were chosen for this remunerated part-time post. One combined his hours with taking on another part-time post as a student counsellor at a local college. Our more recent assistant coordinator, who has had long-term experience in the higher education sector, was also able to do some paid training on the psychodynamic diploma course. The centre also pays the initial interview coordinator. There is remuneration for assessment work, as there is for those on the panel of readers.

Voluntary counselling can be a stable time of gathering experience and inner resources, a launch pad for other work. In many cases (as in mine) it leads to private practice. Others have gone on to counselling in GP practice, to take posts in training or academic work in other counselling bodies. Some have used the experience and new skills to enhance their competence as social workers, in the probation service, the health sector, academic sector or even their acupuncture clinic. Many go on to do further training at some point. Six of our 12 supervisors were once trainees or counsellors at the centre.

It is good to belong to an organization within an ethos I value where I have struggled, learnt and gained much. Some counsellors are at a stage in life when they are able and happy to give a few hours in the week, with the stimulation of the work and the enjoyment of relationships in the centre as their motivation. For others, it is a phase of their ongoing professional development, or it is a mixture of both.

Future developments

The Institute of Education has published a study entitled *Changing Britain, Changing Lives* (2003) which is the result of monitoring over 40,000 people born in 1946, 1958 and 1970. One of its findings indicates a dramatic drop in volunteering and participation in local community life.

The number of people who were prepared to supply voluntary work in the past is diminishing. Counsellors and psychotherapists usually do some unpaid work with clients as part of their training, and these days people are keen to 'make up their hours' to achieve accreditation. The missionary spirit that fired the founders is not extinct. The fact that this centre has thrived for over 40 years is a great success story. Yet with the increasing professionalization of counselling, the financial and time investment required for good training, the desirability of CPD, the demands of family, and other aspects of life, a voluntary counselling service needs to keep an eye on changing trends. Although I have no crystal ball, there is a general sense of cultural change.

The centre recently analysed sources of client referrals, and found that the majority of clients who are able to give the lowest contributions (and therefore need the highest subsidy) tend to be those referred by GPs and other health professionals. In times of financial struggle, this can sometimes give rise to ambivalent feelings about doing the work that the health service apparently cannot. Should there not be some dialogue here?

People need to feel valued. We recognize this for our clients, and we know it for ourselves. Society used to believe that 'it is better to give than to receive', but this has given way to the cult of individual self-realization. James, in his book *Britain on the Couch* (1998), suggests that we are less satisfied and more depressed than in the 1950s, because we all expect so much more. The World Health Organization (2002) does not spare us its frequently printed predictions that by the year 2020, the second most prevalent disease in the world will be depression. We need people trained in the mysteries of 'depression', but – reality-check – do we expect too much? Counsellors may be willing to do voluntary work on the route to self-realization, but what will the next stage be? Voluntary work of all kinds has to find a way to manage this change if it is to survive. The need for help with living our lives is continually here. Work with clients in the Henrietta Meyer room reminds me that she appraised our neurotic traits as being of intrinsic value: 'by producing symptoms the unconscious makes the initial attempt to restore mental equilibrium. It also confirms that our psyche is self-regulating, and that man, by instinct, really aims for inner wholeness.' (1964, p. 61)

Sometimes, if we suspend cause and effect thinking at the beginning of a session with a client, and stay with not knowing, it makes room for new growth. In an organization, any change needs forethought and planning. A realistic appraisal of the real shifts in cultural attitudes and thinking is needed. And always there will be something we do not know: it could be an interesting ride. In the meanwhile there is commitment and rich tradition to draw on.

Ten top tips

Generic and context specific tips:

- Think: what am I trying to achieve?
- Touch base with this initial idea as time goes on to see if you are on course, or whether it needs revision.
- Think laterally. (An American student organization for whom I had taught in the past, asked me to be its counsellor when it found out about my training. I had not even thought of this.) Keep your eyes, ears and mind open.
- Read notices and professional journals for stimulating ideas and possibilities. (It is how I got to write this chapter!)
- Keep networking and enjoy making new friends.
- If you feel overwhelmed by the work, tell a trusted person. These are often growth points.
- Do not be too afraid of 'difficult clients'. With good supervision, this can be challenging and rewarding work.
- Reflect on what your role tends to be within your working group.
- Keep up your paperwork, but don't impose perfect systems on yourself.
- Do something different for your own refreshment of soul.

Can I value the work, myself and others if I am not financially rewarded for it?

Bibliography

Anderson, R. (ed.) (1991) *Clinical Lectures on Klein and Bion*. London: Routledge.

BACP (2002). *Ethical Framework for Good Practice in Counselling and Psychotherapy*. Rugby: BACP.

Calvino, I. (1997) *Invisible Cities*. London: Vintage.

Euripides (1963) *Medea*. London: Penguin Classics.

Freud, S. (1917) 'Mourning and melancholia', in *Collected Works Vol. 11* (1991), *On Metapsychology*. London: Penguin.

Hoffman, E. (1991) *Lost in Translation*. London: Minerva.

Horney, K. (1991) *Neurosis and Human Growth: The Struggle Toward Self-Realisation*. New York: Norton.

Institute of Education (2003) *Changing Britain, Changing Lives*. London University.

James, O. (1998) *Britain on the Couch*. London: Arrow.

Kraemer, S. (1995) 'Parenting yesterday, today and tomorrow', in *Families and Parenting: Report of a Conference*, London, 26 September 1995. London: Family Policies Study Centre.

Mackenna, C. (1999) 'Jung and Christianity – wrestling with God', in E. Christopher and H. Solomon (eds), *Jungian Thought in the Modern World*. London: Free Association Books.

Mathers, D. (2001) *Meaning and Purpose in Analytical Psychology*. London: Brunner-Routledge.

Meyer, H. (1964) quoted in *The Development of Personality in Healing Through Counselling*, ed. W. H. Kyle. London: Epworth Press.

Ruszczynski, S. (1993) *Psychotherapy with Couples*. London: Karnac Books.

Ruszczynski, S. and Johnson, S. (1991) *Psychoanalytic Psychotherapy in the Kleinian Tradition*. London: Karnac Books.

World Health Organisation (2002) *Strategic Directions for Improving the Health and Development of Children and Adolescents*. Geneva: WHO.

3

Counselling for Relate

Elisabeth Long

Few charitable organizations can claim as long a history and as high a public profile as the relationship counselling service, Relate. Founded in 1938, the former National Marriage Guidance Council recognized the diversity of intimate relationships in 1988 and metamorphosed into Relate. The change in name matched a growing awareness and acceptance of the role of counselling, both at a professional and public level. Relate's prominence, promoted through the media and its range of self-help publications, means that it remains a popular choice for those seeking initial counselling training or qualified counsellors looking to specialize in relationship counselling.

A typical voluntary commitment

A mainly voluntary workforce means that the staff's main commitments may lie outside of the agency, and although the work is important to most volunteers from an altruistic and personal point of view, it does not 'keep the wolf from the door'! Time, for the majority of voluntary counsellors, is a precious commodity. Depending on the counsellor's time slot, there may be little physical contact with other counsellors. Group supervision and centre meetings do go some way to making counsellors feel part of a wider organization.

Counsellors are not allowed to work without a receptionist on the premises, and these people are also quite likely to be volunteers. It is their responsibility to administer the appointments and ensure that the counsellor has the necessary paperwork for each new appointment. Counsellors will take care of the ongoing records for existing clients, which will be kept securely on the premises. Increasing professionalization and the data requirements of both the centre and national office mean that the paperwork can be quite extensive.

Voluntary counsellors will contract with their local centre for the number of hours counselling they will provide over a year but the minimum is 135 hours. This varies from centre to centre and depends whether the counsellor wishes to do additional hours (usually paid for more experienced counsellors), or if the counsellor is in training: enough hours to complete their course.

Relate allocates a supervisor to each counsellor. Supervision is a significant part of the counsellor's commitment to their work. Because supervisors are paid employees, they tend to be flexible enough to arrange supervision times to fit in with the counsellor's more limited time. This includes individual supervision and attendance at regular case supervision groups.

Because Relate centres are charitable organizations it is hard to escape from the fact that they have to continually raise funds to maintain their existence. Most funding comes from client contributions. Centre managers and fundraisers spend a considerable amount of time applying for funding and maintaining a relationship with key funding organizations. Although this is largely done without involving the counselling workforce, some smaller funding initiatives do require the involvement of all centre staff. It is not included in a contract, but Relate counsellors can expect to be canvassed for some form of fundraising activity.

It is hard to define a typical day for a Relate counsellor. Would-be counsellors are advised that their commitment to their centre will probably be between five and ten hours per week (Relate). Deduct three hours of counselling, and the remainder of the time is taken up with paper work, reading, training requirements, supervision, group meetings and quite possibly selling raffle tickets to family and friends!

My route in

Like many counsellors at the outset of their training, I felt that the answer I gave at my Relate selection interview to the question why I wanted to become a counsellor was woefully inadequate. I remember mumbling something about wanting to help people, to put something back into the community and personally feeling like it was the right time. I had heard of the agency through a friend who had used the service and was further intrigued by some short Relate courses my partner had undertaken at work. Yet despite studying social psychology at degree level, I was initially sceptical of a service that helped people understand their relationships better. I had after all pursued a career in journalism and PR, which had been more about working at people, rather than working with them.

With the benefit of hindsight it now seems clear that what I wanted then is what I still get from working voluntarily with couples. Briefly, couple counselling provides me with an opportunity to share time with others (both clients and colleagues), as we struggle to make sense of ourselves through our relationships both in the past, the present and hopefully the future.

At the time of my interview I had no clear idea of what personal and professional development lay ahead of me; just a feeling that I was changing and that where I found myself professionally no longer felt right. A career break to start a family allowed me to trust my instincts. I began to retrain as a teacher, but had a strong feeling that I wanted to do something both altruistic and for me. Relate was one of the few organizations I had heard of. I approached them with no real intentions of becoming a counsellor, but after a few months working in the office I was taking every opportunity to talk to the counsellors and borrowing textbooks from the office's library. I had never worked in an environment where people had chosen to be there for reasons other than making money. As a result their enthusiasm for the organization, counselling and life itself was intriguing and infectious. My 'little' voluntary job was becoming far more interesting than I ever anticipated.

I was encouraged by my Relate colleagues to apply for the counsellor training scheme. Initially I had an informal meeting with my local centre manager. This was followed by a selection interview with three committee members and finally a full-day session with eight other candidates, also from a diverse range of backgrounds. It was the most intense and intimate interviewing experience I had had for any job – especially remembering that if I was one of the lucky 65 per cent to get through this process, I was still only a voluntary worker!

At the time of writing I am still a voluntary worker at the same centre. Relate is experiencing ongoing changes that will mean more paid counsellors employed by the service than volunteers. To keep the service going this may become necessary, but I still feel that the real reward of couple counselling is a desire to help others and yourself understand and enjoy the complexities of relationships.

A client story

One of the most disorientating effects of working with couples is that the counsellor from the very first session is entering into an established relationship. Whatever the problem is and however lacking their personal skills and resources are at this current time, the couple hold a hidden world of shared experiences that the counsellor will need to be invited into by them both before therapeutic movement takes place for the clients as individuals.

Being on the outside, looking in was a key feeling for me at Susie and Mark's first session. Susie had made the appointment with Relate following what she had described as an uncharacteristic verbal outburst from Mark. Both appeared to be shocked at Mark's anger, and although he was apologetic and remorseful his attitude in the session was sullen and he contributed little to Susie's explanation of the presenting problem.

Through a stream of tears she told me that she was in the process of leaving Mark after six years of marriage. When he had screamed at her during their argument she felt that he had over-stepped an unspoken boundary and that their relationship was effectively over. Wishing to draw Mark into the session, I asked him if he thought this was the end too. Mark muttered that he wasn't sure and continued staring at the floor.

The argument had clearly been a frightening event for both Susie and Mark. I surmised that the couple had been containing strong emotions, which on surfacing had been uncontrollable and scary for both of them. However, when I attempted to discover what the argument had been about, both clients appeared to struggle to remember. Susie eventually commented that it was about nothing really, as most arguments are. She explained that after the birth of their last child two years ago, Mark had decided to stay at home to look after the baby and their older child who was now four. Susie worked full time as an executive at a bank and had come home tired expecting a meal, which Mark hadn't had time to make.

The presenting problem appeared to be acknowledging the ending of the relationship; but the fact that both clients had come for counselling and both appeared to be colluding in keeping their emotions buried, suggested that the relationship was not quite as final as Susie believed. I completed the session by reiterating our working contract together, with particular emphasis on the limits of confidentiality.

Willi (1982) suggests that we seek partners who we hope will meet our individual need for expression and growth, enjoyment and pleasure. Yet the pursuit of our individuality through our rela-tionships can paradoxically threaten those relationships, leading to an inhibition and blocking of individual expression. It appeared at this first session that both Susie and Mark were blocking each other and that there was fear around expressing their own individual needs.

I had contracted for six sessions, but was not too optimistic that Susie and Mark would return for a second appointment. I felt quite excluded from the couple and although I had obtained the 'bare bones' of their issues, I was left with feelings of frustration and futility. Fortunately a supervision session before our second meeting had helped me realize that my feelings were probably the result of transference from the couple. Gaining this insight helped me remember that the relationship was my client, and that I required both Susie and Mark to jointly recognize and own these feelings.

Just before the start of the second session Susie telephoned to say that she had been held up at work and that she would try and get there later. She told me to start the session with Mark, who added that they had discussed him maintaining the meeting if she was unable to attend.

From the outset Mark was far more responsive than he had been in the previous session. He stated that he was glad to have the opportunity to talk on his own. He shared further details about their personal history. Mark had met Susie the week her parents had emigrated to Canada. He said that they had been 'soul mates' from the outset and had got married within a year of meeting. He felt that the relationship had been fine until the difficult birth of their first child. At this stage Mark's mother had become more involved in helping with childcare, which Susie resented. Mark had been left feeling like a referee between his wife and mother.

I shared with Mark the insight I gained through this exploration of their past. I was aware that the relationship was founded at a potentially vulnerable time for Susie and wondered what impact this had had on the relationship both at the beginning and now. I noted that the couple were at the child rearing life stage that involved investing a great deal of energy beyond their own needs (Erikson, 1950; Sheehy, 1976). The mother-in-law's involvement had appeared to reinforce Susie's inability to parent her own child. Not wanting to engage with these negative feelings following the birth of her second child, she had returned to full-time work.

I was concerned about Susie's absence during this session and was aware that I was only getting Mark's perspective. I helped to remain couple focused by keeping the counselling room arranged to accommodate a couple. I also encouraged Mark to share fully with Susie the content of the session, especially his final comment about feeling better about being able to talk about the past without it starting an argument.

I was feeling more confident that an effective therapeutic relationship could be formed with Susie and Mark. However, this optimism was tested when Mark appeared on his own for the third session and told me that Susie was apparently unwell, but wanted him to continue with our original contract. I was concerned about

Susie's second absence without personal contact from her. I told Mark that I intended to write to Susie, sending her my best wishes and inviting her back for the next meeting. At this point it was important to assess whether we were maintaining our original contract or to look at a range of other possibilities, such as terminating our meetings until both partners could commit to a regular spot or offer Susie some individual appointments. I made a mental note to discuss this with my supervisor.

During this session Mark confessed that after the birth of their first child, he had had a brief affair with a neighbour. He said that it was at the worst stage when his mother and Susie were constantly arguing over the upbringing of the baby and when their sexual life had almost ceased. The affair was long over, and Susie had not known about it. The exploration of this affair led Mark to the startling understanding that part of his decision to stay at home to bring up the children was to prevent this neighbour becoming friendly with Susie and disclosing the affair to her. I felt uncomfortable about having knowledge of Mark's affair and emphasized that although our contract of confidentiality would not allow me to disclose this information to Susie, it could create a block to open and honest communication when we were all together again. We spent some time in the session looking at why he had disclosed this information to me when he was on his own. We also looked at how he could share this information with Susie and then deal with the anticipated outcomes.

Both Susie and Mark came to next session and I invited Mark to describe how he felt the previous two sessions had gone. Although he was less animated, I was pleased to note that he was ready to communicate more and maintain eye contact with both Susie and me. Mark had confessed to Susie about his affair, and had been totally surprised to find out that she had known about it all along. Both now realized that this known secret had been festering away for over three years. Now that it was out in the open an emotional, but frank discussion could be had about why it had occurred and its long-term implications for the future of this relationship.

Unpacking the recent past and connecting it to the couple's beliefs, attitudes, assumptions and needs occupied this session and the next. Mark felt that he was able to express his anger constructively, which then allowed him to get in touch with the deeper fear he felt as the dynamics of the relationship changed after the birth of their daughter. Susie was able to recognize that her feeling of abandonment – that had never been properly explored with the emigration of her parents – had been triggered again. She felt excluded by both Mark and his mother and had distanced herself through work: making an unconscious choice to protect herself from these feelings, but at the same time engaging in a self-defeating cycle that would only magnify them (Mearns and Thorne, 1988).

At the sixth session I reviewed the work to date, and asked the couple if they wished to continue with counselling at this time. Susie and Mark said they had considered this a great deal over the past week, and had decided to finish counselling. I was aware that some major issues were beginning to come to light for the couple and that further counselling would probably benefit them. However, it was clear that the counselling they had received to date had helped them to communicate more honestly and openly. They were optimistic that they could maintain the momentum that their couple counselling work had injected into their relationship. Unlike individual counselling they had jointly entered a process that they could begin to facilitate for each other.

Evaluation

The basic selection, training and ongoing support package offered by Relate ensures that all its practitioners gain a theoretically integrative approach to working with clients, although this is underpinned by psychodynamic and systemic approaches.

Couple counsellors have three main ways to assist couples achieve more satisfying relationships. These are: helping couples renew their sense of hope; changing their thinking processes in relation to their problems and relationships; and developing and using behavioural skills with each other (Bubenzer and West, 1994). The management of a typical relationship with clients could be evaluated and assessed using Egan's three-stage model of counselling (1982). During the exploration stage, clients identify their mutual problems and are encouraged by the counsellor to become involved in the process through assessment and contracting. At the understanding stage, the couple become more aware of how each is contributing to the problems, and by the action stage they can begin to contribute by improving their mutual difficulties.

Research shows that most of Relate's clients have between three and ten sessions (Barkla, 1991), which leads to the assumption that the majority of the counselling work undertaken will be short term, and that any form of assessment and evaluation should bear this in mind.

Relate centres belong to a federation and follow its clinical guidelines. Policies, best practice guidelines and procedures, which affect counsellors, originate at both national and local levels. Centre managers and supervisors provide a synthesis of this material to staff.

Critical evaluation of the counselling work is time consuming and expensive for both the centres and the central office. Centres collect statistical data and occasionally use exit questionnaires to assess the effectiveness of their services to clients. Although these methods of assessing counselling have inherent weaknesses (McLeod, 2003), they do on the whole create an ongoing analysis of the type of clientele attracted to the agency and the value they gain from its services. They are particularly useful, both nationally and locally, to provide data for sourcing potential funding from the government, statutory agencies and trusts.

As an independent organization, each centre is responsible for raising its own funds. Clients supply the bulk of a centre's income through contributions (Barkla, 1991). Other sources of income include funding from local authorities, charitable trusts and centre initiatives. Centre-based activities can vary; but whatever is organized all staff are usually approached to help with the ongoing demand for funding. Without these additional sources, centres face the real threat of closure (Barkla, 1991).

Continuing professional development

Moves in the counselling world to provide a professional, ethical and accountable workforce have resonated through Relate in recent years, leading to a new package of training in 2003 for those wishing to train as couple counsellors, either with or without prior counsellor training experience. The agency now offers a one-year certificate programme for unqualified workers, which can lead to a diploma and master's degree accredited by the University of East London.

The new training programmes aim to develop the role of couple counselling through practice and research into the twenty-first century. Relationship counselling is undoubtedly the core of the organization's business and will remain so. However, there are a number of opportunities for qualified couple counsellors to diversify within Relate's current provision. Perhaps the best known ancillary service offered by the agency is the psychosexual therapy service (PST). Founded in 1974, this service based primarily on the work of Masters and Johnson (Thorburn, 1997) complements the work of the remedial couple counsellor. It is targeted at couples whose relationships are affected by primary sexual dysfunction. PST training is accredited by the British Association for Sexual and Marital Therapy.

Relate's internal counsellor training has an enviable reputation and is arguably one of the oldest counsellor training programmes in the world (Butler and Joyce, 1998). The agency has supported for many years relationship research programmes to underpin internal and external training schemes (Schröder, 1997). Relate's external training service runs a number of Open College Network accredited training programmes for members of the public (including many former clients) and businesses aiming to improve their communication and relationship skills. External trainers are usually attached to a local centre and have a background in training or education with a basic qualification.

One of Relate's newer ventures is the Young People's Counselling Service. This initiative recognized the impact that divorce and separation was having on clients' children, and the general lack of remedial counselling services for young people in most areas. The service has widened its scope to provide support for those affected by parental conflict and targets young people between the ages of 10 and 25. A special training programme is available to qualified counsellors who wish to work in this field.

Conditions of work

Relate's counselling workforce consists mainly of volunteers who provide 135 hours per year to their centre. In reality most counsellors provide a half-day slot consisting of three one-hour sessions per week. Demand for evening counselling is usually greater in most areas, which means that there may be little opportunity for counsellors to choose when they work. Relate counsellors come from a diversity of backgrounds, both personally and professionally.

The diversity of its counsellors is of key importance to the ongoing success of Relate, however, there are some key experiences, abilities, skills and attributes that are regarded as essential for a couple counsellor. These have been listed as:

- An educational background to A level equivalent to cope with the academic requirements of the training process.
- The appropriate management of one's own developmental life stages.
- Having experience of being in an intimate adult relationship.
- Being able to find meaning in one's personal experiences and those of others.
- Being able to contribute creatively to group activities and discussions.
- Having the ability to listen and respond appropriately to others.
- An ability to manage time boundaries, one's own boundaries and other personal boundaries.
- Having an awareness of one's personal emotional life history, resources and limitations and being particularly aware of one's current emotional state.
- Having the emotional well-being to cope with the stresses of counselling.
- Being adaptable and accepting of others' lifestyles and life choices.
- Having a private life that will be supportive of the possible stresses and strains that are part of counselling others.
- Being motivated towards further personal development.
- Having the ability to work within an organizational setting and willingness to comply with the BACP *Ethical Framework for Good Practice*.

(Relate, 1997)

Relate clients refer themselves for counselling; but quite often they have received prompting and information from other agencies, including their GP, social workers, probation officers, teachers and, reassuringly, former satisfied clients (Butler and Joyce, 1998). National standards state that an initial consultation must be offered within two weeks for a one-hour session with an experienced counsellor. It is this counsellor's role to decide with the clients whether Relate is the right organization for their needs and to provide them with details of what ongoing couple counselling will entail. Initial consultation counsellors are specially trained to provide brief, short-term focused counselling interventions.

After this meeting clients who require counselling are added to the centre's waiting list. Once a suitable time becomes available, their assessment information is passed to a counsellor for ongoing counselling. The first session will be arranged by the reception staff, and it is very unusual for counsellors to have direct contact with clients outside their contracted hours. Receptionists and administration staff act as intermediaries between counsellors and their clients, once the initial contract has been agreed.

Counsellors in training will normally carry a caseload of three sets of clients. It is important that the majority of a trainee's caseload consists of couple work, but inevitably single clients will also present themselves for relationship counselling. Counsellors maintain the records started at the assessment session for each case, which are kept centrally in adherence to confidentiality and data protection requirements.

Each Relate centre has an allocated supervisor, who provides individual supervision approximately once a month. Apart from clinical supervision, Relate supervisors provide extra guidance and mentoring to trainees and hold regular group supervision meetings for centre staff. Supervisors can also deliver ongoing professional development training groups for qualified staff. Supervision is part of the counsellor's contract, and its cost is met by the centre. Although this may be seen as a benefit to most counselling practitioners, there could be issues regarding the supervisor's roles within a centre.

Future developments

Relate's longevity in the field of counselling can probably be attributed to its ability to adapt its core training programmes and service to meet the demands of the profession and its clientele. Over recent years there has been a fundamental change in the organization's perspective of itself from 'social movement' to 'service agency' (Schröder, 1997).

Couple counselling will probably remain at the core of the agency's provision, complemented by psychosexual therapy, young people's counselling and external training. Certain theorists view couple counselling as a subspeciality of family therapy (Gurman, Kniskern and Pinsof, 1988), so perhaps it is not surprising that as part of the agency's evolution, it has developed a family counselling service – now being offered in a number of centres.

Other new services are Relate Direct, a telephone counselling service run centrally in Rugby, but with counsellors working from their own homes, and Relate Online, an e-mail counselling service launched in 2002, centrally based, but using counsellors at home responding to e-mailed enquiries. Approaches are being made to national companies to provide relationship counselling for their employees, which will probably utilize a range of face-to-face, telephone and Internet counselling.

Although change is inevitable, are these current and dramatic changes to Relate's traditional ethos both necessary and sufficient? The voluntary sector cannot be excluded from the changes that are taking place within counselling. Relate is recognized as providing a benchmark for professionalism and expertise in the field of couple counselling, but the rise of counselling's profile means that they are likely to be working in both partnership and competition with other agencies and counselling providers.

The changes to the counselling training programme and the expansion of services are necessary steps Relate has to take to meet the developing needs of the profession and retain its level of expertise. This will provide standardized quality assurance and accreditation systems, which are comparable to other counselling agencies. However to maintain these standards, adequate funding is essential. The additional services may supply sufficient income to support the core business of couple counselling; but if they do not, Relate's survival may mean it becomes a fee-paying agency. This will have implications for its future clients, and also for its future workforce.

Ten top tips

Context specific tips:

- Keep updated with Relate through its website: www.relate.org.uk.
- Contact your local centre or look for open days in your local newspaper to take the opportunity to talk to Relate staff.
- Consider whether you have enough time to fit in the five to ten hours per week voluntary commitment Relate will require from you whilst you are in training.
- Relate's selection procedures for counsellors are demanding. Be prepared to complete a detailed application form and to be asked searching and personal questions at your selection interview.
- The interviewers will not be looking for an in-depth knowledge of counselling, but an awareness of the basic principles of counselling may help you at the selection stage.
- Relate are not looking for counsellors with idyllic personal lives, but will be seeking those who have undergone personal change in their lives and are able to use their experiences to empathize with others.
- If you fail to be selected for Relate the decision is rarely final. You can apply again in the future.
- If you have the time, consider offering voluntary help at your local centre. This could be as a receptionist, administrator, committee member, fundraiser and so on, and is an excellent way to find out how the centre runs and keep updated with counselling and Relate.
- The Relate qualifications require candidates to have a certain standard of academic ability. If it is a long time since you did any writing or academic research, consider a short study skills course at your local college to help you with the work.
- Do not ignore the impact and personal insight this work will have on your personal relationships.

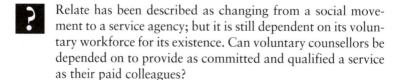

Relate has been described as changing from a social movement to a service agency; but it is still dependent on its voluntary workforce for its existence. Can voluntary counsellors be depended on to provide as committed and qualified a service as their paid colleagues?

Bibliography

BACP (2002) *Ethical Framework for Good Practice*. Rugby: BACP.

Barkla, D. (1991) 'Couple therapy: the agency approach', in D. Hooper and W. Dryden (eds), *Couple Therapy: A Handbook*. Milton Keynes: Open University Press.

Bubenzer, D. and West, J. (1994) *Counselling Couples*. Sage: London.

Butler, C. and Joyce, V. (1998) *Counselling Couples in Relationships. An Introduction to the Relate Approach*. London: Wiley.

Egan, G. (1982) *The Skilled Helper*. Monterey: Brooks/Cole.

Erikson, E. (1950) *Childhood and Society*. New York: Norton.

Gurman, A., Kniskern, D. and Pinsof, W. (1988) 'Research on the process and outcome of marital and family therapy', in S. Garfield and A Bergin (eds), *Handbook of Psychotherapy and Behavior Change*. New York: Wiley.

Hooper, D. and Dryden, W. (eds) (1991) *Couple Therapy: A Handbook*. Milton Keynes: Open University Press.

Litvinoff, S. (1994) *The Relate Guide to Better Relationships*. London: Vermillion.

McLeod, J. (2003) *Doing Counselling Research*. London: Sage.

Mearns, D. and Thorne, B. (1988) *Person Centred Counselling in Action*. London: Sage.

Relate (1993) *Marital and Couple Counselling: Counsellor's Basic Training Notes*. [booklet]

Relate (1997) *Summary Job Description for Relate Couple Counsellor*. [information sheet]

Relate, *At Every Step You Take*. [promotional brochure]

Relate, *The Graduate Certificate: Foundation in Couple Counselling – some notes for applicants*. [booklet]

Relate, *Notes for Prospective Counsellors*. [Booklet available from local Relate centres or from Relate National.]

Schröder, T. (1997) 'Couples counselling', in S. Palmer (ed.), *Handbook of Counselling*. London: Routledge.

Sheehy, G. (1976) *Passages*. New York: Dutton.

Thorburn, M. (1997) *Diploma in Psychosexual Therapy. Counsellor Course Prospectus*. Rugby: Relate.

Willi, J. (1982) *Couples in Collusion*. New York: Aronson.

4

Counselling in a Women's Refuge

Louise Mackinney

For part of my working week I am a counsellor in a well established and resourced refuge for women who have experienced partner violence. This chapter covers my personal way in and responses to this work, and also ways of seeing the issue of partner violence.

A typical day

I arrive at the refuge and go into the office to pick up messages. This is very important because I have not been here for six days. I am self-employed and work here for a day and a half a week. The rest of the time I am in other settings. I see that a regular client is unable to attend today, and somebody has booked a new client into her space. This clearly causes a problem that I will need to sort out later. I will probably have to extend my time here, at least for the next few weeks. I pick up the key for the counselling room and leave the office as quickly as possible. I do not like to be seen to be in the office for too long: this is a residential facility and women may imagine I am talking to the refuge staff about them.

I find I have to rearrange the counselling room because there was a children's group in there last night. I do this and spend a few minutes thinking about the women I am going to see today. I have a new client, and I need to think about what regular time to offer her, as today she has my other client's time. Today I am also seeing a woman who used to live in the refuge, but who has now moved out into her own house. I have been seeing her for 18 months and we are working very deeply on her attachment issues. There are two other women on my list who live in the refuge; I have seen them for six and eight weeks respectively. The last of my five clients for today is a woman who lives in the community, has never lived in the refuge, but has many issues around domestic violence. I have been seeing her for six months.

All of my clients have issues around domestic, or partner, violence. This can include actual physical violence, or simply the manifestations of power and control in an unequal relationship, such as the control of her time or withholding money or affection. It can also involve verbal and emotional abuse, insults or hurtful comments.

I then see my first three clients, with just ten minutes between each client. I find this works for me; I can stay at a high level of concentration if I don't have long gaps between clients. I 'clear' myself between each client by drinking water and washing my hands. I mentally run through the session we had last week. Occasionally I consult my (very brief) notes, which I make at the end of the day.

At the end of the first three hours I take my lunch break. I usually go out to stretch my legs and buy a sandwich from the nearby supermarket. At the end of the day I make my notes, making a brief separate note of the people I have seen today for my invoicing purposes. I then go to the office as the new client I saw today worried me, she seemed to have a very tenuous grasp on reality and was also suicidal. I speak to the refuge manager about a mental health assessment and I also contact the woman's GP, which I have told her I will do. Then I go home.

My route in

Counselling is my third career. I very much hope it is my last, as I think I have now managed to find what I feel most comfortable doing.

I started work in the refuge in September 1995. At that time I had had a reasonable amount of experience as a counsellor and a great deal of experience working generally in the voluntary sector. I had been a volunteer for a large part of my adult life, for such organizations as the Samaritans and Rape Crisis. I had also been involved in the women's movement at local level for some time. The refuge was therefore an ideal choice for me: I had a good deal of experience of the context of the work and also experience of counselling women who had experienced trauma.

My original counselling model was person centred. When I had already been working at the refuge for some time I started an M.Sc. course in integrative psychotherapy at Metanoia Institute. I use an integrative model in working at the refuge. I am particularly influenced by gestalt and by the insights of self-psychology. In working with the women it seems to me that my task is to meet them where they are available to be met (Mackewn, 1997).

By definition, most of the women I work with have experienced trauma and many suffer from what Judith Herman (1992, p. 119) calls 'complex PTSD' (post-traumatic stress disorder). I need to adapt my counselling style to their needs. Paul Lockley (1999) discusses the difficulties of women who have experienced domestic violence in adapting to traditional counselling styles. In particular he discusses the effect of silence as a theoretical tool. My experience also is that I need to be more proactive in working in the refuge than I would otherwise be. Many women who have experienced violence have had silence used against them and therefore can be re-traumatized by clinical distance. The way I think about the work therefore is based on principles of respect for the woman's autonomy, which might be a very new experience for her. I think of my work as being an intersubjective and relational process. I believe that any relationship is affected by both parties and so believe that I am an active participant in the counselling relationship. I need to use myself in this relationship.

My advice to any counsellor wishing to gain paid work in the voluntary sector would be to get plenty of experience as a volunteer first, and to get a good idea of how the sector works. It is necessary to be highly self- motivating. Working in the refuge is actually very similar to my experience of working in private practice.

Client stories

Charlotte is 28 and has three children aged 11, 7 and 3. She has been in a violent relationship for 12 years but she finally left her partner because he started to hit the children. She came to the refuge two months ago. She is amazed at the freedom she has because her partner refused to allow her to go out without him. She was often locked in the house. He insisted that when she watched television with him she should always avert her eyes when there was any suggestion of sexual activity on the screen. He would constantly accuse her of having affairs with people like the postman. Charlotte says she doesn't care about herself but she couldn't let him hit the children. My work with Charlotte started very gently, and the building of the working alliance was slow. She had no real experience of being attended to by another person, as her mother died when she was six and she had been in a series of foster homes since then. Charlotte had been desperate to have a family of her own, and therefore she clung on for a long time to her violent relationship. She blamed herself for the violence done to her children. Charlotte needed positive strokes (Berne, 1975) for her ability to protect her children, then a building-up of her right to make choices now. Our work is still largely in the here and now, as I think that Charlotte does not yet have a strong enough sense of herself to examine many of the difficulties in her past. This may happen later.

Sophie is 54 and has been in a violent relationship for ten years. She has grown-up children who all live quite a long way away. She has had innumerable injuries and first came to the refuge when she discovered her partner had fractured her skull. She went back to him because he said that he would never hurt her again. He will not allow her to have any money of her own. At the moment she comes to see me in secret, and walks three miles, as she does not have the money for the bus fare. Often the refuge managers give her the money for a taxi home. She is exhausted and sometimes injured when she comes to me, but is not yet ready to leave her partner again. With Sophie I sense the despair of being a woman who is no longer young and feels unwanted. She believes that she needs a man to protect her, but finds it hard to accept that he has done the opposite of this. I feel frustration that she is not yet ready to leave, but know she must make this decision herself. When I first came to the refuge I would place subtle pressure on the women to leave violent relationships. When they talked about returning I would suggest we think carefully about this and look at all the options, but I did not do this when they told me they had made a definite decision never to go back. I am very aware of this now, and I hold Sophie's autonomy in mind. I tell her I do not believe that violence is acceptable, but whatever happens and whatever she decides she can come to see me. I worry about her safety.

Sarah is 22 and her partner set fire to their house when she threatened to leave him. She escaped with her three children, all aged under five, and came to the refuge. She is terrified that he will soon be released from prison and that he will find her. He has told her that she will never get away from him and he would rather kill her and the children. Our work is six weeks old and is based on working through the events of the fire. She finds this painful but feels she needs to face some of the issues and make decisions about how to keep herself and the children safe. She is many miles away from him, but still strongly fears he may find her. I think this is reality-based; we also work on practical strategies.

Avril is 28 and has four children. This is the fourth refuge she has been in because her partner keeps finding her and trying to persuade her to go back. She has gone back in the past but is determined not to this time. She has a supportive family but she is a long way from them. Avril is tormented by wondering why her partner was so violent, yet will not let her go. She feels as if she could understand if she were given a reason. We have worked on this, but I know she may never know what the reason was. My work with Avril has now moved into grief work: looking at the death of both her parents when she was a teenager. This is profound work for Avril.

My work with all of these women focuses on helping them to work on their own choices. Many of them do not know what their preferences are on the simplest level, such as whether they prefer tea or coffee. It is essential to build a strong working alliance (Bordin, 1979) and to establish trust. If there are any constraints to confidentiality (such as the revealing of harm to self or others) it is absolutely essential to be very clear about this from the outset. This client group can be easily re-traumatized and it is very important to build a relationship, which is based on fidelity and justice (BACP *Ethical Framework*, 2002).

A difficulty that arises in working in refuges, or in any residential facility, is that women are very aware that the counsellor sees other women who live in the refuge. Sometimes these others will be part of the material for that day, and the challenge is to hold this, knowing that later I may be seeing the same woman who is being spoken about. It seems useful to hold the principle of justice here: that an equal reception is given to all. I believe that the counsellor uses herself in the therapeutic process and therefore my reactions to the client are very important. I believe that counter-transference can give information in the counselling process. This is what Winnicott (1975) calls the objective counter-transference: Clarkson (1995) calls it the reactive counter-transference. There are times when I am very concerned about a woman, and times when I can barely stop myself from falling asleep in the session.

I think that in the context of a refuge the sleepy counter-transference is an interesting one to consider. Jungians would suggest that sleepiness in the counsellor is a response to the presence of the shadow. If we think in terms of personality adaptations or the categories of the *Diagnostic and Statistical Manual of the American Psychiatric Association (DSM IV)*, sleepiness in the counsellor is often associated with the schizoid position, which fundamentally means that the client has cut themselves off from their emotions, obeying the injunction of 'don't feel'. This is a common state for women who have experienced domestic violence. They are frequently desensitized and find it very difficult to connect to any emotions at all. The experience of counselling therefore may be frightening and a woman may have no wish to feel the emotion she has successfully repressed.

At the same time however, the experience of safety in the refuge may help her to begin to take stock of her experience. I think that gestalt insights around isolation and confluence help here. The abusive relationship may well have been a confluent one: the woman experiences herself as being a part of her partner and as being unable to operate apart from him. In the early days of separation she will still 'hear' him and may still conform to his rules. Later, however, she may come to see his absence as a liberation and will experience her separateness. This may, however, then lead to a sense of isolation. The continuum in Figure 4.1 from Sills, Fish and Lapworth illustrates this phenomenon.

Hopefully the contact experienced with the counsellor can model what non-coercive and non-threatening contact can be like, and allow the client to experiment and make new choices in the present.

Evaluation

The refuge where I work has been very fortunate in obtaining funding for counselling from the local council. Every year at funding application time I am asked to give details of the number of women I have seen in the year and the average number of sessions attended. To date, over the eight years I have worked in the refuge, I have seen 410 individual clients for an average of eight sessions each. This average is high for this setting, and especially considering that many women only attend one or two sessions. I am able to operate on a mixture of long- and short-term contracts, so although the average is eight, I sometimes see women for two or even three years. It is important to evaluate my contact with the client and to bring into awareness any preconceptions I may have about how the work should progress.

Counsellors working in refuges also need to evaluate their theoretical thinking about violence, as women can also be oppressed through theory. The very term 'domestic violence' has

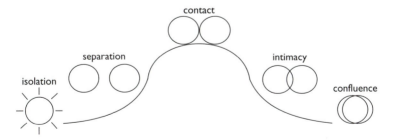

Figure 4.1 The confluence–isolation continuum
Reproduced with permission from Sills, C., Fish, S. and Lapworth, P. (1995) *Gestalt Counselling*. Bicester: Speechmark Publishing.

been criticized because the word 'domestic' sounds cosy, like a domestic animal.

There are many theoretical explanations for partner violence; I feel many of these are not particularly helpful. They include theories of gender-based aggression, theories stating that the absence of fathers in childhood causes men to be violent in relationships (Campbell, 1985), or concluding that it is due to inadequacies in mother–child bonding (Galenson, 1986). A popular theory is Seligman's beliefs on learned helplessness, quoted in Walker, 1978. His rather sad experiments on dogs, which were placed in dangerous situations and prevented from escaping, were used by Walker (ibid) to apply to women in violent situations. The cause of violence is seen as being in the victim and the circumstances of her childhood and adolescence. She is seen as giving power to men, seeing them as incapable of being stopped or thwarted. The 'cycle of violence' is described as including tension build-up, explosion, followed by contrition and a promise not to repeat the behaviour. Women who have experienced violence will recognize this cycle. Walker however, suggests that this cycle, when repeated, leads to a depressive syndrome known as 'battered woman syndrome'. This is marked by passivity, low self-esteem and a reluctance to seek help. The condition can be healed through therapy.

I think that this theory is potentially damaging to women. It does not take into account the fact that women experiencing violence are not helpless, but are often desperately seeking help. Their reactions to violence are normal ones, and I believe that the problem should be located in the perpetrator of violence, and not its victim.

Self-help books such as *Women Who Love Too Much* (Norwood, 1985) also blame women for violent relationships, in this case saying that women become addicted to such relationships because they love too much. I think that even postmodern and phenomenological positions may not be helpful in working with partner violence as they suggest that there is no objective reality and all positions are equal. Normally in counselling I would hold this position, but feel that in working with these issues it is essential to be able to place responsibility where it belongs. I suggest therefore that in this work the counsellor cannot hold a neutral position. Interested readers should consult Chapter 3 of Lockley (1999) for further theoretical discussion of partner violence. I do however need to say a word about feminist theories, as these inform my evaluation of my own practice. The background here is that women face problems arising from oppression in society and sex-role stereotyping. Radical feminist writers such as Burstow (1992) suggest that all women live continually in a context of violence and that the threat of this is used by society to subdue and control. Feminist help therefore focuses on the creation of options and the provision of practical help.

It can be argued that women stay in violent relationships not because of learned helplessness but because of the lack of easily accessible and acceptable alternatives. Increasingly in our society the alternatives that do exist are becoming more known, as domestic violence itself is given a higher profile. Traditionally, in Women's Aid refuges, help was given by volunteer workers, many of whom had themselves experienced violence in the past. There is now a movement towards increased 'professionalism', which can be helpful as long as the professionals concerned hold in mind the self-determination of the individual woman. For myself, as a professional working in a refuge, I think it is essential to keep in mind the possible effect of any theoretical ideas I might hold. I need to evaluate how they help me to honour and respect the efforts of women to find a way to keep themselves and their children safe.

My model

Over my eight years of practice I have developed a way of thinking about offering therapy to women who have experienced partner violence. I think that women often start from a position of disintegration, which needs holding and the experience of safety. This ties in with the feminist position of offering practical help first. From there if women come to counselling they can make choices about their lives which can lead to a decision to change. There will be necessary action and maintenance here. At this point I borrow from the cycle of change (Prochaska and DiClemente, 1982). When this point is worked through there is a further decision about whether to continue in counselling. Here I borrow from Rowan (2000), who talks about two types of therapy: adjustment therapy, to help the person to deal better with their circumstances, and liberation therapy, which is life-changing therapeutic discovery, possibly over many months or years. Either of these choices can lead to integration. Many of the women in the refuge are able to work further on adjustment issues and reach a point where they are happy with their choices, fewer of them are able to undertake deep work on themselves, but some do choose this.

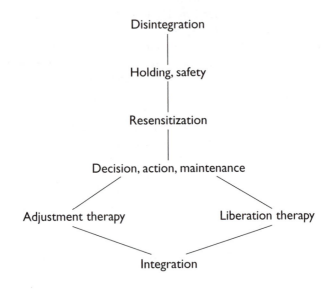

Figure 4.2 A model of therapy for women who have experienced partner violence

Continuing professional development

I am paid by my refuge as a self-employed counsellor, so ongoing professional development is seen as my own responsibility. I also work in other settings, in private practice, and I am senior lecturer in counselling at a further education (FE) college. I therefore see my ongoing development as meeting needs spanning these roles. It is part of the requirement to maintain my British Association for Counselling and Psychotherapy (BACP) registered counsellor status that I undertake at least 30 hours of continuing professional development (CPD) per year. I do this by attending conferences and training events and also by committing myself to longer-term courses. In the time that I have been counselling at the refuge I have undertaken an M.Sc. in integrative psychotherapy, and now a diploma in supervision.

Conditions of work

I see my work at the refuge as part of a feminist commitment that I have held for many years. The refuge where I work is very committed to feminist principles and this is an ideal personal fit for me. I am influenced by the principles of feminist counselling outlined by Eichenbaum and Orbach (1985), Chaplin (1989) and Burstow (1992).

In general the voluntary sector can be a chaotic place in which to work. It is often underfunded and therefore run largely by volunteers or by overworked lone paid workers. It is important that counsellors in this setting understand this and can work with the difficulties that sometimes arise through people trying to help but not always understanding the consequences of their actions. The incident, above, of the extra client being booked in is an example of this. Often counsellors may find that they are trying to find a client for their appointment, only to be told, 'Oh, she left last Tuesday!' Sudden leaving with no opportunity for a 'good ending' is common.

Future developments

Counselling literature has largely disregarded the issues of working with women around partner violence. There is a good deal of emphasis currently in the media around awareness of domestic violence, and I think that it is helpful for counsellors to consider the issues involved. We may also need to question the use of 'normal' counselling practice. I have already discussed the issue that many abused women may find silence a great threat and may need a more proactive counsellor. I have also thought a lot about the use of empathy – and indeed all of the core conditions (Rogers, 1990) – in this kind of therapy. There may be dangers for abused women in receiving too much empathy: immersion in their experience may cause flooding and be simply too much. I think there is a need for what I call 'common-sense empathy', which seems to have common ground with the gestalt idea of 'inclusion': the moving backward and forward between my own experience and that of the client. (Mackewn, 1997, p. 86) This is somewhat allied with what Casement (1985) calls 'trial identification'.

We need to consider further the provision of counselling in the community: for women who are perhaps still in violent situations. This is something that the refuge in which I work is doing, in terms of enabling outreach workers to provide help, advice and support for women still in violent situations. I personally believe that such support is best provided to the woman only. Some counselling around violence in partner relationships advocates working with the two people in the partnership. I think that in most situations this has an adverse effect on the woman being able to express herself and be honest about her feelings.

In writing this chapter I am very aware that I have not referred at all to partner abuse perpetrated on men, or to abuse in lesbian relationships. Both of these are real issues but beyond my scope here.

This chapter gives a very brief introduction to some of the issues involved in working in a refuge, or indeed in any feminist organization. There have been considerable changes recently in how partner violence has been seen and dealt with in the community and in the future these may impact on the way in which refuges are organized. I hope that this chapter has given you, the reader, a sense of the work and an idea of whether or not you would want to be involved in it.

Ten top tips

Generic tips:

- Be patient!
- Volunteer first: this could lead to a paid opportunity.

Context specific tips:

- Find out about the voluntary sector in your area, by attending relevant meetings or talks.
- Be prepared to work independently.
- Seek out good supervision from someone who understands partner violence.

- Think about your views on partner violence and how these fit in with your theory of counselling.
- Challenge your own beliefs about violence and what women 'should' do.
- Consider how you feel about working in a relatively chaotic environment and think about what this may mean for your clients.
- Contact lots of refuges to find out about counselling opportunities.
- Think about what I have said above about 'common-sense empathy'.

? Do you agree that some forms of counselling need to be more politicized, and that the phenomenological method may not apply to working in a refuge?

Bibliography

American Psychiatric Association (2000) *DSM IV TR* (*Diagnostic and Statistical Manual of Mental Disorders*, 4th edn, text revision). American Psychiatric Association.

BACP (2002) *Ethical Framework for Good Practice in Counselling and Psychotherapy*. Rugby: BACP.

Berne, E. (1975) *Transactional Analysis in Psychotherapy*. London: Souvenir.

Bordin, E.S. (1979) 'The generalisability of the psychoanalytic concept of the Working Alliance', *Psychotherapy: Theory Research and Practice*, **16**(3), 252–60.

Burstow, B. (1992) *Radical Feminist Therapy*. London: Sage.

Campbell, A. (1985) 'Beating of wives: a cross-cultural perspective.', *Victimology*, **10**, 174.

Casement, P. (1985) *On Learning from the Patient*. London: Routledge.

Chaplin, J. (1989) *Feminist Counselling in Action*. London: Sage.

Clarkson, P. (1995) *The Therapeutic Relationship*. London: Whurr.

Eichenbaum, L. and Orbach, S. (1985) *Understanding Women*. London: Penguin.

Galenson, E. (1986) 'Some thoughts about infant psychopathology and aggressive development', *International Review of Psychoanalysis*, **13**, 349.

Herman, J. (1992) *Trauma and Recovery*. USA: Basic Books.

Lockley, P. (1999) *Counselling Women in Violent Relationships*. London: Free Association Books.

Mackewn, J. (1997) *Developing Gestalt Counselling*. London: Sage.

Norwood, R. (1985) *Women Who Love Too Much*. Pocket Books.

Prochaska, J. and DiClemente, C. (1982) 'Transtheoretical therapy: towards a more integrative model of change', *Psychotherapy: Theory Research and Practice*, **19**, 276–88.

Rogers, C.R. (1990) 'A theory of therapy personality and interpersonal relationships', in H. Kirschenbaum and V. L. Henderson (eds), *The Carl Rogers Reader*. London: Constable.

Rowan, J. (2000) 'Back to basics: two kinds of therapy', *Counselling*, **21**(2), 76–8.

Sills, C., Fish, S. and Lapworth, P. (1995) *Gestalt Counselling*. Bicester: Speechmark Publishing.

Walker, L.P. (1978) 'Battered women and learned helplessness', *Victimology*, **2**, 525.

Winnicott, D. (1975) *Through Paediatrics to Psychoanalysis: Collected Papers*. UK: Hogarth Press.

5

Counselling in a Voluntary Sector Counselling and Social Work Setting

Julia Layton

My work combines therapeutic counselling with training and supervising both counselling and social work trainees, and job sharing an operations management post. I do this during the three days per week I work at a voluntary sector counselling and social work agency in south-east London.

A typical day

The centre occupies all three floors of a converted Victorian house, with the main office on the first floor. I arrive just after 9 am, and collecting the post on my way upstairs, I greet my colleagues. We deal with any urgent answerphone messages, and generally prepare ourselves for the day. The room is quiet and tidy. Soon there will be three social work students, three counselling students, two associate counsellors and four core staff team members in the building, all busy, with reception work, counselling, client follow-up and referral work, or with management tasks. The noise level will undoubtedly rise!

The entry phone buzzes, and two clients are shown to the tiny waiting room; they will normally be seen exactly on time, for the 'therapeutic hour' of 50 minutes. The post includes referrals from a GP and two duty professionals from the local community mental health teams: the clients referred in this way may have already contacted us to ask for counselling, or this may be the first we have heard of them. Before my first client is due, in my 'reception' role I take three phone calls: a counselling trainee wanting a placement; a local self-help group asking if a couple can refer themselves to the free service, and a very agitated person, who speaks at such speed I can hardly get a word in to respond. She wants an appointment immediately! I manage to discover that her community psychiatric nurse (CPN) has told her he will refer her here for counselling. She urges me to contact him and finally agrees to ring us again at our designated referral time.

I see two clients, one having experienced childhood abuse and domestic violence, the other a young person with a background in local authority care, feeling very anxious about the future. Then I spend one and a half hours supervising my social work student who has clients with problems ranging from depression and self-harm, to the need for help with sorting out a benefits and housing tangle. She is feeling quite angry with one of them, and we talk, amongst other things, about how this may help her to understand how he feels. Lunch is next, though by the time I have fixed one of the toilet cisterns, I have 30 minutes to get a sandwich and chat with trainees and associates before staff supervision. One experienced colleague, working with a person seeking asylum, is very distressed by her client's account of a terrifying ordeal as a child; she needs some supervision time. Another aspect of client work gets us discussing payment: if cost equals value, what is a free service worth? I talk about using a solution-focused approach with a client who found it hard to imagine change: the 'smallest steps' idea really seemed to help. My next client does not turn up, so I write him a letter wondering whether, as he has now missed two chances for an assessment interview, he has changed his mind about counselling. Next, I telephone the CPN as promised; he is not there, but our caller apparently came into their centre at lunchtime. The CPN will ring me, I am told. I feel relieved, as I had been concerned at the woman's obvious distress.

I begin to update my client files with today's contact (in brief, and factually, because our clients have always been entitled to see what is written about them, and the Data Protection Act now enshrines this: client files contain records of all contact, specific action taken and risk situations, together with counsellors' reports, letters, and so on, which are confidential to the agency and kept secure in the filing system). I am interrupted by a client telephoning to speak directly to her counsellor, who isn't available. She sounds angry, and I spend a few moments talking to her before getting a message to her counsellor. It is now nearly time to leave. I have just started my student supervision notes when the CPN I rang earlier telephones and we have a useful conversation about the appropriateness of counselling for his patient at present. I leave the building half an hour later.

My route in

With a background in hospital and education welfare work in the early 1970s, I went on to qualify in social work. I worked part-time as a youth worker, and as a tutor in adult and further education (FE). I also became a volunteer telephone counsellor, and group co-facilitator, for a cancer support group. Whilst teaching adults, I undertook a part-time course in basic counselling skills with tutors from the Westminster Pastoral Foundation, then during my eight years as a part-time FE tutor went on to gain a diploma in counselling and supervision from Roehampton. When a chance arose to apply for part-time counselling work in a newly set-up voluntary sector centre, I felt lucky enough to be in the right place at the right time: I'd had an eclectic counselling training, experience as both counsellor and client, and a useful history of social work and statutory experience, understanding risk assessment and the need for medical and psychiatric consultancy. Since offering placements to social work students brought funding, it was also useful to be able to supervise them. After three years counselling part time, and five years full time, for the centre, I finally applied for, and gained, accreditation with the British Association for Counselling and Psychotherapy (BACP).

The centre was a phoenix, rising from the ashes of redundancy: a larger voluntary organization had shed its counselling and social work staff to concentrate its resources on other mental health services. We had initial funding from the local authority for only three months, so there was great pressure to organize a referral system, and deliver an effective free counselling service, to a diverse range of borough residents whose means do not allow them access to counselling in the private sector. The approaches used in the counselling work were then, as now, as varied as the experience of the workers, but with a leaning to the psychodynamic. My own integrative counselling stance, amalgamating much of the knowledge and many of the skills gained over 30 years, owes something to the (then) psychoanalytically based casework nature of social work training, but also much to the realization in most helping professions that contextual factors (social, economic, political, cultural) mediate all interventions.

It became clear early on that no one approach would do for all, and that a variety of ways of working renders us more flexible and more able to meet a variety of individual needs, in order to be a truly user-centred service. Demand for services constantly outstrips resources; we are the only local service offering long-term counselling, and by definition, if this were all we offered, there would be long intervals when no further clients could be accepted. Early in my work for the centre, I agreed to train in solution-focused brief therapy (paid for by the centre, but undertaken in my own time), and found this filled a gap in my own counselling 'tool bag'. I also attended a short course on single session therapy, since I had observed that a significant proportion of the centre's clients, for a number of reasons, came to one counselling session only. Thus I can use a variety of interventions, including family and couples counselling, group work, and different kinds of short-term individual work. Others in the team also provide such variety, offering in addition a sensitive frontline telephone referral system designed to assess whether counselling is the most appropriate intervention.

A client story

Leonie referred herself for counselling when dealing with the aftermath of living with a violent, substance-misusing husband. She wanted to make changes for herself and her young son (whose behaviour was concerning her) and wanted to become more assertive. Because of her circumstances, and the fact that her son could be assessed as a child both 'at risk', and 'in need', we offered her the help of a trainee social worker, whom I was supervising, who would monitor the child protection and safety issues, as well as provide a 'listening space' to Leonie, and organize crèche provision for her son while she attended the centre. These weekly sessions lasted three months. Soon afterwards Leonie was rehoused, and her husband disappeared.

A year later, Leonie re-referred herself in deep distress. She had been diagnosed with cancer. Her husband had returned 'to look after her', having asked his son on the telephone for the address, and moved in. In her vulnerable and stressed state, and partly because her son had been pleased to see his father, she had been unable to deny him access, and agreed to his staying 'temporarily'. I agreed to see her, and we arranged an open-ended contract of weekly counselling sessions. Leonie used my help to understand her feelings and figure out what she needed to do about her husband, as he reverted to his previous alcohol and substance misuse, and behaved in an unpredictable and intimidating way. The police were called on several occasions, and finally after a physical assault on Leonie, she went to court for an injunction, and her husband disappeared again.

Leonie's illness continued to take its toll, and it was particularly hard while she was dealing with police and the domestic violence unit (DVU) alongside receiving chemotherapy, followed by radiotherapy. Her son became by turns withdrawn and angry with her; he had started school, and was spending a lot of time with his supportive grandmother. Obviously deeply affected by his father's violence, his mother's illness and distress, he was experiencing inner turmoil and conflict. Neither Leonie nor her mother was quite sure how to help him express and manage his feelings, and they were in some confusion about what they could share with each other. There were profound fears for the future, both existential and practical.

Just over a year after I began working with Leonie, and two and a half years after her original referral to our centre, she died. I had

seen her for more than 40 sessions, about five of these with her little
boy. Our last counselling session took place by her hospital bed.
She asked for my help in writing a letter to her son. 'I know what
I want to say to him, but you will know what not to say'. She also
asked me if I would continue to help him for a while. Thus it was
that, having attended her funeral, and with his agreement, I saw
Leonie's son at roughly monthly intervals for almost a year. When
we ended, he had retrieved some of his cut-off feelings, and could
once again cry and show affection for his aunt and grandmother, as
well as demonstrate his anger. In addition, I saw his grandmother
(Leonie's mother) for several sessions of bereavement counselling
some months after Leonie's death.

The work with Leonie and her family happened on several different levels: supportive, practical, empowering and therapeutic –
reflecting the centre's function within the community, and the diversity of its possible approaches and interventions. Her first contract
with the centre had given Leonie an experience of support and
helpful challenge; the second, reliable and steady containment in a
chaotic and uncertain time, and a secure base from which to
explore her fears. Necessarily, the counselling 'frame' had to be
appropriately flexible: I was able to visit when Leonie couldn't
make the journey to the centre, but we adhered to the usual time
and length of session. There was also a 'safe space' to offer counselling to Leonie and her son together. I acted partly as facilitator,
helping them to speak directly to each other about painful things,
and partly as model, showing different ways to communicate,
through drawings, toys and stories.

I was always aware of the social work aspects of the case, particularly when the statutory social worker allocated to the family
went on extended compassionate leave, and was not replaced for
several months. I was able to write reports for Leonie's application
for disabled living allowance, and for a Children Act 1989 Section
8 order, when requested by both Leonie and her solicitor. This
ensured that Leonie's husband would not be able to remove his son
summarily from the care of his grandmother and aunt, should
Leonie die. As I was a counsellor operating from a voluntary sector
agency known to provide both counselling and social work services, this was both possible and acceptable. In the BACP's *Ethical
Framework for Good Practice in Counselling and Psychotherapy*, I
note that 'if work with clients requires the provision of additional

services operating in parallel with counselling or psychotherapy, the availability of such services ought to be taken into account, as their absence may constitute a significant limitation.' (BACP, 2002, p. 5). The centre provided an easily accessible free local service for Leonie and her family, offering a crèche, and visits when needed, as well as more appropriately holistic counselling than the police DVU, the hospital oncology ward, social services, or possibly even the child therapist offered by Leonie's GP.

Leonie's hopes for counselling included developing confidence in herself as a person capable of dealing with the difficulties of her life, of being a good enough mother to her son, and of making sense of thoughts, feelings and experiences, both past and present, in a way which helped her to understand herself better and face the future. Both managerial and external consultant supervision helped me to offer an appropriate service to Leonie, by monitoring my maintenance of boundaries in terms of confidentiality and involvement, and keeping the counselling perspective. My supervisors were able to remind me of knowledge and skills I possessed (for example, in systemic family work, counselling people with cancer, previous direct work with children). They helped me perceive possible projective identification, and offered support when my feelings mirrored Leonie's despair as she realized she was dying.

This example demonstrates the freedom within our work setting to respond to client need in an adaptable and holistic way. The ethos of the centre allows the use of a broad range of skills and knowledge, and also recognizes and values the developmental and emotional needs of its clients and workers sufficiently to protect and 'hold' them, providing the structure that enables this freedom: a structure based on the counselling framework. This has meant giving careful thought to issues of confidentiality, interdisciplinary boundaries, and the use of power. If other tasks like social work or advocacy are undertaken with, or on behalf of, some clients, such interventions are with clients' consent and participation. These often confirm or validate clients' own wishes and actions in an empowering way, and play a significant part in the therapeutic work. The themes of depression and oppression, domestic violence and abuse, substance misuse, illness, trauma and difficult relationships, addressed in my 'client story', are typical of the range of problems brought by many of the centre's clients.

Evaluation

Continuous monitoring and evaluation of our counselling work takes place through managerial and clinical supervision, and also through the quality assurance system. Each core staff member has responsibility for a 'quality' area (for example, finance, service delivery) and has development targets to aim for; trainees are encouraged to become involved in this ongoing work of the centre. The format of the client closing report demonstrates changes and outcomes in the work on ending, and these may be compared with the goals and targets set jointly by client and worker at assessment. It's important to note here that if information from client assessment, interim or closing reports (which all have the same agency format whoever writes them), is taken outside the centre, for example, by trainees for course evaluation purposes, it either has personally identifiable details removed, or permission is sought from the client.

Counselling (and counsellor) effectiveness is further assessed by service users themselves, who, when their counselling has ended, are sent user questionnaires in which they may choose whether they identify themselves. This short questionnaire has questions about referral, waiting time, the counselling relationship and changes experienced 'since undertaking counselling'. Monitoring returns required by our local authority funders indicate numbers of client sessions offered and attended, and also give details of referral sources, age, gender, sexual orientation and ethnic origin, whether low income, and broad types of problems involved, especially those concerned with risk, for example, deliberate self-harm, domestic violence or child protection. There is a weekly supervisors' group, where the learning and expectations of trainees are established and evaluated, allocation of clients to trainees is considered, and concerns are aired within a confidential group.

As we are a voluntary agency without a statutory obligation to work with everyone who refers, it is important to show that we offer equal opportunities and practise in an anti-discriminatory way, looking out for unmet need, particularly where oppression has been experienced. We struggle to balance the need for accountability, transparency and meeting targets, with the preservation of high-quality work, and the reflective space that enables and enriches it. Some service users have rejected, or been rejected by, other agencies because they are seen as difficult to work with. Positive feedback, as well as a distinct lack of complaints, helps to demonstrate that we are providing an acceptable and worthwhile service to most people.

Continuing professional development

Trainees attend a weekly continuing professional development (CPD) group for an hour on Thursday afternoons. It is open to all staff, trainees and associates in the agency involved in service delivery. The centre makes use of the expertise of all its workers in this weekly in-house training, which helps us to develop our skills as researchers and trainers, is less expensive than buying in training, and also offers time for reflection, where people can meet and share aspects of their work. Some sessions will be eligible to fulfil categories 1 and 4 of the BACP's CPD criteria. There is no specific funding for CPD, but expenses may be paid out of a limited training budget for staff to attend relevant external courses, particularly if these can be related to enhanced outcomes for the centre in terms of effectiveness, passing on the results in the CPD group, or attracting further funding. There are times when specific training is offered to management committee, staff and trainees by outside trainers, such as for equal opportunities policy implementation. Some counselling trainees choose to continue their professional development by undertaking additional tasks for the centre, such as referral taking, where there would be some observation and coaching, followed by supervised frontline work. This is a way in which newly trained and qualified counsellors can be assisted to compete more effectively in the job market.

Conditions of work

The core staff team, normally comprising two full-time, and two part-time posts, including those of manager and operations manager, are paid on the basis of a five-day 37.5-hour week, at local authority rates for roughly equivalent work, from the borough's social services budget. We meet weekly for two hours' peer group supervision, and this is supplemented by individual external consultant supervision at our own expense, though time is allowed for this in working hours. An external consultant facilitates discussion of team and agency issues, about three times a year.

Centre staff combine counselling with, variously, training, consultancy and supervisory duties, referral and allocation work, and management and operational matters, including practical housekeeping and environmental issues, ordering supplies and repairs, and keeping financial and administrative affairs up to date. There is no funding for dedicated administrative support, but we are able to pay for a few hours of bookkeeping and accountancy help. It is clear that, as with any combining of roles where there could be conflict at the interface between them (for example, where different professional approaches seem to indicate different responses), I need to be vigilant, and remain aware at all times of my ethical responsibilities and obligations to clients, colleagues and agency. In the BACP's *Ethical Framework* (op. cit.), the sections 'Keeping trust' (p. 6), 'Working in teams' (p. 8), and 'Providing clients with adequate information' (p. 9) give particularly useful guidance for such conflicts, which in fact arise only rarely.

The team sees 50 clients a week, on average, in the free counselling service, and the associates counsel more than 70, often in the evenings. Trainees are an invaluable resource for the centre and its clients, especially when they are reliable, enthusiastic, motivated to learn and committed to their work, and when they enter further into the life of the centre by offering specialist knowledge or skills, for example, to the CPD group. Trainees pay a contribution for in-house supervision, and generally see clients in the free service, during daytime working hours.

Associate counsellors and psychotherapists are qualified practitioners, sometimes on the way to gaining advanced qualifications; they have external supervisors, and charge their clients on a sliding scale according to income. Thus, because they pay room hire charges based on what clients pay them, associates can offer a low-cost evening counselling service for people with low incomes who could not afford the full cost of private therapy. The associates benefit from a flow of referrals, the on-site support of colleagues, and the administrative resources available. Clients benefit from greater choice, and the centre can be an inclusive community resource, lessening the chance that those using the free service will be marginalized. Also, given the holding environment of the centre, and the potential for immediate consultation, and emergency cover for illness and holiday breaks, associates have the opportunity to see more vulnerable clients than they might, if working in isolation. This adds value for clients if it prevents them entering the statutory mental health system.

We make efforts to mirror the diversity of our client population in the wider team, valuing experience of difference as important to us and to the service. This is partly because clients deserve a choice, particularly if they have experienced oppression through racism, homophobia or violence, and partly because we want to help a wide variety of people to develop their employment chances. The centre is oversubscribed by both clients and trainees, so we try to devise fair means of selection, which take into account the needs and resources of the centre at the time, as well as those of the clients, trainees and prospective associates. Some trainees go on to become associates, though progression is not automatic: the breadth and depth of what people can offer, as well as commitment to the ethos and running of the centre, are important.

One of the disadvantages of such a diverse working group is the potential for misunderstanding each other, and our different ways of working. The very busy environment also has its limitations: although reflective space is valued and protected, the opportunities for the informal interaction with colleagues which can often alleviate the stress of working in the mental health field (Brady et al., 1995, p. 11) can actually be experienced as stressful by counsellors who prefer a quiet, calm and reflective atmosphere. A limitation for trainee counsellors is that although the centre can generally contain and help the kind of clients who increasingly refer (or are referred) to the centre since the 1990 NHS and Community Care Act was implemented, they are often rather more vulnerable, or complex to work with, than is suitable for counsellors near the beginning of their training.

The centre is interested in counsellors who are willing to problem solve for the centre, as well as their clients, and who are able to take part in providing training and supervision. Experience of case management, including assessment and risk, and possession of a range of counselling skills are also valuable. Attributes that help counsellors in this setting are resilience and a certain robustness in groups, idealism tempered to a realistic level, and experience of good supportive personal and family relationships. And it seems particularly important to be able to maintain curiosity and manage differences among colleagues in a spirit of ongoing learning.

At its best, the setting can provide the support, stimulation and challenge of a kind of family, with authoritative leadership and the space for allowing diversity, good communication, growth and development. When we attend to the dynamics and processes of the organization, and those between the individuals who work in or attend the centre, we have the chance to learn from each other without anyone owning all the expertise or all the need for help.

Future developments

The service has been operating for 11 years, and will continue to develop. This means responding to changes at all levels: national, local and personal. We undertook project work in the past, for example, with male perpetrators of domestic violence, and with children where there were family alcohol problems. Now we work in partnership, for example, with London Marriage Guidance for couple and relationship counselling, with Professional Advice Counselling and Education (PACE), for counselling on issues of sexuality, and with Stopover, a local housing charity, offering counselling to young homeless people. In the pipeline are other possible partnerships, for instance with a local mediation project.

With emerging emphasis on evaluating the outcomes of counselling interventions, and evidence from the Department of Health's document: *Treatment Choice in Psychological Therapies and Counselling* (2001) outlining the ways in which counselling interventions can be effective (for example, pp. 36–7), it is clear that the future needs to include new ways of assessing the centre's services. We have recently undergone training in 'Improving quality through outcome monitoring' with Patrick Donlan (Q-Trek Social Care Consultancy UK) who reminded us that 'what we do, and what we achieve are two different things'. We hope that using the database to monitor outcomes by qualitative means will help us to become more aware of where our counselling is most, and least, effective. We may need to update our skills in more cognitively-based approaches, which the DoH document mentioned above recommends as being useful, for instance in working with clients suffering from depression, anxiety, post-traumatic stress and eating disorders. Continuing erosion of public sector services through reduction in government funding means that a widening range of service users, experiencing increasingly profound problems, will probably be calling on our services, and we need to be able to offer them the most appropriate and best possible service, whilst looking after ourselves well in order to do so. It is unlikely that our funding will be increased, so we must continue our search for creative solutions, and utilize fully the therapeutic, administrative and life skills of everyone who works at the centre.

Those interested in working in this type of setting need to be able to manage the tension between being flexible and 'ready for anything', and keeping appropriate boundaries which accord with the approach used and the work being done. The realistic position is that core staff have many tasks other than counselling, and ultimately I believe that this is positive: working continuously at the interface of inner and outer worlds, recognising apparently unlimited demand and apportioning necessarily limited resources, is stressful. Windy Dryden and Dave Mearns (Dryden, 1992, pp. 56 and 69) both note in their 'hard-earned lessons' the importance for them of counselling as a part-time activity. It may be that we can be of most help to our clients when we relish the challenge of the different tasks involved in keeping our organization running smoothly, yet dynamically.

Ten top tips

Generic tips:

- Learn quickly about other local resources, so you don't see yourself, or the agency, as clients' only resource for help.
- Be prepared to see very vulnerable clients *and* know your limitations.

Context specific tips:

- Be accountable and responsible: use agency policies and procedures to keep paperwork up to date.
- Be prepared to gain varied experience, but not much money.
- Keep a space for reflecting on your motivation and your role in the team.

- Be creative: dip into the pool of knowledge available in the setting, and think what other skills you might learn.
- Actively look for gaps in the service and think how you could help.
- Get to know as many people in the agency as possible, network, go to meetings and check the noticeboard for in-house and external training events.
- Offer to run a CPD workshop.
- Offer to help with the routine jobs that no one wants to do, but someone has to: you will be so appreciated!

How far should we consider concepts such as 'outcomes', and 'achievements' in evaluating a publicly funded counselling service? Will measuring counselling outcomes reduce the service offered by counsellors to merely identifying and fulfilling target objectives?

Bibliography

BACP (2002) *Ethical Framework for Good Practice in Counselling and Psychotherapy*. Rugby: BACP.

Brady, J., Healy, F., Norcross, J. and Guy, J. (1995) 'Stress in counsellors: an integrative research review.', in W. Dryden (ed.), *The Stresses of Counselling in Action*. London: Sage.

DHSS (2001) 'Department of Health evidence-based clinical practice guideline', in *Treatment Choice in Psychological Therapies and Counselling*. DHSS.

Dryden, W. (1992) Chapter 4 in *Hard-Earned Lessons from Counselling in Action*, ed. W. Dryden. London: Sage.

Dryden, W. and Feltham, C. (eds) (1992) *Brief Counselling*. Milton Keynes: Open University Press.

Mearns, D. (1992) Chapter 6 in *Hard-Earned Lessons from Counselling in Action*, ed. W. Dryden. London: Sage.

Seden, J. (1999) *Counselling Skills in Social Work Practice*. Milton Keynes: Open University Press.

Skynner, R. (1989) *Institutes and How to Survive Them*. London: Routledge.

Section II

HEALTH SECTOR

6

Introduction to Counselling in Healthcare Settings

Pat Seber, Chair, FHCP

Counselling in primary, secondary or tertiary healthcare settings is not new. For over 30 years there has been a body of literature written on counselling in the healthcare sector by experienced counsellors from different theoretical standpoints for example, Marsh and Barr (1975), Pietroni and Vaspe (2000) and Thomas, Davidson and Rance (2001).

From the research, and my own experience, it all began in an ad hoc manner. Counsellors were appointed here and there as someone with an interest saw the need and found the budget to cover the costs. Sometimes it was because of a perceived social need in one particular area. At other times there was pressure from existing healthcare professionals who found that they were being asked to care for the emotional and psychological needs of the patients, as well as the physical ones, something for which they were not trained.

Both doctors and patients welcomed these counsellor appointments. This was due in part to the changes in attitude as to the usefulness of the purely 'medical model' approach to healthcare and a growing appreciation of a more holistic view of health which takes into account the interconnectedness of the patient's body, mood, lifestyle, spiritual nature and environment (Davy, 1999). Western medicine had managed over time to reduce medicine to simply 'the body', leaving other parts of the individual to be cared for by anyone willing to take on the responsibility. This is also paralleled by distrust from patients of some forms of medication, particularly antidepressants, believing them to be addictive (Churchill et al., 2000). All this meant that counselling could be seen as fundamentally different from, yet complementary to, medicine.

The arrival of New Labour led to plans to reform the National Health Service (NHS) outlined in the *New NHS: Modern, Dependable* (Department of Health, 1997). The implementation of these new policies and structures has led to fundamental changes in the ways in which healthcare is delivered including the provision of counselling services.

Given this background if you are considering counselling in healthcare as a career you might ask the following questions.

What is counselling in healthcare?

Counselling opportunities in healthcare are many and varied. Each setting has its own culture and ethos. Basic skills need to be adapted to the particular context in which the counsellor operates and may require specialized training. The Faculty of Healthcare Counsellors and Psychotherapists (FHCP), part of the British Association for Counselling and Psychotherapy (BACP) states that:

> Counselling is a distinct psychological discipline and counsellors employed in healthcare is a distinct professional body not to be confused with any other healthcare worker who may use counselling skills within their role. As such counsellors working in healthcare are the designated professionals, qualified and trained to offer the provision of counselling to patients in the NHS, in accordance with their clinical assessment.
>
> (FHCP, 2003)

Unlike other professions within the NHS counsellors do not yet have national training standards. However the qualification referred to above is a diploma in counselling preferably from an accredited BACP course showing a balance of skills, theory (450 hours) and counselling practice (120 hours minimum) within a training placement. The training placement is essential for the development of the trainee. It is here the trainee puts into practice what they have learned in the classroom. In this situation the technical skills of counselling are sharpened through the exposure of the trainee practitioner to the personality and problems of a *real client*. Here the trainee grapples with the building blocks of the therapeutic alliance upon which the counselling relationship stands or falls.

BACP/FHCP has published guidelines for trainers on placements in healthcare settings. They believe that it is the responsibility of the training establishment to support student counsellors on placements through mentoring and counselling supervision (Sharman, 2003). Supervision is a requirement of the professional bodies for the protection of the client and the well-being of the counsellor. The priority for both the profession and training establishments should be to train counsellors to the highest possible standard to enable them to work in any environment without restriction. This means that *all* counsellors, not only those in healthcare, should know something about risk assessment and common mental health problems, such as depression and anxiety, as well as the appropriate counselling interventions and medical treatment and this should be reflected in the training curriculum. As with all other healthcare professionals, counsellors who obtain work in a specialist area after qualifying, will find that the specialist training can best be provided 'in-house' on the job and tailored to meet the specifics of patients (clients, customers, users).

Where are these counselling opportunities to be found in healthcare settings?

These range from the GP surgery, to the hospital ward, into the community through hospices, the voluntary sector and private healthcare providers. In each of these places counsellors can be found working as part of a team to improve the health of the individual. The National Health Service is the largest single employer of counsellors in the country. The Primary Care Trusts, Mental Health Trusts and Hospital Trusts are the employing bodies and within these the majority of counsellors are to be found in primary care.

In 1993, in England and Wales approximately 31 per cent of general practices employed an 'on-site' counsellor (Sibbald et al., 1993). By 1998 this had risen to 51 per cent (Mellor-Clarke, Simms-Ellis and Burton, 2001). It would be fair to say that most counsellors working in this context are likely to be 'generalists' (although there are exceptions, that is, drugs and alcohol) dealing with a wide variety of presenting problems. The GP counsellor offers counselling usually on a one-to-one basis to patients whose symptoms range from mild to severe depending upon the complexity of the problem. Research material frequently states that counsellors work (only) with clients who have 'mild to moderate (mental) health problems' but in my experience this is not a true representation of what counsellors do. Colleagues and I see many people who are more towards the severe and enduring end of mental health difficulties. Indeed it is not unusual for a psychiatrist to refer a patient back to the GP with a recommendation that the patient is seen by the in-house counsellor. The diversity of people and problems all make for a very interesting and exciting working life.

In hospital settings the counsellor will become more of a specialist in one particular area, through working on a specific ward or department such as maternity and gynaecology, coronary, oncology, A & E and of course psychology where the degree of distress of patients is often acute. That psychological distress, as well as physical pain, is generated through trauma or physical illness such as losing a baby or having a life-threatening illness is more readily accepted than it was. Therefore offering counselling alongside medical treatment when these situations occur frequently produces a better outcome for the patient.

In the voluntary sector the hospice movement has been a key area in which there has been an acceptance of the need to provide psychological intervention to the dying and their relatives. Increasingly, paid counsellors are being used in hospices to support the excellent work of the volunteer counsellor.

Elsewhere in the voluntary sector there is a great variety of organizations working to help those suffering as a result of disability, illness or a life event, from autism and heart disease to sexual abuse. They often bridge the gap between what the statutory bodies can provide for patients and what patients may actually need. Many of these organizations offer the placements already mentioned to counsellors in training while employing a professional counsellor to provide services to clients, and where appropriate train and supervise the volunteers.

Finally, the private sector has seen an expansion of counselling services relating to abortion, plastic surgery, genetics and fertility as well as a wide variety of private hospitals including those specializing in treating addictions.

Given that there are a wide range of places and institutions where counselling takes place it is worth looking at when and how this is provided.

When and how is counselling provided?

When counselling is offered to patients, it is very much governed by the location in which the counsellor is working. The majority of counsellors who are engaged in the NHS are part time and work during the hours of 9 am to 5 pm. In certain situations counsellors may be part of a team that is on call 24-hours a day to provide a service to rape victims or the relatives of the seriously injured or dying. In the voluntary sector there is a wide variety of service delivery times and locations, reflecting the complexity of the sector. For example it may be that counselling is provided in the evenings because the majority of the client group are at work during the day. The private sector tends to deliver services at similar times to the NHS.

Counselling services in the NHS are often provided by a health-care trust and are therefore embedded in the local structures. They may be independently managed counselling services or form part of a multidisciplinary team including members from other professions. The voluntary sector has a wide variety of delivery systems, from large agencies providing major services on contract to the NHS, to small charities where there is one counsellor working alone with only his or her line manager to relate to. Whatever the mode of delivery, all counsellors should have clinical supervision from a qualified counselling supervisor to ensure ethical practice.

More details about how counselling is delivered is to be found in the chapters following this introduction. Here counsellors in two different NHS settings give you an opportunity to be a 'fly on the wall' and observe their daily routine.

But who are these healthcare counsellors and how do you join them?

As has been stated elsewhere in this book, counselling owes much to the trail-blazing of the voluntary sector. The profession has moved on but women still make up the majority of practitioners employed in healthcare, and many of them have come into counselling as a second career. The steady increase in the number of men, and people from black and minority ethnic (BME) communities joining the profession is welcomed as it makes us more representative of the population at large. Hopefully with better pay and terms and conditions of service, a career in counselling will be something to which many aspire.

The introduction of managed counselling services has lead to the recruitment of counsellors ranging from newly qualified counsellors to service managers. The latter tend to be experienced clinicians with audit and research experience and the ability to manage a team of individuals plus a budget of perhaps upwards of half a million pounds. The majority of these counselling jobs are found advertised in local and national newspapers and specialist journals such as the *Counselling and Psychotherapy Journal* and the *Healthcare Counsellors and Psychotherapy Journal* produced by BACP and FHCP.

Why should anyone choose counselling in healthcare as a career?

Not for the money alone! In a recent survey it was found that there are many ways to be contracted in the NHS, and the hourly rate for a self-employed practitioner could be as little as £8.00 before deductions. Employees' pay ranged from £14,000 to £25,000 for a whole-time equivalent (WTE) depending on qualifications and experience (Seber, 2003).

In 2004 the government will implement the *Agenda for Change* if the current negotiations are acceptable to staff and management. This is the greatest change to the health service since its foundation in 1945. At the heart of the change will be terms and conditions of service, and they will affect most health service workers including counsellors. Instead of the existing system of being paid according to your job title, in future you will be paid according to how much the job is worth. It will be equal pay for work of equal value (Unison, 2003).

There are therefore exciting things happening within the NHS and to the counselling profession. Counsellors are being offered further opportunities to develop and manage services within the medical setting. More and more counsellors are conducting research into the cost-effectiveness of counselling to both employer and patient. As the lead body for counselling, BACP is aware of the government's future intention to *regulate in some way* the profession of counselling and psychotherapy. In addition we are working alongside other professionals and their governing bodies to bridge the gap between the professions. The launch of the Health Professionals Council in 2003 saw the uniting of professions previously considered on the edge of medicine within one body.

These are some of the reasons I think a career in healthcare counselling offers exciting opportunities for job satisfaction in the future. Over the last 25 years I have worked in a wide range of settings in the NHS (currently in primary care) and in the voluntary sector. I have learned a great deal about myself through the generosity of patients who have willingly allowed me into their lives. I hope I have also contributed to their well-being. I would choose this career again.

Bibliography

BACP (2003) *FHCP Grading Criteria and Pay-scales for Counsellors in the NHS*. Rugby: BACP.

Churchill, R., Khaira, M., Gretton, V., Chivers, C., Dewey, M., Duggan, C. and Lee, A. (2000) 'Treating depression in general practice: factors affecting patients' treatment preferences', *British Journal of General Practice*, 50, 905–6.

Davy, J.A. (1999) 'Biopsychosocial approach to counselling in primary care' in R. Bor and D. McCann (eds), *The Practice of Counselling in Primary Care*. London: Sage.

Department of Health (1997) *White Paper. The New NHS: Modern, Dependable*. London: HMSO.

Marsh, G. N. and Barr, J. (1975) 'Marriage guidance counselling in a group practice', *Journal of the Royal College of General Practitioners*, 25, 73–5.

Mellor-Clark, J., Simms-Ellis, S. and Burton, M. (2001) *National Survey of Counsellors Working in General Practice: Evidence for Growing Professionalism*. Occasional paper. London: Royal College of General Practitioners (RCGP).

Pietroni, M. and Vaspe, A. (eds) (2000) *Understanding Counselling in Primary Care: Voices from the Inner City.* London: Churchill Livingstone.

Seber, P. (2003) 'Counsellors' pay and conditions in the NHS: an update', *Healthcare Counselling and Psychotherapy Journal*, 3(2), 19–21. Rugby: BACP.

Sharman, K. (2003) *Guidance on Good Practice for the Management of Counselling Placements in Healthcare Settings.* BACP Information Sheet DG3. Rugby: BACP.

Sibbald, B., Addinton-Hall, J., Brenneman, D. and Freeling, P. (1993) 'Counsellors in English and Welsh general practices: their nature and distribution', *British Medical Journal*, **306**: 29–33.

Thomas, P., Davidson, S. and Rance, C. (eds) (2001) *Clinical Counselling in Medical Settings.* London: Brunner-Routledge.

Unison (2003) *The Agenda for Change.* www.unison.org.uk.

7

Counselling in a Primary Healthcare Setting

Sue Santi Ireson

For the last 11 years I have managed a counselling service in a GP practice located in the centre of a town in south-east England. When the practice achieved fundholding status in 1991 the GPs decided that counselling might be an asset to the surgery and I was employed to set up the service, which now has myself and another counsellor working in it. The GPs became enthusiastic advocates for counselling during the painful changeover from fundholding to primary care groups and then to primary care trusts. For the past two years or so, the trust has had counsellors working in every practice.

A typical day

A day at the surgery starts with me collecting the 'counselling referral box' from the reception area. Our referral system involves a doctor giving a patient a referral card, together with a leaflet that explains about counselling. It is intended to help patients make their own decision about whether or not they wish to see a counsellor. I see this process as a kind of triage, where patients are deciding whether or not counselling sounds helpful for them.

Working in a GP practice means that we see clients who otherwise might never have accessed counselling. We meet people with a wide range of issues: depression, stress and anxiety, relationship problems and difficulties, abuse, traumatic childhood histories, loss and bereavement, illness and disability, substance misuse, issues around conception, fertility, abortion and stillbirth, gender issues, sexual problems, sexual identity problems, life transitions, eating disorders, cultural issues, mental health problems, and so on.

I work for a total of 11 hours a week at the surgery. Of this time, eight hours are face-to-face contact with clients. One hour is set aside for the task of statistical returns and other requirements, which may be tutorials with a new registrar or meetings with the primary care trust or other external bodies. One hour a week is earmarked for note writing and filling in the clinical outcomes in routine evaluation (CORE) forms, and we also have an hour set aside for a counsellor meeting. This hour is a time when doctors, health visitors and nurses know that they can find us to talk through a client referral if they wish. We also discuss clients and case management and other relevant topics during this time. The remaining eight hours are in three sections: three hours on Wednesday mornings, four hours on Thursday afternoons and two hours on alternate Saturday mornings. (This is not my favourite time to work!)

The client hour is 50 minutes, which leaves a ten-minute gap between one client and the next. We now have an appointment system which indicates on our computer screen when the client has arrived, so we don't have to waste time going out to the waiting area to check. The same system allows us to note when the client leaves. The time between clients is earmarked for making and receiving phone calls and our receptionists are now, after careful training, usually very careful to contact us only during these gaps.

On the way up to my room I may get stopped by one of the GPs with 'Oh by the way, I've just referred someone to you.' If I have time I will have an 'on the hoof' quick chat about the patient and the reasons the doctor has referred. Sometimes these 'on the hoof' consultations are when the doctor is unsure about whether to refer a patient or not. Part of my job includes offering tutorials to new doctors and registrar doctors, and I encourage them to see me as a resource.

Once I am in my room the computer appointment system shows me who is due to come in that day. For new patients, and for those who are completing their therapy, we are required by the local primary care trust to complete a CORE assessment form. This is a tick sheet clients fill in, and it gives a snapshot of how they are feeling at the moment. These forms are not my favourite activity. They take a good 15 minutes to process after the client has gone, and involve manually counting responses in four different categories, doing some mathematical calculations (thankfully with a calculator) to get mean scores, evaluating the client's mental state and noting the client's main problems. I appreciate that the primary care trust needs this evaluation as it enables them to make some sort of quality assurance, but they are time-consuming and I often end up doing them in my own time. However, on the plus side, some clients find it helpful to compare their first CORE form with the one they fill in at their last session, so they can see evidence of how much they have moved on. (For more information about CORE see the section on evaluation of the service.)

We now have a dedicated room for counselling. Until five years ago we had to use the surgeries, which could be uncomfortable for some clients because we could be in a room where they regularly saw their doctor and it was not always easy to establish the difference between the kind of relationship they have with their doctor and the therapeutic relationship I want to build with them.

We have three comfortable chairs in our room and a small library of helpful books, which we lend from time to time. We have a 'Do not disturb' sign on the door and mostly this is carefully observed. (It took quite a while for us to establish that 'Do not disturb' really meant just that. In doctor's surgeries it seems quite common for other professionals to 'just pop in for a second', and one or two members of staff found it very difficult to accept that this was not appropriate.)

When a new patient starts, the first task may be to acknowledge how nervous they are feeling about coming for counselling, and to outline the boundaries of confidentiality within the surgery setting. Some of our clients are extremely uninformed about counselling and may not really know why they have been referred. At our request we get very brief referral notes (if any), for example, 'family problems' or 'stress at work'. Before the patient comes in, I look at his or her notes on the computer screen to see what kind of issues he or she has brought to the doctor. This may or may not be informative. Information about major life events, births, deaths, losses, traumatic events, illnesses and so on may help me to understand what the client has had to deal with in his or her life. The notes don't always help, but can provide a quick route in which is sometimes helpful when counselling sessions are limited. We are not strictly confined to a particular number of sessions: this is left to our judgement, but most people receive between six and eight sessions.

My route in

I began my life in the counselling world as a volunteer in a provincial youth counselling agency in 1976. Back in those days we were trained in an embarrassingly short time: one residential weekend and ten evenings. Within a year or so I had become a team leader and a trainer on the volunteer training programme. I began to realize just how little I knew, and enrolled for a diploma course in humanistic counselling at the local university.

Over the years I continued to supplement my training with as many courses as I could afford to attend – and I joined a transactional analysis (TA) therapy group. This was quite daring at that time because within the agency the view was that if you needed to have therapy you weren't suitable to be a counsellor. (I am pleased to say that these views have long since been abandoned in this agency.)

In 1986 I was offered a part-time job as a director of a small youth counselling agency in a nearby town, and I worked there for eight years with a brief to professionalize the agency and develop its role in the community. The job was terribly badly paid: my wages were calculated on the same rate as sessional unqualified youth workers, but the local authority paid for some management training which was helpful, and I continued to attend personal and professional development courses and to have individual therapy. In response to need in the local community I developed various initiatives and built good links with social services and the community health team. On a national level I had also become involved with what was then the British Association for Counselling (now the British Association for Counselling and Psychotherapy: BACP) in the workgroup developing codes of practice. I also joined the executive committee of the Personal, Sexual Marital and Family division (now called Personal Relationship and Groupwork Division). This gave me a valuable contact with a much wider network of counsellors as well as challenging me to think more widely about counselling issues. During this time I was invited to become editor of the journal, *News and Views*, and learned on the job how to use a computer. I worked as editor until 1997, when I was elected chair of the division.

One day I happened to pick up the local paper and noticed that a local doctor's surgery was advertising for three counsellors. Feeling very excited I called for an application form and was duly offered an interview. I discovered later that my CV had been sufficient to ensure that I had been earmarked as the candidate who would be the manager of the counselling service, and I was appointed to start a month before the other two counsellors to get the service set up.

This was an amazing opportunity to talk with the doctors to discover what they wanted from a counselling service, and indeed what they understood of counselling. I discovered that they had read good reports about the benefits of counselling to doctors' practices, and as fundholders they were keen to take the initiative and try it. But they weren't really sure what counselling was exactly, nor did they know how the service would work and how exactly we would achieve results. This gave me the opportunity to advise them about what would be the most effective use of their new service, using my experience from the youth counselling service. The service has matured from there, and they now (ten years on) view the counselling service as a valuable support to their work.

During the early years we had several discussions about what confidentiality meant within the surgery. In the main, the GPs were willing to accept that the content of clients' stories would not be revealed to them, and gradually as they perceived that the work was helpful to their patients they grew less and less anxious about believing they should know these kind of details. We worked together on developing our own code of practice within the surgery for issues of harm and self-harm, and I believe every counsellor who works in this setting should discuss this issue and formulate a strategy for these issues before starting work. We also had to look at what happened if a GP wanted to 'section' one of our clients. Client notes are not made available to GPs and are kept in a locked filing cabinet in the counselling room. We keep them for five years then shred them.

A client story

Anne is 46 and was referred for counselling because she was suffering from depression and panic attacks. She was rather overweight and although it was autumn seemed to be dressed for the Arctic. Her eyes were rather staring, but she gave me little eye contact. She sat heavily in the chair, and did not really respond to my wondering if she was feeling a bit anxious. When I asked her what had brought her to decide that she would like counselling (to remind her that this was a choice she had made), Anne told me she had come because the doctor told her to. I gently told her that the choice about counselling cannot be the doctor's, and asked her if she knew why the doctor might have thought counselling might help her.

Anne: It might be because I get depressed. And I'm tired all the time.
Me: I wonder what you are so tired of and so depressed about?
Anne: I don't know. [She looked at me challengingly, almost as if she wanted to know why I wasn't telling her what made her depressed]
Me: If you did know, what do you think it might be? [This is one of my classic ways of helping clients to get past 'I don't know']
Anne: I don't know.

The referring doctor had told me Anne was a miserable woman and wished me good luck with her, and I began to see why the doctor had formed this opinion. This client obviously needed help, but it was difficult to engage her in the process. I didn't believe that she didn't know, but I wondered if it was 'safer' for her to not know and give the responsibility to someone else. I needed to try a different tack and find out how Anne dealt with her difficulties. I suspected that under the flat effect of the blanket of her depression was a good deal of unexpressed emotion. I asked her about home and work, and discovered that she had left home to join the Army, then had married when she was in her early thirties. After leaving the Army she had had a daughter, now ten. Anne had found coping with her quite difficult and had therefore decided that she would not have any more children. She had not worked outside the home since her daughter was born. Life seemed to be too much for her; she was only just keeping up with housework and the demands of her husband and her daughter. She had vague ideas about getting a job but felt too tired to think about it.

When asked about her childhood Anne revealed that she had lived in terror of her mother who was never satisfied with anything Anne did and would sometimes beat her unmercifully. When I commented that this was a very abusive way to treat a child, Anne said flatly, 'Well, I was very naughty.' It was hard to see this woman, who had told this story without a flicker of emotion in a flat unemotional voice, as ever having had the energy to be 'naughty'. I emphasized that this was physical and emotional abuse and that nothing she had done could have warranted such treatment. Momentarily Anne's eyes met mine and her face changed. I felt that she was engaged with me.

Me: How did it feel for you when your mother flew into a rage?
Anne: I don't know.
Me: What did your body feel like when she flew into a rage.
Anne: I used to feel really frightened. I would hide. Sometimes I would hide under my bed all day and not come out until it was dark.

My question about how it felt when her mother raged had been too hard for Anne just then. So I asked her how her body felt: often where the person has had to repress the emotion it is much easier for them to recall the physical effect of that emotion. This is where the counsellor's work and that of the doctor overlap. Unexpressed and repressed emotion becomes somatised, that is, expressed in a physical way.

Slowly Anne started to recognize how she withdrew into depression now in much the same way as she had once hidden under her bed. Anne also recognized that she had panic attacks when she was unsure of herself and feeling pressurized.

We talked about the lasting impact that Anne's abusive childhood had had on her, identifying that the beliefs of her childhood that no one was to be trusted and the world was an unpredictable and dangerous place were still subconsciously informing her behaviour today. Anne began to be able to identify when she felt threatened by observing the bodily symptoms: headaches, panicky feelings, lethargy or difficulty finding words. She learned how to evaluate the current situation to measure whether or not it was really threatening.

We also considered how Anne's lifestyle was contributing to her feeling of lethargy. We discussed her sugar consumption and her lack of exercise. She identified for herself that she felt worse when she ate bread. (I frequently discuss diet and exercise with clients: overconsumption of sugar, caffeine and refined carbohydrates often make people feel quite poorly.) Choosing an aerobic activity which will raise the heart rate for ten minutes a day dramatically increases a sense of well-being by reducing stress chemicals and raising seratonin levels. With Anne's permission I spoke about this to the doctor, who agreed that diet might have a connection with her feeling so tired.

Speaking to the doctor about management of the patient is one way in which counselling in the doctors' practice differs to counselling in private practice, where usually the counsellor only speaks to the supervisor about the client, and then the client is not identified. This could potentially present a difficulty that can be avoided if there is good contracting at the outset of the counselling relationship. If the counsellor believes that it would be helpful for the client to have the doctor know about some of the issues being discussed, but the client disagrees, then the counsellor has a dilemma, but in practice this has never happened to me.

Another client, Angela, was referred by the doctor because she was suicidal. Her history was one of appalling abuse, physical, sexual and emotional. Angela found it very difficult to trust anyone and often tried to play off the doctor, the nurse who saw her when she had cut herself, and me against each other. It seemed that the best we could do for Angela was to be sure that we all knew what had been said so that she could not 'divide and rule'. This was made explicit in the gentlest possible way to Angela, modelling for her a kind but firm parenting of the sort that she had never received. Gradually, Angela began to work on the issues of her lonely life rather than try to make us distrust each other. Such cooperative handling of a client would not be possible in a private counselling setting, and is an example of how carefully negotiated contracts with all the boundaries clearly defined can provide a safe and therapeutic containment for the client, which then enables her to empower herself more effectively.

Evaluation

From the first year I was employed in the surgery I collected statistics on age, gender and referring doctor, together with numbers of sessions, cancellations and unattended sessions. I also collected information about the major problems our clients brought to their counselling sessions. I devised ways of showing this information in graphs and pie charts so it was easy to read. This information was printed in colour and presented to all the doctors annually. In the period when primary care groups were first being formed and were trying to decide on equal provision across the area, my statistics were also used to demonstrate the effectiveness of the counselling service.

Our primary care trust has recently begun to use the CORE system, which was developed by the Psychological Therapies Research Centre at Leeds University. This system has been developed in consultation with groups representing psychiatry, clinical psychology, psychotherapy and counselling. It can be used both for evaluation of the treatment and also for service audit purposes. Information is processed by the centre in Leeds, and complete patient anonymity is assured. The information can be collected either on the computer, using special software, which is then analyzed at the university, or manually using forms. Our primary care trust has opted for the manual system.

This involves a tick sheet that the client fills in and which gives a snapshot of how they are feeling at that moment. The 34 questions enquire about the person's subjective sense of well-being, his or her problems and symptoms, life functioning and risk to self or others. These questions are asked during the client's first therapy session, and then again during the last session.

The data collected is sent to the primary care trust, which then sends data gathered from all its counsellors to the centre in Leeds for analysis. This enables them to get an informed feedback about how clients progress as a result of their therapy.

Continuing professional development

The surgery provides some allowance for continuing professional development – about £200 per annum and a week of study leave. In 1996 I did a diploma in counselling in primary care at Bristol University. This meant an investment of my own, and my study leave did not cover the day a week attendance requirement. However, the course has stood me in good stead; the contacts I made there have been invaluable, and the focus towards working in medical settings gave me insights which I really value. Further, the research I did for my dissertation on the presentation of somatised sexual abuse to the GP has led me on to further research, several teaching assignments (one in India) and a commission to write a chapter for a book.

BACP's Faculty of Healthcare Counsellors and Psychotherapists (FHCP) is concerned with counselling in medical settings, and organizes an annual conference. Conferences organized by the Counselling in Primary Care Trust provide interesting workshops and valuable opportunities for networking. Opportunities sometimes present themselves at local psychiatric hospitals (both NHS and private), and these are often free or at quite low cost. I have found it helpful to develop my knowledge of psychiatric conditions and to understand what treatments are offered in the secondary and tertiary care fields. An area of study I have interested myself in is how to work with the 'borderline personality disorder'.

Conditions of work

Unlike most other counsellors in our primary care trust, those at my surgery are employed by the surgery itself. We have five weeks' paid holiday, a training budget, payment during sick leave and a contract of employment. However, this situation is rather unusual. Most counsellors working in primary care seem to be self-employed and expected to finance their own supervision and training. Of those I know, we are paid less than most, but we receive the benefits of being employed and are thus more protected.

When I first started working at the surgery I had to explain that supervision was an essential requirement for our work, and that it would not be possible to work within the BACP code of ethics without it, so work done at the surgery must be properly supervised. This is not a concept that is particularly well understood in the medical setting (unfortunately) but it was agreed. We have two paid hours of supervision a month, together with two paid hours set aside for it. My supervisor works in a psychiatric setting; her training in counselling is psychodynamic and Freudian. This works well for me, as she is able to help me look at issues in another way. She also has an excellent understanding of psychiatric disorders, knowledge that I am sometimes very glad to draw on to help me understand more difficult clients.

Opportunities and limitations of working in a GP practice

I have sought opportunities to become involved in the wider picture of counselling: recently I have been part of a group, mostly consisting of psychologists working in secondary care, that was convened to draw up guidelines for doctors referring to the psychological therapies. This opportunity came about as a result of networking at a conference put on at the local psychiatric hospital. These kinds of opportunities are almost never advertised, they have to be sought out. However, one of the difficulties of working part-time is that extra activities of this sort are unpaid, but it was a challenge and it was interesting to be working with professionals from other settings. But I recognize that this creates a difficulty which becomes permanent unless a lead is taken at primary care trust level.

The work within the healthcare setting can be limited by the 'tribalism' of the different professions and specialities; primary care trusts could take a lead into breaking down inter-professional suspicion and defensiveness. Informal contacts can be made by the individual most effectively, but a structured approach to developing and strengthening such links would be more effective.

Career progression routes and pathways

For counsellors who are prepared to diversify into training and supervision, there are some possibilities of developing their career. I have devised and run a range of training courses and seminars: listening skills for registrars and GP returners; sexual abuse and its toll on the survivor; listening skills for receptionists; dealing with angry people. I have run supervision groups for new doctors and registrar doctors that have been very successful in helping them cope with the psychological demands of working so closely with people. These were not part of the original job but have been a way of developing my work, and indeed have got me work in other surgeries where I have put on these courses. Networking and offering to do courses and seminars, writing papers and responding to particular opportunities are all ways of forwarding your career. These opportunities seldom present themselves, so finding them involves marketing yourself and your course or group.

There is enormous scope for group work: anxiety and stress management, bereavement, anger management, sexual abuse survivors and eating disorders to name but a few areas of work that could be well managed by counsellors, maybe working across several surgeries at a time.

Resources and resourcing

The Department of Health's *National Service Framework for Mental Health* (1999) notes that 25 per cent of consultations in doctors' surgeries relate to mental health, and that 90 per cent of mental health care is provided from primary care. These figures emphasize the importance of counselling services to doctors. The framework sets out guidelines and timescales for the implementation of appropriate mental health services. Primary care trusts are trying to meet these requirements but there is constant tension within the trusts in their effort to provide top quality services with the financial resources at their disposal.

What I enjoy about working in this setting:

- I love working in the team. The contrast to working privately with individuals works really well and gives me a balance.
- I like the challenge of the wide range of clients, many of whom would never access counselling privately.
- Access to a wide range of professionals.

Difficulties of working in this setting:

- The frustration of the lack of overall structure and management by the primary care trust. Rather than just funding it, I would like the trust to develop counselling as a broad-based service, which is integrated throughout the provision of psychological therapies.
- The uncertainty of continuity of employment.

Future developments

Specific training for work in a GP practice will become increasingly important. Here are some suggestions to follow up:

- Join a professional body. BACP can be contacted at BACP House, 35–37 Albert Street, Rugby, Warwickshire CV21 2SG. For those involved in counselling in healthcare settings join the specialist division, FHCP. Membership of this group offers a regular journal and access to training opportunities. You can buy their journal without becoming a member (enquiries to BACP as above).
- Counsellors and Psychotherapists in Primary Care, Queensway House, Bognor Regis, West Sussex PO21 1QT is a smaller but very active group that provide a journal and training activities. It also offers advice and support to counsellors working in primary care.
- Consider taking a diploma in counselling in primary care or health settings. These are offered at a range of universities. In addition, the Counselling in Primary Care Trust has a range of information about training for counsellors in issues particular to work in general practice, including conferences, short courses and post-graduate diploma courses. Contact Dr Graham Curtis-Jenkins, Counselling in Primary Care Trust, 38 Richmond Rd, Staines, Middlesex, TW18 2AB. Tel: 01784 441782.

Ten top tips

Generic tips:

- Take good care of yourself: if you don't, you will burn out.
- Offer training, seminars, reports and groups in addition to counselling work.

Context specific tips:

- Join a professional body concerned with counselling in healthcare settings.
- Attend staff training days so you understand the team culture
  and get to know your fellow professionals and let them get to
  know you.
- Understand the most common forms of anti-depressants.
- Be flexible: sometimes the GP needs support with difficult clients
  who may not always be open to a classic counselling relationship.
- Network! Make contact with other counsellors working locally
  in healthcare settings as well as professionals in community
  mental health teams and at your local psychiatric hospital.
- Use a supervisor familiar with counselling in primary care.
- Be prepared to educate GPs and other professionals who may
  be unclear about what counsellors do.
- Be firm about working conditions. It is not reasonable or effective
  for a counsellor to see clients in the way doctors see their
  patients, one straight after another with maybe 20 in a morning,
  but doctors and practice managers may not understand this.

 Counselling in primary care is a multilayered role. Will this
suit my working style?

Bibliography

Bor, R. and McCann, D. (eds) (1999) *The Practice of Counselling
in Primary Care*. London: Sage.
Core System Group (1998) *CORE System (Information
Management) Handbook*. Leeds: Core System Group.

Corney, R. and Jenkins, R. (eds) (1992) *Counselling in General Practice*. London: Routledge.

Counsellors in Primary Care (2001) *Professional Counselling and Psychotherapy Guidelines and Protocols*. Bognor Regis: Counselling in Primary Care.

Department of Health (1999) *National Service Framework for Mental Health: Modern Standards and Service Models*. London: Department of Health.

Department of Health (2001) *Choosing Talking Therapies?* London: Department of Health.

East, P. (1995) *Counselling in Medical Settings*. Milton Keynes: Open University Press.

Gregory K. (2001) 'Integrating counselling within the mental health services', in K. Etherington (ed.), *Counsellors in Health Settings*. London: Jessica Kingsley.

Hudson-Allez, G. (1997) *Time Limited Therapy in General Practice*. London: Sage.

Kates, N., Crustolo, A-M., Farrar, S. and Nikolaou, L. (2001) 'Integrating mental health services in primary care: lessons learnt', *Families, Systems and Health*, **19**(1).

Mellor-Clark, J. (2000) *Counselling in Primary care in the Context of the NHS Quality Agenda: The Facts*. Rugby: British Association for Counselling and Psychotherapy.

Pietroni, M. and Vaspe, A. (2000) *Inside Counselling in Primary Care*. London: Churchill Livingstone.

Pietroni, M. and Vaspe, A. (2000) *Understanding Counselling in Primary Care – Voices from the Inner City*. London: Churchill Livingstone.

Rance, C. (ed.) (2001) *Clinical Counselling in Medical Settings*. London: Brunner/Routledge.

Santi Ireson, S. (2001) 'Somatised presentation of sexual abuse to the GP', in K. Etherington (ed.), *Counsellors in Health Settings*. London: Jessica Kingsley.

Sharman, K. (2002) 'Southeast Sheffield PCT Counselling Service one year on', *Healthcare Counselling and Psychotherapy Journal*, **6** (Oct.), 20–2.

8

Counselling in a Secondary Healthcare Setting

Jill Brennan

I'm a counsellor in a clinical psychology department based in an inner city general hospital site and employed by the local city-wide mental health and social care trust.

A typical day

08:30. I arrive to a fairly empty car park. In the clinical psychology department secretaries' office, I collect post, messages and the office key, and check my desk diary against the central diary. While my computer is booting up, I make a brew in the department kitchen, chatting and joking with colleagues. We are part of a team and I'm aware that the quality of our service, ultimately including our safety at work, depends on our communication with each other. Back in my office I scan messages, post and intranet e-mails, discarding what is irrelevant and recording on my clipboard tasks arising from the rest.

08:50. I locate files for clients 1 to 3, stilling and focusing my mind on my 'cockpit drill': tissues, clean board, chairs, ambient sound, temperature and ventilation, board pens and prepared documents.

09:10. Client 1 arrives late (car park full). He is tense and unsure. We chat quietly for a few minutes and then begin drawing up his genogram (a diagram of a person's family tree). As well as four major bereavements within the past two years, the exercise reveals the death of a sibling in childhood. He stares at the board. 'When you see it like that you can see why it all feels so bad...' He cries and relaxes a little. We begin talking about the most recent death and agree to talk some more.

09:50. I walk client 1 to reception. Back in my office, I note down key points of his session and skim my next client's file.

10:00. Brenda (secretary) announces client 2. I check the office and collect client 2 from the waiting room. She rises slowly, pulling herself up on her stick. Progress along the corridor is slow. As client 2 lowers herself gingerly into a chair, I remark that life looks painful today. The floodgates open. Client 2 has been unable to do any of the things we agreed on at our last session. This is the fault of the 'bloody SS' who have rejected her renewal claim for disabled living allowance (DLA). Her welfare rights worker has lodged an appeal and will shortly be in touch to request a report. Noting the smell of alcohol, among others, I ask if she has been drinking. Client 2 admits she has had 'a drink'. I acknowledge that she has made a big effort to get here today. However, the plan we agreed on to help her improve her quality of life includes doing 'home-work' tasks and excludes drinking alcohol before sessions. Perhaps we need to take another look at the plan. I offer client 2 an early appointment, which she accepts, then launches back into her tirade against the DSS.

10:25. Client 2 is still complaining loudly as we return to the reception area. I sign forms to enable client 2 to reclaim her bus fares from the admin centre in the psychiatry building. Returning to my office, I open the (frosted and caged) window and the door, and spray air freshener. I write up, sign, date and time session notes for clients 1 and 2 and prepare for client 3, who is due at 11:00, then dip into the list of 'admin' tasks on my clipboard. Today's admin list includes:

- writing a letter to a GP discharging his patient who has moved out of area
- updating my caseload monitoring database ready to do my monthly Korner statistics for departmental records
- reading minutes/briefing notes for the psychological therapies quality committee (part of our trust's clinical governance structure) and local health and safety committee meetings
- collecting and filing case notes returned from the typing system
- shredding rough notes
- rereading case notes for a care programme approach (CPA) review meeting on Thursday
- making an internal referral to community mental health team (CMHT) 'A'.

11:25. Client 3 has not appeared. (While waiting, I have reread his notes and decide to allow him 24 hours to contact us before writing to his GP to suggest discharging him. I record his non-attendance in my diary and his notes.)

11.55. I call CMHT 'A' requesting support for a vulnerable client I screened yesterday. The mental health practitioner on duty initially thinks the case more suited to a primary care team. After further discussion, I agree to write a referral letter for the CMHT's next allocation meeting, since I can't attend in person.

12:00. I dash to the Women's Royal Voluntary Service (WRVS) café in outpatients to buy a sandwich.

12:15. Weekly business meeting/lunch in the department's group room.

Today's agenda includes:

- discussion of waiting list management options
- finding office accommodation for trainee psychologists
- dates for mandatory fire, back care and 'breakaway' courses and a workshop on the needs of asylum seekers
- department's kitchen rota.

12:55. Back at my office, I find and skim client 4's file. Cockpit check.

13:00. I collect client 4 from Reception. She shares further thoughts on last week's session, elaborating on her experiences as a second-generation member of an Asian family and their impact on her self-esteem. We create a 'map' of some of the tensions and contradictions implicit in these experiences. I ask how she has coped. Client 4 focuses on her resources, and we begin to consider what might constitute optimal coping. Client 4 agrees to continue the exercise as 'homework'.

13:50. I escort client 4 to reception and check my pigeonhole. It contains an apologetic message from client 3 requesting a further appointment, and a bundle of case files returned from typing. I put the message slip in my 'in tray' and update client 4's notes, then sort the files by day of next appointment into my office filing cabinet.

14:05. As I'm preparing for client 5, a psychotherapist from the nearby psychodynamic psychotherapy unit calls with a query about a client I referred last week.

14:15. Client 5 is on time. The short-term memory problems and epilepsy he has suffered since his head injury have sapped his confidence. He tells me he feels overwhelmed. I suggest we look at the current stressors and review his coping plan. Top of the list are manipulative calls from his mother-in-law. We look at what already works, and what doesn't. I ask whether anything we have done before might help here. He thinks of the flashcards by his phone which have helped him to say 'no' to sales calls without humiliating loss of temper. We review skills work already done on assertive communication and prepare some cards to help with handling calls from 'mum'.

15:05. I show client 5 out and begin his session notes. (My memory is better earlier in the day, which is one reason for allowing more time between afternoon appointments.) Attaching details of an appointment to client 3's file, I put it into the typing system.

15:15. Tea break. I close my eyes and breathe calmly, then do a couple of T'ai Chi warm-up stretches. A colleague drops by to tell me about a possible counselling referral.

15:30. No sign of client 6. The secretaries say the car parks are packed due to a conference at the postgraduate centre, so she may be parking. Meanwhile I catch up on reading (a paper on cultural variations in depression).

15:40. Client 6 shows up, breathless. I give her a moment to visit the toilet and get some water. Client 6 has made a list of questions that have troubled her about a childhood experience described in her last session. We consider the implications of her questions from various perspectives: her own as a child, a police-woman's, a compassionate friend's. (I remain alert for active child protection issues. Though nothing arises in this case, I would have a duty to report a child at risk to the child protection team.)

16:30. I walk client 6 to the reception area. Returning to my office, I finish writing up today's case notes and file them. I then draft a letter about my vulnerable assessment client for discussion at the CMHT 'A' allocations meeting on Monday. Before shutting down the computer, I check my e-mails and finish tomorrow's admin list.

17.01. Closedown routine. (Tidy desk, close window, water plants, lock up and leave.)

Box 8.1 Some terms commonly used in mental health settings

Community mental health team (CMHT): team of medical, mental health nursing, social work, support workers, occupational therapy and psychological therapies practitioners, and psychiatrists, who assess the needs of those with acute severe mental health prob-lems, and who may offer intensive crisis support or longer-term care to highly vulnerable patients. Secondary care service, despite the name.

Primary care team (PCT): Multi-disciplinary teams who serve patients with mental health needs in primary care.

Primary care: GP surgery based services.

Secondary care: Hospital-based services.

Psychiatrist: Medical doctor with additional training in diagnosis, management and prescribing for severe mental illness. A minority of UK psychiatrists also have substantial psychotherapy training.

Clinical psychologist: Psychologist usually with a doctorate in clinical psychology and/or chartered status with British Psychological Society.

RMN: Qualified mental health nurse.

Nurse therapist: RMN with specialist psychotherapy training.

Mental health practitioner: Experienced RMN or social worker member of CMHT; may or may not have some psychological therapies training.

Care programme approach (CPA): system under which all patients are given an initial assessment leading to a detailed care plan, naming the worker responsible for overseeing the plan and those agencies/individuals who deliver planned care. This plan is periodically reviewed at a meeting for all those involved, including the patient (CPA review).

My route in

In 1997, I took the post of temporary counsellor in a clinical psychology department, which was then an integral part of an inner city general hospital. My post was created when waiting lists were running at record levels, qualified and experienced clinical psychologists were hard to recruit to the area, and the budget was limited. Initially I was offered only short-term contracts. After renewing my contract twice, management finally agreed to make my post permanent.

When recruited, I was writing up my MA in a counselling research project while working as a day centre coordinator for the mental health charity where I had previously done an advanced diploma placement. I also worked as a freelance counsellor/group worker for GPs' surgeries and as a group worker/facilitator for colleges and businesses. I was then in the process of applying for British Association for Counselling and Psychotherapy (BACP) accreditation.

Teams recruit 'temps' in the hope that they will fit as smoothly as possible into the running of their system. So I think that my prior familiarity with clients with mental health and medical issues, medications and the variety of presentations of common mental health problems of all degrees of severity will have been significant in my appointment. Also, my extensive up-to-date knowledge of local voluntary organizations was an immediate asset to the department.

Perhaps surprisingly in a department specializing in cognitive-behavioural therapies (CBT), integrative counselling training made me quite a good candidate. Based around Egan's skilled helper model, my pragmatic problem management approach with a firm bias towards action has a natural affinity with the structured and action-oriented cognitive-behavioural therapies. At the same time, it's flexible enough to offer a distinctive alternative to classic CBT.

It certainly helped that my advanced diploma/MA course had encouraged me to read widely in the psychological therapies literature, to have experience with a variety of therapy models and to be prepared to be proactive in finding a common language with colleagues.

Colleagues were openly sceptical of my abilities at first. I seemed to be thought of as some form of assistant psychologist, competent to handle only simple cases but puzzlingly old to be in such a role. Looking for information leaflets describing counselling, I found one which stated that qualified counsellors typically hold a one-year certificate and could handle straightforward, short-term cases! Since then, through presentations to departmental meetings, and less formal discussions with colleagues I have tried to dispel some myths about counselling and its applications. In turn, I have discarded some of my own prejudices about clinical psychology and cognitive-behavioural therapy.

Adult psychological therapies provision has changed considerably in the past six years. Historically, our department has taken referrals from a wide range of sources, including GPs and primary care workers (about 60 per cent), and medical consultants, psychiatrists and other professionals (about 40 per cent). Its caseload mix reflected all the various interests, specialisms and professional links of department personnel over the years. In the early days I saw a very mixed clientele, including in-patients on the psychiatric wards, in-patients on general and surgical wards, out-patients who had previously been patients in both these settings, and out-patients referred from GPs and other external agencies.

Since our department became part of a specialist mental health trust three years ago, its caseload has increasingly consisted of complex cases, including those of people with severe mental illness and/or long-term mental health problems and their carers.

Most of my work is now done with out-patients visiting the department, which is in a separate building on the edge of the hospital campus. However, I still very occasionally work on both the psychiatric and medical wards with in-patients. Although my colleagues (clinical psychologists and nurse therapists) have clinics in GP surgeries in the locality, unlike other counsellors working in similar units, I have not been asked to do so.

A client story

In this setting, it's almost impossible to offer a representative clinical vignette. My caseload is both wide ranging and shaped by the setting and by the role that counselling plays here.

In adult psychological therapies, counselling is still a minority profession in process of establishing its value in the mainstream. So it is very important for me to study what I do and whether or not it works for clients. In my first three years in the post, for example, I routinely audited my client's presenting problems by type and number per client.

Most cases seen in the department are complex in some way. In simpler cases, patients may already have been diverted to practice counsellors or the voluntary sector, have recovered or have simply given up waiting. I routinely work with people with multiple social, physical and mental health problems due to the pressures of inner city life; demographically, they are more likely to be the victims of crime, to commit suicide, to have poor physical health, and to be caught in debt and poverty traps.

Knowledge of local systems and an ability to communicate with other professionals and agencies is essential for effective helping here, together with an awareness of the special needs of, for example, homeless people and asylum seekers. In the psychiatric system itself, difference has traditionally underpinned definitions of psychopathology (for example, Fernando, 1995) and political issues have been magnified by the technologies of treatment. (It is less than 50 years, for example, since this hospital used to 'treat' people for homosexuality!) Awareness, including self-awareness, of the implications of working with diversity of all kinds is therefore essential in this environment.

In some cases, client and/or referrer ask specifically for counselling. In others, for example, where the primary problem is bereavement or loss, counselling may be the therapy of choice.

Our department is committed to providing high-quality evidence-based CBT, and to engaging in research projects to develop cognitive therapies. Some patients referred for group CBT or for research projects prove at assessment not to fit protocols but are clearly distressed; in such cases, counselling can be a useful and humane alternative.

There are also those who are, for one reason or another, unable to make good use of the time of a cognitive-behavioural practitioner on an individual basis (for example, those who are not 'psychologically minded'). In such cases a counselling intervention may be more appropriate.

Table 8.1 Analysis of problems raised at assessment
for counselling 1997–2000

An analysis of the cases of 128 of my clients who engaged in counselling at least until their penultimate agreed session (between 1997 and 2000), revealed that the proportion reporting distress related to particular issues was as follows:

Problems with symptoms e.g. insomnia, depression	65%
Loss and change [other than bereavement]	51%
Relationships with partners or friends	39%
Family [including adoption, parenting etc.] issues	37%
Bereavement	34%
Victimization e.g. rape, domestic abuse, CSA[1], assault	34%
Work/workplace issues	8%
Surviving in society [debt, welfare, housing, environment etc.]	19%
Existential, spiritual or moral issues	13%
Experiences in the medical/psychiatric system	13%
Addictions [alcohol, street/prescribed drugs/gambling etc.]	13%
Cultural issues	12%
Carers' issues [not included in Family]	11%
Lifestage issues	11%
Other [likely to identify client/client withheld from record]	16%

Note: These figures are based on issues raised at assessment. Clients brought a mean of four problems, and in some cases as many as 11.
1. CSA – sequelae of childhood sexual abuse

Good practice

Since starting work in an adult mental health environment, I have extended and adapted my understanding of 'good practice' to fit with prevailing conditions and definitions. For example:

- *Record keeping.* Traditionally, confidentiality in counselling remains strictly between client, counsellor and supervisor. In adult mental health generally, and in work with clients with multiple needs in particular, confidentiality is understood as existing within a care/service team. Counselling notes are stored and handled as psychology case files so, in logging sessions, I must remember that a client's notes could be read by admin and clerical workers or by any department clinician or assistant who may subsequently see the client. My view is that this is not inconsistent with humanistic practice, provided that my client is aware of and comfortable enough with this level of confidentiality from the outset.

- *Risk of suicide or homicide.* Sadly, people with severe, complex and/or enduring mental health problems are more likely than the population as a whole to commit suicide or damage themselves in the attempt. Some of those referred to us have problems with aggression and could harm others. It would be unwise, working in this context, to forget these possibilities. Sometimes, then, it is necessary to do a formal assessment of risk, and if need be, to disclose that risk to others. I explain this to clients at the contract stage. If such intervention appears necessary, I will talk my concerns through with my client and with my supervisor or an experienced colleague before taking appropriate action.

- *Child/vulnerable adult protection issues.* Very occasionally, the issue is risk to vulnerable third parties, such as when a client identifies ongoing child abuse. In such a case, all workers have a duty to disclose to the appropriate authorities. As with the above, consultation is essential.

- *Medication.* It is considered normal for clients in this setting to be taking psychoactive medication(s). Knowledge of the effects of common medicines can be key to understanding what is happening for some clients. I may communicate with the GP or psychiatrist responsible for prescribing, for example, if a client has stopped taking medication that may be warding off disabling symptoms, or if a client has symptoms of tolerance of long-term medication and needs help in withdrawing. The criterion is quality of life: if medication prevents my client from becoming suicidal or psychotic, I will tend to endorse it; conversely, if a client has tolerance related anxiety symptoms, I will argue for slow withdrawal under medical supervision.

- *Using interpreters.* It makes for some awkward dynamics at times, but the growing proportion of non-English speakers on our books is equally entitled to counselling!

- *Caseload management.* I routinely monitor my caseload (referral dates, first appointments, current status, referral route, practitioners and agencies involved, and so on), then submit a monthly record (Korner statistics) of the numbers of appointments offered, new clients seen, clients referred from different parts of our catchment area, and current waiting times. My clients benefit in that I can keep track of a caseload of between 50 and 80 individuals, without forgetting where any one case is up to.

So systemic factors as well as the needs and interests of the triad of client, counsellor and supervisor determine good practice in counselling in this setting.

Evaluation

Our department routinely collects baseline questionnaires (for example, the Beck anxiety and depression inventories (BAI and BDI)) and with some clients, I repeat these questionnaires as outcome measures. I also use questionnaires to determine whether a client's symptoms meet threshold criteria for referral to a colleague (for example, Yale-Brown obsessive-compulsive scale (YBOCS) for obsessive-compulsive disorder).

However, there are questions about whether it is valid to assess outcome this way (cf. McLeod, 2000). Also, as far as I can determine from the literature, few if any of the measures currently in use have been validated cross-culturally, which is interesting, given the ethnic mix of our caseload.

That said, evaluation is built into most effective helping. Goal setting is an essential part of assessment. If a client cannot identify therapeutic goals, then I would question whether counselling was a suitable approach for this client in this setting.

Typically, my client and I develop 'measures' of change which are subjectively meaningful to the client. (One client measured his recovery from depression in solved daily crossword clues!) Review of goals and measures is built into the counselling process at intervals, so evaluation of a sort is integral to my counselling approach.

Of course, goals vary. A client confused about what kind of help would be useful might engage in counselling with the goal of developing therapy goals. For some, realistic aims might include minor improvements in quality of life, for example, reduced alcohol intake. Such personally significant changes might not show up in routine psychometrics. A very vulnerable client might have a goal of staying alive.

Counselling is process, too, so evaluation includes taping and reviewing with my supervisor, and writing up challenging cases as retrospective case studies.

Continuing professional development

The NHS's member organizations run mandatory training courses, which are updated annually, for example, confidentiality and 'breakaway' training.

Most trusts also offer optional courses to promote staff CPD. Since counselling is not recognized as a profession in the NHS, these tend to be geared to professions such as nursing. However, in-house training programmes are a source of free or cheap training which can enhance, for example, computing skills. Participating in NHS consultations brings opportunities to network and to update knowledge of the mental health system.

Once a year, I discuss my personal development plan (PDP) with my line manager, an experienced clinical psychologist and cognitive therapist. As yet, there are few precedents for CPD for counsellors in the NHS, other than training to be something else. I use BACP criteria for continuing accreditation in planning CPD activity including workshops offered by nearby universities, BACP and the British Association for Behavioural and Cognitive Psychotherapies (BABCP).

Although the department has very limited training budget – I'm funding my own doctorate – management have allowed me time off to attend a taught doctorate in counselling at Manchester University and conferences, workshops and other activities consistent with my PDP. This has included time to be involved in committee work with the BACP and BABCP.

Naturally, I am expected to show evidence of the value of all this, for example, by appearing in print and presenting conference posters and papers.

Although the department supports CPD activities familiar to nurses and psychologists using a medical model (research, publishing, and so on), developmental activities such as personal therapy are regarded with frank suspicion. I sometimes use annual leave to do therapy workshops. I also take care to look after my mental, spiritual and physical health on a routine basis.

Conditions of work

I'm not a nurse, an occupational therapist, a psychologist or a social worker, so for employment purposes in the NHS I do not have a professional pay scale. On the basis of my experience of teaching in adult education and of business management, I am classified as 'A & C' (admin and clerical) by trade.

Being assigned a non-clinical grade has been unexpectedly problematic. I am now paid substantially more than in my first year, thanks to seniority and recognition by management. However, full-time clinical work can often be more emotionally and intellectually demanding than clerical work. My leave allocation, therefore, does not fully reflect the stressful nature of my job. Study and personal development eat into annual leave time, too.

Although on an individual level, colleagues are respectful enough, arguably the most negative aspect of having no pay scale has been the implicit invalidation of my professional identity as a counsellor.

Attitudes towards supervision in the psychological therapies have changed a great deal in the past decade. It is now generally thought essential for all therapists to have routine supervision (although there is still some disagreement about what that entails). However, when I joined the department things were different. The requirement for all counsellors to have clinical supervision throughout their career was an anomaly in a psychology setting. Because I insisted on external supervision, I self-funded for a year. After that, my employers agreed to pay. Despite the cost, I wanted to stay with my supervisor, an experienced counsellor with many years' experience in psychiatric social work. I am certain that I would not have learned to survive in adult mental health without supervision of this quality.

Ironically, although initially my supervisor and I worked for different organizations, our employers then amalgamated to form the new mental health and social care trust. Since we work on different sites and in separate parts of the trust, we have agreed to continue in supervision, although now funding is internal.

Future developments

Old hands in mental health say of changes in the NHS that if one waits a couple of decades, everything gets abolished ... and then is eventually recycled as a new idea! The NHS as an institution is particularly vulnerable to political whim: so much depends on who is in power, and what they promised in order to get there. Here are some of the changes in the pipeline that could affect counsellors in settings like mine:

- *New pay structure.* At the time of writing, a radically new common structure of pay and conditions is being negotiated between NHS management and unions. The intention is to do away with the parallel professional structures and disparities in pay and conditions, which exist at present in the NHS. Unfortunately, counsellors in secondary care are neither influential nor well organized. Will we have an adequate voice in the job evaluation process to determine where on the common scale counsellors are placed? On the other hand, the system could allow counsellors greater career progression if they are prepared to train for it.
- *Priority for severe mental illness.* A combination of scarce resources and government concern with the containment of the severely mentally ill drives secondary care towards an ever-narrower focus on patients with psychosis. This is an area from which counselling has generally been excluded, although there is

little or no convincing research into applications of professional counselling with this population. An opportunity for pioneers, perhaps?

- *Computerized record keeping, monitoring and outcome measurement.* I understand that the trust is currently working on a computerized record keeping system, including statistical monitoring, routine psychometrics and centralized case notes. This will be challenging in a number of ways, including the confidentiality issues raised by wider access to notes. However, I am optimistic that what we lose by placing limits on the privacy of the consulting room we may gain in improved communication within the therapeutic team.

Ten top tips

Context specific tips:

- Be persistent. Don't give up the day job. Building up a relevant portfolio of experience and knowledge will take time and dedication.
- Look after yourself. Find a range of effective ways of managing stress and build them firmly into your lifestyle before you start.
- Open your life to career opportunities. Study Wednesday's *Guardian* and the *Counselling and Psychotherapy Journal* jobs pages and make use of every chance to network.
- Educate yourself. Read the literature on common psychoactive medications, mental illness, common mental health problems and physical health problems with psychological consequences (for example, diabetes, stroke). Not everything you read on the web can be relied upon, but more reputable sites offer definitions, outlines of debates and references to relevant literature; use common sense and always read a range of references to get a spread of opinion.
- Know your client group. If you are not already a health professional, develop plenty of 'hands-on' experience of working alongside the kind of people you want to work with as a counsellor. THIS DOES NOT COUNT AS COUNSELLING EXPERIENCE, but it will give you some insight into the world that your clients inhabit and the way the system impacts upon them and their care.

- Be realistic. Be prepared to work for peanuts initially. Remember, this does not mean you are a monkey. But you may have to prove your worth to people who have no reason to suppose what you do is of value.
- Be assertive and prepared to patiently and politely argue your case, repeatedly!
- Find a supervisor with plenty of good clinical counselling (not clinical psychology or psychotherapy) experience, plus a sound understanding of the healthcare system – they're hard to find but invaluable!
- Listen carefully to colleagues and adapt your practice to the smooth running of your environment as far as is reasonable and ethically OK.
- Be prepared to say no. Other professionals may attempt to refer 'heart sink' patients for indefinite 'support' with no clear goals. Ask yourself: Will this really help? Is this what counselling is for?

 What do you believe/know about:

- antidepressant or anxiolytic medication
- electroconvulsive therapy (ECT)
- borderline personality disorder
- alcohol abuse
- domestic violence
- bereaved parents
- people who abuse children
- pain
- disability living allowance
- deliberate self-harm
- post-traumatic stress?

Bibliography

Davies, D. (1997). *Counselling in Psychological Services*. Milton Keynes: Open University Press.

Department of Health website: www.dh.gov.uk/

East, P. (1995). *Counselling in Medical Settings*. Milton Keynes: Open University Press.

Fernando, S. (ed.) (1995) *Mental Health in a Multi-Ethnic Society.* London: Routledge.

Hetherington, K. (2001). *Counsellors in Health Settings.* London: Jessica Kingsley.

McLeod, J. (2000). *An Administratively Created Reality: Some Problems With the Use of Self-Report Questionnaire Measures of Adjustment in Psychotherapy Outcome Research.* http://www.shs.tay.ac.uk/shtjm/

National Electronic Library for Health. www.nelh.nhs.uk

Proctor, Gillian (2002). 'The NHS in 2015: science fiction or scary possibility?', *Healthcare Counselling and Psychotherapy Journal,* **2**(3), 2–6.

Section III

EDUCATION SECTOR

9

Counselling in a School Setting

Linda Sheffrin (Chevin)

I took up my present position at Carisbrooke High School in May 2000 where, with the support of a part-time colleague, I have set up a student support centre for children with social, emotional and behavioural difficulties. I counsel regularly, and I run social skills groups for these children. My caseload of students includes some who have statements of special educational need (SEN) for social emotional and behavioural difficulties. All have various learning or social and emotional needs. For the statemented students I hold annual reviews to check progress and am responsible for the individual education plans of all my students on the SEN register. Though my colleague and I use counselling skills on a daily basis to help us deal with a range of issues, therapeutic counselling is always done on a strictly formal basis, when we decide it is an appropriate intervention. With parent/carer consent we usually contract for an initial six sessions, and review progress in the fourth or fifth session to decide whether or not to continue. These sessions are arranged weekly with fixed appointments lasting between 30 and 40 minutes.

A typical day

I arrive at the centre at 8 am in the hope of catching up with some paperwork. A parent rings me to ask my advice on strategies of how to deal with her teenage daughter who is frequently rude and is coming home far too late in the evenings. I empathize with how difficult teenagers can be and suggest ways to compromise. We agree on a meeting with all three of us present so we can attempt to resolve some of these difficulties. By the time we finish speaking, children ranging in age between 13 and 16 are arriving at the centre. They find it helpful to chat with us before school about their lives outside. It grounds them and prepares them for the day ahead. One lad needs a 'behaviour contract'. He and I agree on two positive targets to achieve in each of his lessons. He receives a point for each tick against the targets, marked by his teachers. Twenty points will earn him a reward. It is an uphill struggle for him. Yesterday he earned three points but two were deducted for poor behaviour. A long-term absentee turns up unexpectedly. He has just turned 16 and has been banned from living in the parental home. I help him fill in his benefits form and make various phone calls. I also arrange to see some staff so that he can complete his coursework in the centre.

After registration the three support assistants who are working today check their timetables with me. While they disperse to their respective classes I see my first student for counselling. He is a boy who is constantly abusive to peers, causing so much disruption in the classroom that he is frequently put in isolation for his own safety. It is a touching moment when I ask him if there is anyone in his life that he never verbally abuses: 'My grandmother' he states without hesitation. When asked what makes her different he answers: 'Because she loves me'.

I have to write up a file note on the parental phone call, and make some notes following the counselling session. I am just about to begin when a colleague comes into the office. She tells me a student has disclosed some violence at home. I see the child in question, who repeats the allegation. I have to contact the teacher in charge of child protection. She is tied up with a parent and asks me to contact social services. They arrange to come into school this afternoon and interview the student with me present. I have to log the call, and now have two file notes still to write as well as my counselling notes.

I am just finishing the first file note when I am interrupted by one of the behaviour support assistants. She tells me that one of our students has barricaded himself in a room in the student support centre. He is refusing to come out. I talk to him through the door. He is upset because he thinks he will be excluded again. It seems he was caught at the shop at break time and swore at one of the supervisors. I explain to him that if he comes out we can sort out the problem. I remind him that no student is excluded just for being off-site. It is his reactions when told off that trigger the major incidents leading to exclusion. He listens. I give him a couple of minutes to think about coming out of the room so that we can talk. He moves the chair, which he had used to jam the door handle, and quietly comes out. We talk a little longer. I now have a third file note to write, and manage finally to complete the first before the lunch break.

After lunch I have another counselling session, before meeting one of the nurse therapists from the child and adolescent mental health team (CAMHS). She has been working with one of our students who has reintegrated into mainstream education following a year out of school. This boy is a school phobic who has also been experiencing some agoraphobia outside school. The therapist has been working with him and his parents. We discuss how the centre can best help the student. We agree on some self-esteem building, some sessions on anger management and a modified timetable. So far the reintegration has been successful. The boy attends four days a week and has even managed to go to mainstream lessons in three different subjects.

After lunch a social worker with a female police constable comes to interview the child who disclosed violence at home. The child does not want to go ahead with a prosecution. This means that social services and the police are limited in their ability to help. They can do no more than arrange a child protection conference with a view to putting the child on the at risk register.

The social skills group goes well. We are role playing some situations where the students have to use their newly acquired assertiveness skills. This has been a revelation for the more aggressive students in the group as well as the more passive participants. One girl finds it difficult to understand why it is wrong to call a teacher 'Your Majesty'. She was only being 'polite'. Another student tells me he has been banned from all his social and religious education lessons. When I ask him why he tells me, 'I got angry and picked up a table. But it's not really fair. I wasn't going to throw it.'

Towards the end of the afternoon a head of year reports that one of his students has been self-harming. We face an ethical dilemma here. We know that confidentiality cannot be absolute, but clearly we need to make a decision in the best interests of the child. The student is claiming home is at the heart of the problem, yet we have a duty to inform the parents that their child is self-harming. We resolve the situation by enlisting the advice of CAMHS which is already working with the family, and we manage to gain the student's consent to inform the parents.

I always ensure that the children are aware from the outset that I cannot promise total confidentiality, and that if they tell me something that makes me feel they are at risk, or that someone close to them is at risk, I have a duty to pass on the information. I promise them that I will always do this openly and with their consent. It is a challenge, as it could mean that a child will not disclose. My experience so far is that most children who are desperate enough to disclose, do want something done about their situation. It took one of the children I worked with 36 sessions before she eventually disclosed the violence at home.

A girl wanders in and asks if I can spare her a few minutes. She tells me she has been told that she has obsessive-compulsive disorder, and wants to know what this is. Her symptoms corroborate the diagnosis. The girl consents to my ringing her mum. I advise the parent to take her daughter to the GP who will most probably refer the girl to the CAMHS clinic. My training helps me to recognize severe disorders that need to be referred on for psychiatric intervention.

At the end of the school day I complete all my file notes and counselling notes. I have to send out various memos to staff. I still have five more individual education plans to write, and preparation for a couple of annual reviews. They can wait until tomorrow.

My route in

I began teaching modern foreign languages in 1974, having spent four years at university to gain a BA (Hons) 2:1 in German, and a year studying for a postgraduate certificate in education. I taught in mainstream schools full time until 1995 with a career break of five years during which I had two children.

In 1995 a succession of traumas in my personal life led me to take a risk and consider a career change into counselling. I began a six-month RSA certificate course in counselling alongside continuing full-time work. I saw this as a taster, and indeed it led me towards my decision to qualify as a counsellor. I embarked on a part-time, two-year BAC accredited diploma course.

This commitment involved my moving to a part-time position in a different school, working four days a week. Towards the end of the course I had to counsel on a Saturday morning in order to make up my required counselling hours. On three days per week I was finishing as late as 9 or 9.30 pm, which was quite a struggle on top of a full working day. In July 1997 the struggle proved worth it, as I gained a diploma in counselling (with distinction). The course was eclectic, and covered integrative, cognitive/behavioural, multimodal, person-centred and solution-focused ways of working, broadly following Gerard Egan's *The Skilled Helper* (5th edn, 1994) as a framework.

In January of the year that I qualified, I applied for, and was offered, a part-time post (four days per week) with Kent County Council's Behaviour Support Service. I was employed as a counsellor in four different Kent Schools. I also did a lot of multi-agency work and became heavily involved with CAMHS and social services. In addition to counselling, I was contracted, as part of a team of three teachers, to deliver behaviour management training to staff within those schools.

When I had completed my diploma, Kent County Council employed me full-time. I went on to do an advanced certificate on 'children with emotional and behavioural difficulties', writing a school focused research project, which tackled the benefits of counselling in improving children's learning and emotional literacy.

I have found the eclectic course has fitted in very well with the type of counselling needed in the setting. 'An effective eclecticism must be more than a random borrowing of ideas and techniques from here and there' (Egan, 1994, p. 14). 'Client centred helping means that the needs of the client are the starting point, not the models and methods of the helper ... Eclecticism is the practice of helping people by drawing thoughtfully from a range of skills' (Egan, 1994, p. 21). Since qualifying I have been on several courses in solution-focused therapy, which fits in very well with my training model, and enhances my work.

A client story

I have chosen to use a composite mixture of material so as not to identify any one student. The boy (I shall call him Karl) is one of five brothers, three older and one younger. When I saw him initially he was in Year 8 and aged 12. He was referred to me because he exhibited severe emotional and behavioural difficulties in the classroom. Around the site he was extremely abusive to peers and could be violent if his anger was triggered. As part of the initial assessment of Karl, I met his family, and heard their side of the story.

At home he was always getting into fights with his brothers, usually because he was protecting his younger brother from the older two. Mum reported that Karl was difficult, moody and uncooperative, and seemed different from the others. Where they were boisterous and loud, Karl was frequently withdrawn. They talked about him as 'over-sensitive' and said that the older brothers were constantly picking on him because of his sensitivity. In the classroom Karl was clearly very intelligent, but was not achieving anything like his potential. He was disruptive, loud, attention-seeking and always responding with his fists or with verbal abuse when teased. He was frequently called 'gay' by other students, as they perceived his sensitivity in this way. Karl could not bear the tag and inevitably became aggressive in response.

Karl engaged really well in the counselling sessions. Over the next four weeks, using person-centred core conditions (Rogers, 1951), we were able to establish a relationship based on trust. Susannah Temple (1996, pp. 81–5) alludes to the effectiveness of non-directive counselling in schools. She talks of the few positive messages some children receive through their life experience. 'For some therefore, the very fact of having someone to listen to them and show them empathic understanding and give them wholehearted non-judgemental acceptance can be enough to raise their self-esteem. "This form of counselling rests on the humanistic assumption that when their needs are met, human beings tend to grow and flourish in their own best way" (Maslow, 1970).'

I worked with Karl to gradually rebuild his self-esteem. He began to value himself and see his differences from his brothers as positive. Given the opportunity to express his thoughts and feelings about his situation, Karl gained insights into his character and began learning some strategies on how to deal with his difficulties. Karl told me that he was very fond of his grandfather and would often visit him for long talks. It seems that this relation was able to bring out Karl's sensitive nature and offered him respite from his tumultuous home circumstances. Sometimes Karl arrived at the sessions so angry about something said to him earlier in the day that he needed an opportunity to work through his anger. On one occasion we walked around the field talking until he felt better.

Six weeks on, Karl disclosed to me that his father was violent towards him. Around the same time Karl's elderly grandfather, who had become terminally ill, finally died. Karl felt isolated outside school. Karl's inability to cope with his grief may have been an added trigger to his disclosure. He showed me bruises, which had been inflicted on him by his father from punching and kicking. Karl knew from the outset of the counselling sessions the implications of disclosing such information. He had no problem with my contacting social services, which I did through the teacher in charge of child protection at the school. Social services stepped in at this point and Karl was placed on the at-risk register. I was able, thanks to the school's cooperation, to attend the core group meetings. It emerged that the whole family was under extreme stress. Karl's father's job as shift worker involved long and unsocial hours. His mother found five boisterous boys more than she could handle. His father's response to the situation was extreme anger, which often spilled over into physical violence. It seems that he himself had been in care as a child and a lot of his violence towards Karl was learned behaviour. Social services worked closely with the family while I continued my one-to-one work with Karl.

Karl gradually learned how to manage his stress more effectively. Social services worked extensively with his father on his own childhood issues. The work with Karl was particularly effective because it was not limited to school. On several occasions I was able to help his mother with strategies on how to manage Karl. She had been very negative with him almost as habit, and she was eventually able to try a more positive approach with him, using praise and rewards. Because social services were working with his father, a change in Karl's home circumstances gradually began to have an impact on his behaviours at home and in school. When my work with him finished nearly 12 months later, Karl was developing into a mature boy who was learning to take responsibility for his behaviour.

In this particular case, working in a multi-agency way helped Karl and his family towards change. Had I been counselling Karl in isolation I doubt that that we could have achieved the same outcomes. The school was happy for me to work as long as was needed, because they could see measurable change in Karl's behaviour. At the time my work with him began he was very close to permanent exclusion. One year on, he was still coping in mainstream education. Though CAMHS was not directly involved with Karl I had regular supervision from the nurse therapist there, whose guidance and help was invaluable through some harrowing work with Karl.

Evaluation

I work with a colleague who is also a trained teacher and counsellor. She works two days a week and I work full-time. Within our team we also have three behaviour support assistants (one of whom is full-time) and a coordinator. In this setting our brief is very clear. We work with individuals and with groups of students to improve attendance and reduce the frequency and length of fixed-term exclusions. Our ultimate aim is to prevent any permanent exclusions, and we have achieved this so far. The fixed-term exclusions for our cohort in our first year were reduced by 42 per cent. Our targets are achievable and measurable.

When a student is referred to us, we do an initial assessment, which looks at the 'make up of the child'. We look at the following areas: the environment, the behaviours (including common patterns, antecedents), student's ability, beliefs, values, identity and self-esteem. As part of the initial assessment we usually link with the parents or carers.

Following the assessments we offer all or some of the following where appropriate: regular counselling, a modified timetable to include a programme of off-site alternative educational provision, a place in a small social skills group to improve peer relations, raise self-esteem and develop assertiveness skills.

The heads of year have regular feedback from staff on students who present with difficulties. Children of all levels of ability are referred to us via the heads of year. Referred students may be bright and able, may have special learning needs or may have statements of special educational need which could include learning and/or behavioural needs. In most cases the children's self-esteem is very low when they are first seen. As they begin to value themselves, there is often a marked improvement in their behaviour and frame of mind. With the heads of year we review each student individually on a fortnightly basis to monitor progress.

The head teacher at the school is committed to the idea that a student support centre can enhance the achievements of all referred students by helping raise student self-esteem and thereby re-engage them in learning. From our employer's point of view our effectiveness as counsellors is measured by our success at keeping children in mainstream education. From our point of view we track and monitor student's increasing confidence and improved social skills. We speak to their form tutors and subject staff, and ask for regular pastoral progress reports to help us measure the improvements. We also ask students to fill in evaluation sheets so that we can monitor their perception of the support offered. Following in-depth departmental discussion we move students from the 'active intervention' list to 'monitoring only'. When students are being monitored we arrange to see them periodically rather than weekly for an informal 'check-in'.

The centre is open to all students (referred or otherwise) in the morning and afternoon breaks and during the 40-minute lunch break. The students enjoy coming to the centre for their lunch break. We have an ethos of mutual respect, where students feel safe and valued. They know the rules. These are few in number and are very basic: respect each other verbally and physically, respect property. The students respond well to the firm boundaries, and those who cross them are rarely banned for more than a day, and then welcomed back. It seems to work well. As a staff we 'model' good behaviour while eating and chatting. For some students it is the only time they have an opportunity to sit around a table for a meal and to socialize. The setting is therapeutic for the students, and the staff are committed to its success.

Continuing professional development

Schools have budgets for staff training. We receive regular information about training courses in counselling and behaviour management. As long as our requests are reasonable, we are encouraged to go on courses, which we then evaluate and feed back to the senior management team. We have three 'performance management' meetings with our line manager per year, which include discussion of our training needs.

Conditions of work

In teaching children the skills to tackle their personal difficulties and life events, I see the opportunity to help raise self-esteem and empower children to improve their social interactions and feel happier. Children can be helped to see they can change their responses, which can enable them to take a more optimistic view of the future.

There are limitations to do with time and confidentiality. Counselling slots with adults are made regularly and are usually 50 minutes. In a school setting this is a lot more difficult to achieve and is not always desirable. Most children can concentrate on this kind of work for 30 minutes at most. The slots also have to fit around lesson times, breaks, lunches and numerous bells. There are timetable restrictions (such as two-week timetables in some schools), which make this very complex. A lot of time is wasted when children forget their slots, and are perhaps not in the classrooms that are on their timetables.

Although we try not to be disturbed during counselling sessions, in a school context there are sometimes crises to be resolved which do not easily await the end of a session. If a child comes into the centre angry he or she can be violent or aggressive. Sometimes I am the only one around to deal with it. I usually find that the students are so grateful for the full attention and time that they are given, they can accept the rare interruptions.

Confidentiality is tricky. Schools are in loco parentis and have a duty of care. They are accountable to the parents. They cannot really refer students without parental consent. Counselling is normally discreet. Sometimes it is relevant and even occasionally helpful to the school situation for it not to be! Heads of year often need information that sheds light on behavioural difficulties. However, information cannot be disclosed without the child's consent. Child protection is an additional major issue when tackling confidentiality with children.

Supervision is not always easy to organize. When I worked with the Kent County Council Behaviour Support Service, we had regular supervision from a nurse therapist with CAMHS. The local education authority did not have to pay for this as CAMHS recognized that we kept its waiting lists low, being able to deal with a lot of the less serious cases 'in-house'. At Carisbrooke we have recently set up a similar link with CAMHS which has agreed to offer regular supervision for our more difficult cases. For routine cases we work on a basis of co-supervision between the two fully qualified counsellors on our team.

Having a dual role as counsellor and teacher in charge of the support centre is not easy. I have to make use of my own 'internal supervisor' to ensure that I can adhere to this important role distinction.

Without qualified teacher status, career progression in education is limited. There are currently opportunities with the Connexions organization to train as a personal advisor. This is a new initiative, and the training is going on throughout the country in each education authority. The training for unqualified teachers is over a ten-month period and the sessions are one day per week. For qualified teachers training can be completed in ten days. The salary ranges from £11,000 to £24,000 per annum depending on experience and qualifications. Counselling skills are useful in this field. Advisors act as the link person and coordinator for youngsters aged 16–19 who may be experiencing personal difficulties.

Experience working with children could lead to a counselling role within the NSPCC. Social services are also looking for educational social workers with counselling experience, though a diploma in social work is usually required.

As a counsellor in a school setting you need to be able to relate equally well to adults and young people. You need to be empathic to teachers' problems in dealing with difficult youngsters. It will achieve little if you only take a child's eye view of situations, although having empathy with young people is vital too. Some knowledge of family and group dynamics may help you step back and see conflicts as a whole picture, and this may facilitate solution building. Ability to communicate and work confidently alongside a range of other professional colleagues is also a significant part of the job here.

You need to have strategies and skills that help children manage their anger and conflicts and be able to put them across to the students; I find assertiveness skills particularly useful. You need to be able to communicate with young people without patronizing them or alienating them. Employers would value evidence of experience of work with young people in other capacities, as well as work with parents and appreciation of your own learning from experience as a parent.

It is essential to be able to deal with more than one situation at a time without losing focus. Knowledge of child development, child protection procedures, other agencies, CAMHS, social services, child protection conferences, core group meetings and the education system is also crucial.

As well as at least a diploma in counselling, it is desirable and adds to your credibility with teaching colleagues to hold a teaching certificate or a diploma in social work.

Future developments

Goleman (1996, p. xiv) can foresee a day when mainstream education will routinely include development of intra and interpersonal competencies such as self-awareness, self-control, empathy, listening skills, conflict resolution and cooperation. Current research in this area promotes emotional literacy (Goleman, 1996, Appendix F: Social and emotional learning: results). Virginia Makins also quotes Rob Long, an educational psychologist with Devon County Council: '"You can work on their (children's) emotional literacy", he says, "and help them see their difficulties as challenges they can overcome" ... above all he wants to promote the importance of the emotions and self-esteem, at a time when the official focus is on curriculum and academic outcomes' (Virginia Makins, 1999).

There are some local education authorities (LEAs) who employ counsellors in their schools. Other schools purchase time from a local counselling service, for example 'The Listening Ear' in Bournemouth, which is well established and provides a service of fully qualified counsellors who receive good supervision. The LEA commends that service to schools, and three of them use the service regularly. You can find out an individual LEA's policy from the full directory of LEAs (see references).

Ten top tips

Generic tips:

- Reflect on the positive outcomes each day and avoid dwelling on the negatives.
- The work is extremely demanding and sometimes harrowing, so find a balance in your life of work, rest and play to replenish energy levels.

Context-specific tips:

- Ensure you are familiar with the local authority/school child protection procedures.
- Familiarize yourself with picture/story work if you choose to work with younger children.
- An additional qualification (for example in teaching or in social work) will greatly enhance your likelihood of finding a job in a school setting.
- Look for work in a school where the head teacher supports emotional literacy.
- If you have no teaching qualification, expect that you will have to work in more than one school to make the job up to full time.
- Be prepared to offer a counselling service to staff as well as pupils.
- If you are working in the field of behaviour management, make sure you hear the views of all parties and beware of premature judgements.
- Recognize that there will be some students who are not ready to accept your help and will as a consequence reject it.

A girl you have been counselling discloses violence at home. She understands that you must pass this on to social services but she says that is a waste of your time, as she won't tell them anything. How will you handle this?

Bibliography

Egan, G. (1994) *The Skilled Helper* (5th edn). California: Brooks/Cole.

Furman, B. and Ahola, T. (1992) *Solution Talk Hosting Therapeutic Conversations*. New York: Norton.

Goleman, D. (1996) *Emotional Intelligence*. London: Bloomsbury.

Jones, K. and Charlton, T. (eds) (1996) *Overcoming Learning and Behaviour Difficulties*. London and New York: Routledge.

Lawrence, D. (1998) *Enhancing Self Esteem in the Classroom*. London: Paul Chapman Publishing.

Makins, V. (1999) 'Star of the Show at Special Needs North; Opinion; Editorial', *Times Educational Supplement*, 23 April.

Maslow, A. (1970) *Motivation and Personality* (2nd edn). London: Harper and Row.

Newton, J. (2002) *Guidelines for Counselling in Schools*.

Rhodes, J. and Ajmal, Y. (1995) *Solution Focused Thinking in Schools*. London: BT Press.

Rogers, C. R. (1951) *On Becoming a Person*. Boston: Houghton Mifflin.

Temple, S. (1996) In K. Jones and T. Charlton (eds), *Overcoming Learning and Behaviour Difficulties*. London and New York: Routledge, pp. 81–5.

A full directory of education authorities can be obtained from:

The School Government Publishing Company Ltd, Darby House, Redhill, Surrey. RH1 3DN. Tel: 01737 642223. Fax: 01737 644283.

Connexions Service National Unit, Department for Education and Skills, Moorfoot, Sheffield, S1 4PQ. info@dfes.gsi.gov.uk

10

Counselling in a Further Education Setting

Lindsey Neville

Evesham and Malvern Hills College is a general further education college. 'Further education is everything that does not happen in schools and universities' (Kennedy, 1997, p. 1). In 2001/2002 it had 594 full-time students and 7919 part-time students. It operates across two sites, 35 miles apart. The primary role of the college counsellor is to support teaching and learning through the provision of a confidential counselling service. It is part of a package of student services which focus on improving retention figures at the same time as enabling students to maximize their educational opportunities (Association for University and College Counselling (AUCC), 1999).

A typical day

The day begins with an informal approach by Mike, a lecturer, who meets me on the stairs and wants to discuss a student who has confided in him. We make an arrangement to meet at lunchtime, to discuss the matter in confidence. I find Emma, a student I know well, waiting outside my office. Emma has needed a great deal of support in the transition from school to college and makes contact several times each week. Over the weekend she has had a row with parents. I spend 20 minutes listening to her feelings about the row, and trying to help Emma see her parents' perspective. Half an hour at the beginning and end of the day offers students like Emma immediate access to the service. Staff might also drop in, with either their own concern or concern for a student.

I use the time until my first assessment session of the day to listen and respond to telephone messages. Students are able to refer themselves to the service and anonymously reserve an appointment by filling in a timetable on the door. Other than ongoing clients, I rarely know who to expect. First-appointment clients are offered a 30-minute session to give them information about the service and to assess appropriateness for counselling. Helen, 16, has just discovered that she is pregnant. She is very tearful and frightened and would like to be able to talk about what she is going to do. I arrange to see her at the end of the day.

Helen is immediately followed by Jane, a 33-year-old student who has just found out that her husband of ten years is having an affair. Jane is shocked and I offer her four sessions to explore her feelings. In a five-minute space I am able to make quick notes on the new clients. Then Susan arrives. She is a member of staff in the middle of a series of six sessions following her return to work after a long period of stress-related illness. We spend the session exploring practical ways in which she can minimize her stress response.

An hour is then set aside to respond to client e-mails. E-mail counselling proved very popular following its introduction in 2000, particularly with students for whom access was an issue. This might include those in rural areas, students from the smaller site, students with physical disabilities, those with caring responsibilities and those who feel more comfortable, at least initially, talking anonymously. Young men are particularly high users of the service.

Darren is a 17-year-old male student, who has only made contact by e-mail:

> I'm finding it really hard to attend college lately, there is just too much going on in my head, it takes all my willpower just to get out of bed in the morning, I know it's no real excuse for missing lessons but I just find it so hard to get through a whole day pretending that everything is all right when clearly my life is too complicated to deal with, I just want to hide from everything and everyone but I'm afraid of being chucked off my course if this carries on and I really don't want that because I do enjoy it, I just can't concentrate at the moment.

Anne, a 40-year-old part-time student, is only able to access the service every three weeks and so used the e-mail service as a way to reflect on her understanding of the sessions:

> I think I feel slightly awkward and self-conscious about some of the things I told you today which I probably wouldn't tell anyone normally because I feel so embarrassed about it. I wanted to communicate with you about last week's session and its effects. I think the session was very beneficial because afterwards I kept returning to the idea about everything involving risk. Whilst thinking about it I started feeling truly liberated like I had just shrugged off a straitjacket. It changed my state of mind throughout the day and night. It was wonderful.
>
> I'm struggling again now, but am also conscious of that liberation and want to find it again and develop it. A few points occur to me ... when I was in my teens and twenties I took more risks but I didn't perceive them to be risks. I expect I didn't think a lot about it. I'm not certain, but I can see that I have been trying to create a 'risk-free' zone, which is agonizing, frightening and dull. It's only through 'talking' with you that I can see about taking calculated risks ... I don't think I've previously thought about it so clearly or from that angle.

Mike arrives for the meeting we arranged earlier in the day, and we discuss ways in which he can support his student using listening skills. I offer information about support agencies appropriate to the case.

Lisa, a mature student I have been seeing regularly for several months following the breakdown of her marriage, phones to say that she won't be able to make her appointment as her son is unwell and off school. She uses the call to update me on what has been happening to her since the last session and we reschedule the appointment for the following week. These unexpected spaces in the schedule offer an opportunity to make brief notes or, in reality, gulp coffee, grab a sandwich or dash to the toilet!

Once a week I run a counselling session at the second site in Malvern. The college is 45 minutes' drive away, which creates a welcome opportunity to enjoy some emotional space. The service here operates as a drop-in session for the first hour followed by pre-booked appointments.

Claire, a student with learning difficulties, uses the drop-in to speak about difficulties she is experiencing with other students in the group. I teach her some strategies to help her integrate with the group. The first of the pre-booked appointments is taken by Rob, a 19-year-old student who is beginning to confront a drug problem. We are working towards enabling Rob to access the services of a specialist drug agency. A member of staff has booked the second appointment to discuss her difficult working relationship with a colleague.

Following my return to the main site I have time to update my notes on those I have just seen before my second meeting of the day with Helen. The day ends as it began, with an opportunity for clients to 'drop in'.

My route in

In common, I suspect, with most counsellors, my journey into counselling has been partly accidental. I began my professional life as a teacher. While at college I became the sabbatical president of the students' union, which involved me for the first time in the emotional issues affecting other young people. During this time a college friend committed suicide. Looking back, his death was the beginning of a growing awareness of the importance of talking therapies in helping individuals cope with difficult areas of their lives.

I went on to teach for many years in both special and secondary education. After ten years, seeking variety and change, I accepted a post as the education officer for the local branch of the British Red Cross Society. During my seven years with the charity the local authority offered a variety of free training places to voluntary agencies. I was allocated a counselling skills course. I loved the work and decided to fund myself through the next course with the same training provider. With a Royal Society of Arts (RSA) certificate in counselling skills for education and training, I looked around for what might be my next step in counselling, exploring opportunities with several different voluntary organizations. I applied to Relate and was fortunate to be accepted to train as a couple counsellor. Throughout training, and after completing the Relate certificate in couple counselling, I continued to work part-time while couple counselling as a volunteer.

I probably would have continued to combine part-time teaching with volunteering had it not been for a number of personal issues that arose at about the same time. My employer made my post redundant, and the offered alternative did not seem an attractive proposition. I had a major operation, my father died and I celebrated a 'significant' birthday. These events heralded a change in the professional direction of my life, and happily coincided with the advertisement for a college counsellor at Evesham and Malvern Hills College.

My success at interview may have been attributable partly to my professional qualifications as a teacher, rather than my experience or qualifications as a counsellor. In further education, particularly smaller colleges, multitasking is highly valued. My post incorporated other student support responsibilities in addition to the key role of providing a confidential counselling service. For the first few years of my employment I was responsible for the college accommodation service, the students' union and equal opportunities. Gradually, through negotiation, and as a result of growing client demand, these additional responsibilities were reallocated.

My theoretical approach has its roots in the three-stage model of counselling. The core activities of the three-stage model particularly lend themselves to the, usually, focused short-term work of both Relate and the college setting. The diverse nature of the client group necessitates a flexible approach and may lead me to adopt a more eclectic approach in some circumstances. The person-centred model enables me to put at the centre of the work, the acknowledgement that each of us is born with the resources to cope effectively with all that life involves (Rogers, 2002). My task, as the counsellor, is to help clients to rediscover their abilities, and to identify and try out new ones. My relationship with the clients is crucial in achieving that outcome.

A client story

John is a 19-year-old student with a physical disability and learning difficulties. John felt he needed someone to talk to, and was able to ask his tutor to arrange an appointment with me. John and I had never met before. He was very anxious and asked whether his tutor could accompany him.

I began by acknowledging the effort that John had made to arrange some help for himself, and gave some explanation of what counselling is. I acknowledged the presence of the tutor, and we spoke about confidentiality. It became clear that the tutor's role was introductory, to ease the first session for John. As John became more relaxed with me I began to understand his speech a little better. This was to become much easier as the sessions progressed. This first session involved developing rapport with John and setting up the contract.

John arrived very promptly for his next session, and appeared less anxious than I had expected, as the tutor had telephoned me to say that John had decided to come alone from now on.

The first thing that I noticed about John in this second session was his sense of humour; he was very witty and quick to poke fun at himself. Even at this early stage it felt like a defence mechanism. I felt that it was too early in our relationship to share this with him, and I stored this away for a later session. He seemed reluctant to focus on his reason for arranging the sessions. I gently expressed my feeling that this must be very difficult for him, acknowledging his discomfort. Gradually John began to tell me that he had recently had money stolen. He suspected a flatmate. He appeared very upset by the theft, and I reflected his distress. John told me that he knew who had stolen the money, but that he could not forgive – he kept repeating, 'Once a thief, always a thief'. A pattern had arisen in this initial work, in which John always asked me for reassurance that he was right. I always used it as an opportunity to encourage him to explore what he thought, and the evidence for it. He seemed to have a number of sayings that did not seem congruent with his pattern of language. Gradually, as our relationship developed, John was able to give me an insight into his past that was to move the work on.

Throughout the work there was a need to work through, in supervision, the frustrations caused by John's speech impairment. Supervision gave me an opportunity to express frustrations around the speed of the work. I needed to ensure the accuracy of my understanding of what John had told me, and discovered that very frequent summaries achieved the accuracy that I was seeking, and reaffirmed for John that he had been heard. This was something that he later told me had been the key enabling him to unlock early pain. For me it was a reminder of the value of ensuring that clients feel they have been heard.

Over the next four weeks John slowly told me his history. He was the eldest of three boys. His father drank heavily, did not work to support the family, and when drunk was violent. The family seemed to have a very spartan existence. The parents argued violently and it appears that they were unable to cope with John's special needs. John was happiest at school, but one day he returned home to find that his mother had left. To this day she has made no contact with him. Eventually John was taken into foster care, where he stayed until he was 16. He returned to the local area recently to attend college. Contact with his father is almost non-existent. His only fond childhood memory was of an aunt. In supervision I was able to speak about the sadness that I felt for John, and to acknowledge the anger that I felt at the treatment he had received.

As a trusting relationship developed between us I was able to gain an insight into John's very lonely existence. He always tried to present a social life that was very active and full of friends. He used humour repeatedly. Using immediacy, I was able to share with him my earlier concerns, and gradually a different picture emerged. John was enabled to reveal his vulnerability. In an effort to meet people John had developed the habit of spending each evening in the pub: he had found that drinking helped him to feel better. It eased his isolation. He had recently begun to recognize that he was becoming violent, easily falling into arguments with others. He had been stealing to be able to afford his visits to the pub. As we talked about the drinking and I offered him new information about the effects of alcohol, he said, 'Once a drinker, always a drinker'. I was able to make a tentative link, and guessed that these were phrases used by the aunt that had stuck in John's mind. It seemed important to challenge the basis for the theory, but John was resistant to the challenge. I wondered whether in challenging the phrase John perceived me to be putting the one positive image from his family, that of his aunt, in a negative light.

At this stage in the work I felt very stuck. I felt that the counselling had progressed well. I had established a good relationship with John, but could not see a way to move the work on. I decided to take the case to supervision before I next saw John. In talking the case through with my supervisor I was able to identify a degree of transference in the relationship. I had picked up John's stuck feelings, and was also colluding with him, in that I wanted to preserve for John his positive image of his aunt. Through supervision I was able to acknowledge previously recognized 'rescuing instincts'.

As a result of supervision I decided to help John to look at why his aunt might have said that about drinkers. John guessed that it might have been because her brother (his father) had a drink problem that he had never overcome. It had caused him to become violent and had been responsible for much of the pain in both of their lives. I left a long pause after he had said this and then told John that I believed it could be different for him.

John and I moved on from this point to focus on facilitating a change in his drinking behaviour. The work has been slow, six months have passed since our first session and we still meet regularly for the support that John feels he needs to effect change. I encouraged John to speak with his GP, and he is also working with John in a supportive capacity. This was vital in ensuring that John had some source of support during the college holidays, when he does not have access to the college counsellor. One of the key areas of more recent work has been to facilitate the reframing of some of John's 'right and wrong' judgements of himself to 'better than, worse than'.

Evaluation

The Office for Standards in Education (OFTSED) carries out inspections of post-16 non-higher education and training under

Part III of the Learning and Skills Act 2000 using the common inspection framework. The framework evaluates the access learners have to relevant, effective support on personal issues.

The annual survey, undertaken by AUCC, is used to collect data on the state of counselling in further and higher education. It reports a steady increase in the proportion of seriously disturbed students using the service since 1995–96. Fifteen per cent of all counselling clients in further education (FE) and higher education (HE) presented an issue linked to suicide (AUCC, 2002). Internally, the same system is used to collect and record data for the purpose of management reports. This data identifies a number of the key concerns for students using the service. Despite these pressures on the service, FE has on average a far higher number of students per counsellor than other institution types (AUCC, 2002). The number of people with mental health problems in FE has risen (FEFC, 1996) at a time when counsellor/student ratios are worsening.

There are self-led opportunities to develop further understanding about the client base, which can be used to inform practice. I undertook a small research project to explore what contributes to 16–19-year-old student unhappiness. (See Table 10.1.)

A research project into self-esteem amongst a group of 16–19-year-old students highlighted a link between self-esteem and experience of loss before the age of 10. This was used to develop a series of group sessions for students who self-referred or were referred to the group by a member of staff.

Continuing professional development

There are many opportunities within the setting, with funding usually coming from a designated staff development budget. Sometimes this will involve a percentage contribution towards the cost, and occasionally full costs. My employer is fully supportive of my professional development. During my six years at the college I have successfully worked towards British Association for Counselling and Psychotherapy (BACP) accreditation and United Kingdom Register of Counsellors (UKRC) registration. As a way of dealing with the professional isolation I was also supported in completing a B.Sc. (Hons) in health studies at the local university. Further support is available in the form of short courses. Internal

Table 10.1 Causes of unhappiness in 16–19-year-old Evesham College students	
Relationships	**%**
Boyfriend	20.36%
Girlfriend	49.70%
Partner	33.53%
Father	44.31%
Mother	8.38%
Stepfather	28.74%
Stepmother	30.54%
Brother(s) Sister(s)	54.49%
Friend(s)	52.10%
Behaviours	
College work	22.75%
Appearance	19.76%
Violence	69.46%
Drugs	71.26%
Smoking	55.69%
Part-time work	6.59%
Money	27.54%
Weight	47.71%
Sex	58.68%
Gender issues	21.56%
Alcohol	37.13%
Other	3.59%

Source: Neville (2001)

staff development days run regularly within the college and can be freely accessed by all staff. These might include anything from information sessions on pensions, substance abuse, and sexual health to full computer courses or 'drop in' information technology development opportunities.

Diversity in my work and personal development has been achieved through teaching on a number of further and higher education programmes. Further development could also be achieved by becoming involved in other areas within the colleges. Keen volunteers are always sought to become members of college committees. This is an excellent way to ease the isolation and gain an insight into the work of the college.

There are opportunities to become involved in leading staff development sessions to raise awareness amongst tutors of the role of the counselling service and the kinds of issues that students bring to the counsellor.

Conditions of work

'Isolation, frustration and anxiety are occupational hazards of being a counsellor/therapist' (Dale, 2002). This isolation is often compounded in FE as most institutions only employ one counsellor. There is no one readily available with whom to discuss areas of common interest. This adds to the intensity of the work. Clients directly access the counsellor; there is no receptionist with whom they book sessions. There are no opportunities for a daily debrief, or lighter exchanges between clients.

Evesham and Malvern Hills College does pay for regular supervision in line with BACP guidelines, but it cannot be assumed that all colleges financially support supervision. When I took up the post at the college there was no supervision provided by the organization. However, the senior management team listened to my views on the importance of supervision and its relationship to my own health and well-being. Supervision, within BACP guidelines, was then provided. I approached this solitary working environment by contacting all college counsellors within a 25-mile radius of my own college and inviting them to join me in a network of further education colleges. The network exists to provide opportunities for counsellors in similar circumstances to support each other. We meet together regularly to discuss matters of common interest.

For reasons of confidentiality and the potentially delicate nature of the work, my line manager is the college principal. This affords an opportunity to directly access the decision-making bodies within the organization and offer feedback on the emotional climate within the institution. However in other FE colleges the counselling service may be part of student services, and line management is through the head of student services.

College counsellors are usually paid on a term-time-only basis. This has the benefit of providing regular opportunity for respite from counselling, and a chance to recharge batteries. However, it does inevitably have financial implications, as college holidays are unpaid. Salaries are usually on a clerical scale rather than in line with the lecturers' scales of pay as recommended by BACP (Palmer, 2002).

The amount and variety of available client work is endless, making it ideal work for anyone needing to build up his or her counselling hours. Clients can be anything from 14 years old upwards.

It is very easy for boundaries to become unclear in institutional counselling. It is common for the counsellor to be called for to deal with immediate situations such as students or members of staff crying. Both students and staff will seek out the counsellor in times of particular stress and it is often difficult to remember where one heard a particular piece of information. Social relationships at work can become very strained. It is challenging to maintain the integration and separateness necessary to deliver a quality service. This is best achieved though maintaining ethical boundaries.

Confidentiality is a vital feature of the counselling service. Issues of confidentiality can be complicated in this sector as there are three different categories of students who may need special consideration. 'Increased flexibility for 14–16 year olds', the Department for Education and Skills (DFES) programme which began in September 2002, created a new dimension to the provision of a further education counselling service, given that it introduced the potential of work with students under 16. Counsellors need to ensure that clients within this group are of sufficient age and understanding that they may be treated for all intents and purposes as if they were 16 (Bond, 2002). An awareness of the Children Act (1989) and 'Gillick' competence (this relates to the young person's ability to fully understand the choices that they are making) will therefore be useful in ensuring that these responsibilities with regard to confidentiality are met.

Future developments

The vision for the future of the sector suggests that it needs to 'promote opportunities for support staff to advance in their careers' (DFES, 2002, p. 39). Currently there are few opportunities for counsellors to progress. In larger colleges progression might be possible within a small team of counsellors. Otherwise, progression would undoubtedly mean moving out of the sector.

Funding is a crucial factor in the problems of the sector, with FE having lost 38 per cent of its real budget since the mid-1990s (BACP, 2002).

Recent initiatives in further education, such as widening participation, impact upon the client work, and a range of support services for students are now seen as crucial in maximizing student learning (Kennedy, 1997). Within FE today there exists a mix of vocational and academic options pursued by 14–19-year-old learners, which begins to break down barriers between schools and colleges (DFES, 2002).

There appears to be an emerging partnership for the support of young people. The Connexions Service, rolled out nationally in 2003, aims to help teenagers make the transition from school to further education and the job market, and occupies a key role in supporting and signposting 14–19-year-olds. College counsellors will need to become part of the support package that helps young people to overcome barriers to participation and achievement (DFES, 2003).

Much of the work is adolescent task-oriented, with eating disorders, self-harm, self-esteem and family breakdown central issues for the further education counsellor. Any special interest in these issues will be beneficial. It is often difficult to separate the counselling work from welfare issues, and an understanding of financial and benefit matters together with an extensive knowledge of local and national referral agencies would be advantageous.

Information technology has had a major impact on the work in recent years, with students able to book appointments by e-mail and access online therapy (BAC, 1999). Consequently, intending counsellors hoping to secure work within the further education sector would be well advised to work towards a high level of IT literacy.

Ten top tips

Generic tips:

- Establish a supportive professional network.
- Create a database of referral agencies.
- Ensure that IT skills are up to date.
- Develop personal strategies for coping with the emotional intensity of the work.
- Join the British Association for Counselling and Psychotherapy (student membership is available).

Context-specific tips:

- Gain experience of working or volunteering with young people.
- Get involved with other areas of the work in the college, for example, equal opportunities, student consultation, health and safety.
- Read widely, particularly around the theoretical frameworks of adolescence.
- Develop an information and knowledge base around issues of substance abuse.
- 'Value added': consider acquiring/developing additional skills such as first aid, sign language or a foreign language.

 Given the rising suicide rate amongst young people generally since the 1970s, what part can a college counselling service play in improving the mental health of its students?

Bibliography

AUCC (1999) *A Report from the Heads of University Counselling Services Degrees of Disturbance: The New Agenda*. Rugby: BAC.
AUCC (2000) *Categorisation of Client Concerns*. Rugby: BACP.
AUCC (2002) *Annual Survey of Counselling in Further and Higher Education*. Rugby: BACP.
BAC (1999) *Counselling On Line...Opportunities and Risks in Counselling Clients via the Internet*. Rugby: BAC.

BACP (2002) *Student Mental Health – Wall to Wall Support?* Press release, 25 November.

Bell, E. (1996) *Counselling in Further and Higher Education.* Milton Keynes: Open University Press.

Bond, T. (2002) *Confidentiality Guidelines for College Counsellors in Further Education and Sixth Form.* http://www.bacp.co.uk/members_visitors/members_login/info_sheets/info-sheet-E6.htm accessed 09/03/03

Catan, L., Dennison, C. M. and Coleman, J. (1996) *Getting Through: Effective Communication in the Teenage Years.* BT Forum.

Dale, H. (2002) *Am I Fit to Practise as a Counsellor?* http://www.bacp.co.uk/members_visitors/password/members_login_page2.htm (accessed 9 Mar 2003)

Davies, J. (2000) In P. Aggleton, J. Hurry and I. Warwick (eds), *Young People and Drugs in Young People and Mental Health.* Chichester: Wiley.

Dearing, R. (1997) *Higher Education in the Learning Society.* London: HMSO.

DFES (2002) *Success for All. Reforming FE and Training: Our Vision for the Future.* London: DFES.

DFES (2003) *14–19: Opportunity and Excellence*, annexes. London: DFES.

Further Education Funding Council (FEFC) (1996) *Report of the Learning Difficulties and/or Disabilities Committee.* London: HMSO.

Kennedy, H. (1997) *Learning Works.* Coventry: FEFC.

Lees, J. and Vaspe, A. (eds) (1999) *Clinical Counselling in Further and Higher Education.* London: Routledge.

Neville, L. (2001) *Mental Health of 16–19 Year Old Students at Evesham College*, unpublished.

Palmer, I. (2002) *Guidelines for the Employment of Counsellors* http://www.bacp.co.uk/members_visitors/password/members_login_page2.htm. (accessed 28 Mar 2002)

Rana, R. (2000) *Counselling Students: A Psychodynamic Perspective.* London: Macmillan.

Rogers, C. (2002) *Client Centred Therapy.* London: Constable.

Stanley, N. and Manthorpe, J. (eds) (2002) *Students' Mental Health Needs: Problems and Responses.* London and New York: Jessica Kingsley.

11

Counselling in a Higher Education Setting

Maggie Reid and Kevin Rodgers

Photograph taken by Judith Railton

We, Maggie Reid and Kevin Rodgers, work in a college of higher education (HE), Liverpool Hope, with university status. (Our degrees are currently awarded by Liverpool University.) We provide an example of a small counselling service set up to serve approximately 7000 students, helping them achieve their potential in HE. The team – three counsellors and a secretary/receptionist – is embedded as permanent staff within the institution. HE institutions vary in size, with the larger ones employing a core team of staff who counsel students and staff too, as well as sometimes managing and supervising a group of 'associate counsellors'. These can be voluntary or hourly paid.

Maggie will firstly give you a flavour of the hands-on counselling work in this setting by describing a 'typical day', followed by a case vignette, then Kevin, as head of service, will give a managerial perspective and look at some operational matters. We will both also describe our route into our current roles. We work together and meet regularly as a team to ensure the smooth running and development of the service, and also discuss our input and reaction to college wide initiatives. Feeling part of a small unit can be supportive, stimulating and fun. It can also sometimes feel a little claustrophobic when we are in the depths of a semester and stress levels are highest.

A typical day

Sun streams into my room and at 9 am I look, from my warm enclave, onto frosty white all-weather astroturf. It is February. The *Hope Virtually Daily* webpage on my computer greets me with news of sundry college events. Reading my e-mail, some of which relates to lecturing I am also doing here, I have a sense of belonging to a vibrant community. I say 'Hi' to Joan, the service's secretary. Joan initially receives clients and assigns them an appointment and counsellor. Today I have one new client, three regulars and a supervisee, and it is my turn to cover our daily 'emergency slot'. Having located all relevant notes for the day's 50-minute sessions, I prepare to receive my first client at 9.30 am.

At 26, Sandra is a single parent of three young children she finds difficult. Sandra fiddles with her fingers, but now doesn't bite them, as she tells me she's pleased with the way she's been standing up for herself recently. She had been abandoned by her second husband, and currently suffered chronic depression alongside an abusive relationship with a female partner. She came conscientiously to counselling last semester for four weeks to work on her confidence. Now we are consolidating that work. With widening participation, we get many mature, working class, local clients who are the first generation to attend HE. The clash of cultures, together with any financial and family problems, often makes for intolerable pressure. The next client is due at 10.45 am so I have time to complete records and brief notes, which are kept in a securely locked filing cabinet.

The next client's record sheet tells me Angela is 19 and has been referred by her GP who has a regular weekly surgery on campus.

She does not arrive. Joan asks if I can fit in a client who is currently with her. Claire explains through tears that she has abandoned her final teaching practice after a crisis of confidence. She made herself come back to college after a week at home. Highly anxious and desperately lost, she wails, 'What's wrong with me?' By the end of the session, she has admitted to questioning her choice of career for some time. We agree our working contract, arrange next week's meeting time, and she departs looking tired but relieved.

After a coffee I'm ready for my midday client. Deirdre saw me in her first year, presenting with multiple problems including an eating disorder, depression, social difficulties and a history of family sexual abuse. Having attended a hospital psychotherapy group while in her second year, she returned to me. She is close to deciding to take a break from her final year of degree studies, the pressure being too great. Deirdre is the kind of client who 'spills' over. After discussing and agreeing to her request for me to write letters of explanation and support to tutors, at intervals, I now find myself regularly consulted about her worrying behaviour by them and others. Elsa Bell (in Lees and Vaspe, 1999, p. 10) describes how useful it can be for some students to witness a counsellor and tutor working together so that they can introject a more positive 'parental' model than they have perhaps experienced at home. Yesterday I got a call from the academic in charge of halls of residence saying the cleaners were concerned about Deirdre leaving bin bags of vomit outside her door. There is a tension between serving the client's interests as well as those of the community. It is important to negotiate appropriate boundaries with all concerned. Eileen Smith (in Lees and Vaspe, 1999, p. 139) talks of the need for a counsellor in this setting to have 'clear but permeable boundaries' to accommodate the prevailing emotional climate in the individual, institution and wider social context.

There are a steadily increasing number of clients presenting in HE with chronic severe mental health difficulties (HUCS, 1999, section C). I find they test boundaries and present huge demands on the counsellor in this setting. Excellent supervision is a must. Some larger institutions employ a mental health coordinator, or the counselling services work closely with a community psychiatric nurse for the more psychotic cases. Most, like Hope, have a mental health policy.

A welcome lunch break means I leave my room to meet a colleague and friend for lunch.

Refreshed, I return to receive Sylvia at 2 pm, an Indian student at Hope for her degree. She went to her GP because of breathing problems and was referred to counselling. She has anxieties about academic work, living in hall and being apart from her French boyfriend and maintaining the relationship. She is showing signs of disturbed eating behaviour. We continue to build trust together. We have a low-key open contract (*AUCC Newsletter and Journal Special Issue*, November 2002, p. 38). Many young students do not like the idea of 'contracts' so perhaps avoiding that term and using a more flexibly structured 'working arrangement', which is still sufficiently therapeutically 'holding', works better in these cases.

At 3 pm I supervise a counselling trainee on placement with our service.

At 4 pm Andrew walks in, red in the face and shaking. He was mugged last night, his money and mobile phone taken. He was already stressed by his final year academic demands, alongside personal pressure to get a 2:1 degree, plus a tight money situation, and this has tilted life to crisis point. He offloads, also pointing out he has no idea of what is coming next for him at the end of this academic year. This trauma has added to a common theme seen here: the pressures associated with transition out of the HE community into the adult world beyond. Addressing anxieties, desires and generally preparing for the process helps many students about to leave college. It is also, as in Andrew's case, about a developmental transition from late adolescence to adulthood. It involves both losses and gains with all their accompanying feelings and thoughts, integrated with an adjustment to self-concept.

Maggie's route in

I trained to teach secondary age children and gained teaching and lecturing experience in school, FE and HE sectors. Having completed an M.Sc., following my B.Ed. (Hons), and now with a diploma in counselling, I was looking for a way back into the education world where I felt more comfortable, in my early anxious counselling days.

Having succeeded through the formal application and interview procedure, here I was, stepping into my room as a permanently employed half-time HE student counsellor now sorting out details of my filing system and decorating the wall with a soothing Monet. My counselling Rogerian/humanistic training was acceptable and my life experience fitted the bill.

Each academic year consists of two semesters – 15 weeks each – during which I work a three, or mostly a four, day week. Therapeutic momentum is often interrupted because it is nearly a vacation break or a coursework hand-in period is pressing (difficult to meet when a client is feeling full of pain). So I needed to develop a particular sensitivity to the pacing, progress rate and shape of the work. It is not appropriate to facilitate deep work when an exam is looming. Students need to be highly functional and in their 'adult' state at times like this. I have become used to facilitating clients to deal with mini endings and beginnings, as they handle the therapeutic gaps moving from semester to semester and year to year of a typically three-year undergraduate course. I have also developed and trained in short-term ways of working that are highly focused. The average number of sessions for clients in HE colleges is 4.3, new universities 5 and old universities 5.3 (AUCC *Data Report*, 2002). Now I am integrative and my blending of approaches reflects the leanings and needs of the client. I have topped up my training over the years to equip me with other skills such as art therapy, solution-focused brief therapy (SFBT), group work and specific approaches to phobia and traumas.

A client story

Emma, a young looking 22-year-old, from a local working class family, walked into the room in April of her first year at Hope, looking tense and closed-in. In a monotone 'dead' voice, with little sustained eye contact, she described the pressure of juggling 19 hours' paid work per week, academic demands and the difficulties of living with her stepmum and dad and younger sister. She was tired all the time. Her (biological) mum had chronic clinical depression and Emma chose not to see her much. She feared she was going the same way as her mum. She felt angry with her dad. There were rows at home – shouting and verbal abuse – and her sister was going wild. Her stepmum was ineffectual and Emma could no longer stand the responsibility of trying to hold it all together. I followed up allusions, to discover that at times she felt suicidal. She had had a job after A levels, and this had helped her realise there was more to life – hence the degree course. She talked a great deal about her dream of escaping the family, living in a place of her own. She felt trapped, lonely and unsupported. However she was here at college, tentatively clinging on to the motivation to do the degree even in the face of no one at home understanding or caring. She was upset. How could she keep it going? It was all too much.

She came for three more sessions, during which she talked of her feelings towards her dad and her longing to be heard by him, at the same time recognizing the futility of this. I did not explore but listened. She admitted finding it a struggle to make friends, and her loneliness was underlined by the fact that her only close girlfriend had recently got engaged. Emma felt cut out. She wanted to feel more confident and to live elsewhere.

At this stage acknowledgement, validation and support helped Emma stay on course and continue to believe in herself. She had offered a goal. Given the situation was not going to change, she decided the first step towards this goal was to get support for herself. She had an aunt she could speak to a bit. Simply recognizing this fact helped her at this point. She stopped coming to counselling. In truth, I felt we had not made much psychological contact, our relationship was minimal and only a small impact had been made on Emma's situation. I was wrong. Emma was feeling her way. The intuitively paced process matched Emma's stage. Had I done anything more, in hindsight, it would have been 'solution forced' and she would have been frightened off.

In the autumn of her second year she returned to counselling, finding academic work a struggle and belief in herself wavering. She questioned whether she deserved to get the degree. Depression was palpable and suicidal ideation recurring. She was considering withdrawing from college. She felt unbearably isolated, her sense of inadequacy and inability to cope blocking her entire life strategy. Negative thinking had set in and energy was extremely low. Despite all this she had made efforts to contact a tutor about her psychology course. Encouraged to give it up and do English instead, she had found a better way forward academically. Grasping this 'exception', I decided to use SFBT, an effective approach with young people in this demanding environment. (I had vital support from my SFBT supervisor and a peer group 'Solution Focus North West'.)

What did Emma know about herself that kept her 'on track' for her big goal: her own place? She learned (though the process required sensitive timing and care; tricky to get consistently right) to acknowledge and reinforce her personal qualities and strengths, developed over all her experience of life so far. She had tenacity, vision and inner determination. We discussed what it took to keep these going in the face of all the home difficulties. We externalized (O'Connell, 1998, pp. 80–2) the suicidal thoughts, questioning how she got back on track when they pushed her around so much. She turned from a 'visitor' to 'customer' (Berg and Miller, 1992, pp. 22–5) and our therapeutic relationship engaged. Throughout, the 'fit' with her world and pace had been crucial and often not easy. Bill O'Hanlon discusses this process and talks metaphorically of brushing just ahead of the curling stone (O'Hanlon and Weiner-Davis, 1989). She steadily increased her 'tool bag' of coping strategies. Setbacks occurred and when she felt low she was able to do breathing exercises, take herself to a mental 'safe place', even, as time went on, talk more to one aunt she liked. Her self-confidence was growing. We looked at achieving her hypothetical future through small concrete current steps.

Then in our last week before the Christmas break of five weeks, she walked in looking terrible, scratches all over her red blotchy face. A fight with her sister had ended with Emma punching her. Then, on her return after the break, she described her devastation when, during the holiday, her nan blamed her for her mum's problems. It seemed her aunt was unable to support her. She decided not to speak to her nan. She also had major difficulties with her new English module. She had read the wrong books and was unprepared and behind. A draft essay had been criticized too. Stress was sky-high. It was at this time that she spontaneously labelled an inner 'little self' who felt 'squashed'. In the face of all this, we looked at how she was getting through at all. She realized her 'little self' *was* there, though feeling squashed. It was tricky to make sure my responses were a 'fit', as well as just ahead of the overwhelmingness.

We worked at various levels. For example, Emma admitted that she had always been told her mum's depression started post-natally after her birth, so she blamed herself anyway. With 'adult' knowledge we reframed this more logically. We looked at her choices not to speak to her nan, and fighting with her sister, as her strong bid to resist the family culture. How did she learn to want better things for herself in the face of all this? And how did she manage to put that degree of trust in her own judgement? How did she manage to hold on to her dream?

By early March, Emma was feeling a little better. She arranged meetings with key college people in which it was mutually agreed that she should interrupt her English module and continue it at a later date. She felt tremendously supported by college staff. This spoke volumes about how she approached them. By the end of March she told me she felt 'lighter', 'more optimistic'. We looked at how she had achieved this and what she needed to do to maintain it. Eventually we began to look, in detail, at what would convince her she did not need to come to see me any more. Emma identified skills and self-concept changes, and bridged these to her overall goal. She measured how convinced she was that she could do more of this, by awarding herself 7, on a 0–10 scale. Good enough.

We discussed relapse prevention. What did she need to do to keep herself on track? She could now trust me – could she replicate this with someone else? What would she need to discern about someone to place her trust in them? Emma's ability to trust and open up to others was underdeveloped. Counselling had created a 'ripple' in this stagnant pond, however, through her acknowledged trust in me.

In finally evaluating the counselling experience itself, Emma told me she had gradually eased herself into talking about herself, which she found difficult. She felt facilitated by my 'non-judgemental, unbiased' presence. She liked being able to talk about her whole life: university, home and so on. Someone else seeing, but not getting involved in, the whole picture helped. Emma said she decided to commit to the counselling process because she knew she really needed to sort out the 'trust' problem. Now she felt she really did have choices, and finding a way of staying on course to gain her degree added to this. She recognized and cherished her own open attitude, which had initially developed when she had had to grow up so fast on her mum's departure, and eventually she could harness to look for a graduate job. She liked the tools she'd learned because they gave her a sense of control. She gave me a final card that read: '... Thank you for helping me rediscover and better my "little me"...'. Emma felt she had learned to trust me and take in my support, and that this had started to be generalized, for example to tutors and others in college.

My learning from this case is how difficult it is, but also how important, to be patient and trust the counselling process. Suicide was a recurrent theme. It was like walking a knife edge at times, to be just ahead with this. Supervision helped me trust the process and remain sensitive to the skill of 'pace' and 'fit'. I also learned that setbacks, such as the one after Christmas, can lead to an even greater leap forward, when resolved.

Kevin's route in

My teaching background spans 12 years, from a Catholic boarding school in Liberia, West Africa to head of a sixth form for 200 students in Liverpool. While living in New York for a few years, I completed a Master's degree in psychodynamic counselling in 1987. In the UK in the 1980s, counselling in schools was virtually unheard of, whereas in the United States it was already well established. In fact, one of my training placements was in a high school, working with 16–17-year-old 11th grade students. After graduating, I did not feel ready to embark upon a career in counselling right away and decided to continue in the profession in which I felt more experienced.

I returned to teaching in Liverpool and did some voluntary counselling for a local organization. In the early 1990s I was faced with an important career choice: to consider applying for headships, or to make a complete break and seek employment as a counsellor. The pastoral dimension of my work with sixth formers appealed to me more than the disciplinary role, so I decided to take a year's sabbatical to pursue further training in psychotherapy in London, with a view to discerning the future. The *Guardian* and the *Times Higher* proved invaluable resources for jobs and I applied for four posts, all in HE. At that time there seemed to be a wide range of counselling opportunities from which to choose. In June 1992, a part-time counselling post became available at Liverpool Hope University College. This was in response to an increasing demand by students for counselling. This enabled me to test the water before embarking upon full-time counselling. I soon knew that I had found my niche and, after a year, was offered a full-time position. In 1998 I was appointed head of service.

Evaluation

As a manager, accountability is crucial: one needs to both justify and explain the work of the service, which to an outsider may seem somewhat mysterious. Accurate statistics are an important tool in this regard. We are also guided by our professional body, the Association for University and College Counselling (AUCC), which has produced some very helpful benchmarks for recognizing best practice in educational institutions. The service's annual report provides an opportunity to reflect upon the quality of service delivered and covers several areas: the suitability of the physical resources; training and professional development undertaken by the team; statistics; an action plan; and operating targets for the following academic year.

In 1999 we purchased a database, Inform (Cambridge Counselling Resources Ltd, 1999), which is designed specifically for further and higher educational counselling services. This enables the efficient collection and analysis of counselling statistics. It is easy to use and requires minimal IT expertise. With Inform it is possible to extract a vast amount of information as everything is saved automatically. It provides a comprehensive overview of the clients, their problems and severity, the number of interviews received, clients on the waiting list, students at risk, courses undertaken, ethnicity, as well as general information about contact addresses and so on. In terms of management, its usefulness extends further: it is possible to keep track of the caseload of each counsellor – the number and type of sessions each week – individual, group work, supervision, cancelled or did not attend (DNA). It is also possible to establish the levels of severity that each counsellor is dealing with at any particular time.

From September 2003 the service will introduce CORE-PC (Clinical Outcomes in Routine Evaluation) as an additional tool. CORE-PC is a total-solution computer software package that is now being used by well over 100 services to provide a standardized and low-cost solution to CORE system data collation, management and reporting. In addition to other functions, it is used to identify risk assessment, which gives a clear indication of the severity of clients as they present to counselling. It also allows monitoring of any clinical and reliable change that occurs as a result of the counselling, and the significance of this change is assessed statistically because it is compared with national results across a variety of settings. So it evaluates three important factors: the client, the clinical effectiveness of the counselling and the performance management of the counselling service. Thus it will provide a more objective and clinical evaluative tool than Inform, which focuses more on the particular statistics of relevance to the HE setting, in addition to providing valuable information which can be used in the annual report.

Proper record keeping is a mark of professionalism. Consequently, brief notes of each session are recorded on an official sheet. Formal notes on clients are, generally speaking, the property of the college, and therefore remain within the service. As students now have a legal right to see their notes, they are written in an objective and factual manner. Case notes and records may also be required as evidence in any kind of complaint or legal action and cannot be destroyed after a problem has arisen, without breaking the law. Clients' files also contain any correspondence that has been sent or received.

In our service, the secretary keeps details of each client who contacts the service. This includes his or her name, an identification number, the date when the first contact was made, the time when an appointment is offered and the name of the counsellor. If a client makes a particular request at that time (for example, to see a specific counsellor), this is noted. These records are kept securely locked in cabinets within the secretary's office after the information is transferred to a database (password protected). Some of the information provided when a student registers with the service (for example, age, gender, course, and so on) contributes towards general statistics used for annual reports.

The brief confidential notes that record the counsellor's understanding and perceptions of the sessions may also include background information. If a counsellor has any points of particular concern, these are noted. The notes are kept locked in a cabinet in the counsellor's room until counselling ends. They are then filed in securely locked cabinets in the secretary's office and are retained for six years. After this time they are carefully destroyed.

Feedback from users of the service is important for the counsellors themselves, as it enables them to reflect upon their practice; it also provides accurate and objective data for management. At the end of counselling, each client is given a brief evaluation form to complete and the counsellor records his or her evaluation on the client's record sheet. This gives the opportunity for both to assess independently and subjectively, how effective they judge the counselling to have been. Since evaluation forms are anonymous they may also be used for an internal or external review of the service and for inclusion in the annual report.

Continuing professional development

An educational environment lends itself to continuing professional development (CPD). You need to be selective about choosing from the wide variety of lectures, presentations, seminars and performances that are available. Some have direct relevance to counselling, psychology and personal development whereas others are of a more general interest and afford an opportunity to meet with colleagues and to participate in the life of the institution. Occasionally I meet students and/or clients at such events, and this may give a different perspective of their talents: not always evident in the counselling room. In these situations, however, there is often a tension in managing the boundaries, and as counsellors in educational settings, we need to give this serious consideration. Sometimes it is more appropriate to stay away from certain events in order to protect and preserve the integrity of the counselling relationship.

Continuing professional development of the team is a priority and accounts for a major part of the budget. Provided we have suitable accommodation counsellors, unlike lecturers, require very little equipment or other resources. As the most important instrument needed for efficacy in our daily work is ourselves, CPD and supervision are the most effective ways of achieving this. Clearly, CPD does not always have to be costly in time or money. Relevant journals and articles can be read as part of daily allocated 'administration' time or when a client cancels unexpectedly.

BACP has published some guidelines and requirements for CPD in order for each team member to maintain his or her accredited counsellor status. These incorporate a wide range of possibilities such as short courses on professional issues, seminars and conferences, committee work and meetings, encouraging the development of others and personal development. Most of these are very manageable within an institution of higher education. As counsellors, we are frequently invited to participate in various educational endeavours, often requiring us to take an active part in events such as workshops and seminars. As a manager, it is sometimes a difficult balancing act to know where to draw the line in terms of such involvement, both within and outside the college. Our team is multi-talented and our skills are frequently in demand. Having tried various ways to allocate time and money to CPD fairly, I have reverted to allocating a specific sum and number of days to each counsellor and then leaving it to the individual to choose how to utilize and apportion this most effectively.

Conditions of work

At Hope our terms and conditions of work are comparable to those of academic teaching staff. Full-time staff are employed for 35 hours a week with 30 days' holidays, on academic pay scales which rise broadly in line with inflation each September. In addition to this, the college closes for several days at Christmas and Easter. All permanent part-time members of staff are paid on equivalent academic scales and are also entitled to take bank holiday and privilege days on a pro rata basis. Fortnightly supervision of the counselling is included as part of the working contract and is paid by the college.

Career progression within the service is somewhat limited. Since I became head of service in 1998 there have been several prospects for a change in direction within the college, while maintaining a foothold in counselling. One recent example was a half-time post as director of student services. This position involved overseeing the work of careers, chaplaincy, international students, students with disabilities, resident tutors, student accommodation and my own area, counselling and health. Many aspects of the role would have been both relevant and challenging and would have necessitated liaising with a range of students and staff. However, it would also have presented a role conflict and the probability of blurring professional boundaries when dealing directly with essential disciplinary matters relating to students. In order to maintain confidentiality within the therapeutic counselling relationship, there needs to be a degree of separateness, which must remain distinct from other aspects of student services. Inevitably there could have been times when the prioritizing of roles would have resulted in an understandable clash of interests.

An HE setting suits my background, experience, qualifications and skills. Essential attributes that an employer would want from a counsellor working in an HE setting are likely to include the ability to work as part of a team, in addition to having knowledge of working with young adults. Personal experience, and a sound understanding of academic demands and lifestyle, is indispensable. It is crucial that a counsellor is able to offer some flexibility in the way he or she works. The specific counselling orientation is probably less important than these other attributes and most services employ counsellors with a range of approaches and skills. Accreditation with a professional body is important as it affords counsellors professional credibility when working alongside other academics. A willingness and ability to network with counsellors in similar settings, as well as with colleagues, tutors and managers, is essential. On occasions it is necessary to act on behalf of students. In many institutions there is an expectation by management that counsellors will respond appropriately to major or minor crises. At Hope, I am a member of a critical incident team comprising nine people which would convene to respond to any major incident.

Our department is often invited to comment upon, or contribute to various policies on matters relevant to student mental health and welfare. As a consequence of the Government's policy of widening participation in HE, counsellors in this setting have to deal increasingly with students experiencing mental health problems that are not dealt with adequately elsewhere within the institution. Funding for education is a constant problem and, as employees of the college, we, like other staff, may need to justify our salary by demonstrating our commitment to and effectiveness in student retention. Consequently, we monitor the number of students who on first contact with us, are considering withdrawing from or interrupting their studies, and at the end of counselling, we record the number that decide to stay on their course as a direct result of counselling. From a political/management point of view, this can readily be translated into justification of our salary.

Future developments

As I write this chapter, two recent documents have been published which will shape the future of HE over the next decade. The first is the government's white paper *The Future of Higher Education* (2003), which sets out its aims for widening access, to persuade students from non-traditional backgrounds to take up HE. As an incentive to attract applicants, there will be no up-front fees. Only after graduation when the person is earning a substantial salary will he or she be required to pay this back. The second document supplements this: the Higher Education Funding Council for England (HEFCE) *Strategic Plan 2003–2008 Consultation Paper*. This sets out a broad vision for the development of HE. Three areas that are likely to have a significant effect upon counselling in HE are (a) the challenge that widening access will present, (b) increasing student non-completion and (c) lifelong learning.

With widening access, it is likely that the number of students with mental health problems will increase. NHS services are already overstretched, and within an institution there will be an expectation that the medical, counselling and/or disabilities services will deal with such students. Those with mental health problems often take up a disproportionate amount of time and frequently involve numerous people: resident and academic tutors and other support staff in student services. Confidentiality and boundary issues need delicate handling in these circumstances.

The proportion of mature and part-time students has increased significantly in recent years. These students often bring valuable attributes which enhance the learning environment but equally, they may bring a greater number of complex and longer-term relational and financial problems which are not a direct result of transition to HE but do impact upon the students' ability to succeed in their studies.

I remain optimistic that the work of counsellors in HE is valued by management and that, for the foreseeable future, employment opportunities will be available. Our work supports the government's vision and commitment to student retention. Counselling services need adequate staffing in order to implement the institution's mission statement, the requirements of the Disability Discrimination Act (1995) and the obligation of its 'duty of care'. Counsellors support tutors in their pastoral roles and assist management in dealing with crisis situations, for example, death, attempted suicide, violence or other critical incidents. Such support is not easily found elsewhere in an institution, and thus the availability of counselling adds indispensable value to the whole student experience.

Ten top tips

Generic tips:

- Enjoy the small as well as big rewards as you witness client movement.
- Develop an expressive outlet: creative, physical, spiritual, intellectual, political or, best of all, playful. Counselling is relatively physically static and also involves a persistent degree of self-inhibition/control.
- Keep reflecting on, questioning and developing the way you work. Counselling is a complex evolution of skill, knowledge and style.

Context specific tips:

- Have a complete break from counselling in your working day: it will help concentration. Meet with colleagues for coffee or lunch, for example.
- Don't get isolated in your institution or be 'precious', attend events organized for staff and/or students and this will also keep you up to date with what's going on so that you can consider how to respond to institutional changes in an appropriate way.
- Maintain a good relationship with the students' union, resident tutors, chaplaincy and other student support staff and perhaps offer help with any initiatives or endeavours of mutual interest.
- Regularly appraise the users' and institutions' requirements of the counselling service and publicize any relevant changes made, seeking advice and/or opinions from colleagues and students regarding their perceptions of new ventures undertaken, publicity, and so on.
- Work to embed yourself and your service into your institution, for example, give an occasional lecture or run a course on a topic which will capture the imagination; keep senior management informed of any developments, innovations and achievements in the service.

- Preserve your professional integrity but be prepared to talk to colleagues about your counselling role and ask about their roles, so encouraging ongoing dialogue.
- Network to keep fresh, up to date, stimulated and supported. After some experience you could consider becoming an active member of AUCC by joining a committee.

 What makes an understanding of the issues involved in transitions particularly pertinent to counselling in HE?

Bibliography

AUCC (1998) *Advisory Service to Institutions: Guidelines for University and College Counselling Services*. Rugby: BAC.

AUCC (2002) *Annual Survey of Counselling in Further and Higher Education Data Report 2000/01*. Rugby: AUCC.

Bell, E. (1999) In J. Lees and A. Vaspe (eds), *Clinical Counselling in Further and Higher Education*. London and New York: Routledge.

Berg, K. and Miller, S.C. (1992) *Working with the Problem Drinker. A Solution Focused Approach*. USA: Norton.

Butler, C. (2002) 'Counselling needs better marketing', *AUCC Newsletter and Journal Special Issue* (Nov.), p. 38.

Cambridge Counselling Resources Ltd. (1999) *Inform* (1st edn). University of Cambridge.

Cambridge Counselling Resources Ltd. (2000) *Inform* (2nd edn). University of Cambridge.

DfES (2003) *The Future of Higher Education*. Government White Paper.

Heads of Counselling Services (HUCS) (1999) *Report Degrees of Disturbance: The New Agenda. Section C*. AUCC Publication.

HUCS (2002) *Survey into Medical, Psychiatric and Counselling Provision in HE*. HUCS.

HEFCE (Higher Education Funding Council for England) (2003) *Strategic Plan 2003–2008 Consultation Paper*.

O'Connell, B. (1998) *Solution-Focused Therapy*. London: Sage, p. 80–2.

O'Hanlon, B. and Weiner-Davis, M. (1989) *In Search of Solutions: A New Direction in Psychotherapy*. USA: Norton.

Smith, E. (1999) In Lees, J. and Vaspe, A. (eds), *Clinical Counselling in Further and Higher Education*. London and New York: Routledge.

Websites
BACP divisional website. www.aucc.uk.com
General information and advice for students or those concerned about students. www.studentcounselling.org
Heads of University Counselling Services website. www.hucs.org

Section IV

WORKPLACE SECTOR

12

Counselling in a Workplace Setting

Caroline Jones

At the time of writing this chapter, I worked for Birmingham City Council Social Services department as a workplace counsellor. There has since been a major local authority reorganization.

A typical day

My day normally starts with settling in and getting organized. I like to arrive early and well before my first client is due to arrive, so I have time to ensure that my room is ready and to pick up my telephone messages and e-mails. Today, I have a message to say that my 10 am client (Kath, work-related stress) cannot attend as her child is ill. I ring her and we provisionally set another date and time next week. My diary shows that I now have appointments at 8.30 am (Iqbal, bereavement) and 11.30 am (Pauline, work-related stress/alcohol) this morning. I am meeting a friend for lunch, returning to the office for appointments at 2.30 pm (Vicky, a first session as this is one of my dedicated appointment times for new clients) and 4 pm (Sharon, anxiety). Another message is from a distressed client (Neeta, returning to work after a long absence) seeking an emergency appointment. We had agreed at our previous session that she could do this, if necessary. When I contact her, she is unable to make 10 am so we agree to meet at 5.30 pm for a 30-minute session. We already have an appointment booked in a fortnight's time.

Some workplace counselling services may have support staff to handle this kind of task, but, in this service, once the reception staff have passed on information about a new referral, the counsellors are responsible for all subsequent communication. Five years ago, a typical day would also have included responding to requests for a first appointment. At that time, employees selected a counsellor and rang directly for an appointment. This system was changed when a second part-time counsellor was recruited and a telephone reception point was set up to allocate new clients as fairly and efficiently as possible. At that time, a new publicity leaflet was issued widely throughout the department, with photos and information about each counsellor. Clients can still choose the counsellor they want to work with if they are prepared (occasionally) to wait longer for their first appointment. Many are happy to accept the first convenient available appointment. I have six or seven appointment times a month allocated for new clients.

I have another couple of messages, about appointments next week, requiring a response and I plan to deal with these later on. The advances in telecommunication technology make this task easier than it used to be. These days, the availability of message-taking facilities and the wide use of mobile phones make it easier to speak directly or leave messages if necessary. Even so, leaving messages for clients does need careful thought, in case these are overheard by others in the household, and information needs to be conveyed in an intelligible but discreet way.

The British Association for Counselling and Psychotherapy (BACP) recommends that counsellors employed full-time do not see clients for more than 20 hours per week, with the proviso that variables such as the experience and competence of the counsellor and the complexity of the work and variability of the clientele are taken into account (BACP, 2000). The target set by our current line manager is up to 16 sessions a week. As I am a part-time counsellor (having reduced to a three-day week in the late 1990s), my caseload is adjusted pro rata. I hold up to 10 or 11 (60 minute) sessions a week. I space appointments out over the course of the day. In this setting in particular, it is preferable that clients do not pass each other when arriving and leaving in case they know one another. Having space between sessions also allows me to debrief, update my diary and records, and prepare for the next session. Counselling sessions usually take place at my office, but occasionally it is more convenient for the employee (and the employer) if the session is held in a room at the workplace. Very occasionally, when an employee is on sickness absence with a physical or psychological condition that makes leaving the house impossible, a home visit is allowed. An outreach session can take up to three hours, taking travelling time into account, therefore these have to be planned carefully. I enjoy the challenges of counselling away from the office and these days, safety protocols are in place for all work away from the office. I have to notify the team (see below) where I am going and when I will be back, and carry a mobile phone and alarm provided by the department (see also Conditions of work).

Today I do not have a meeting and the longer gap I now have at 10 am gives me time to prepare for meetings that are scheduled within the next week or so and to do other tasks. Team meetings (currently this service is part of the departmental health, safety and welfare team), line management supervision and counselling supervision are regulars. Other tasks include:

- collating the monthly statistics
- reviewing and updating my own publicity materials and handouts such as my personal information sheet
- reading the news bulletins that are produced by other sections of the organization
- preparing background material for the team annual report (this normally contains statistical data and other information that the organization may wish to know)
- continuing professional development (CPD) such as professional reading

- case notes and other recording
- a regular review of my contingency plans in the event of unplanned emergencies.

I have plans for lunchtime today. On other days I might have a walk, or relax with my feet up, or go shopping – whatever the choice, having a change of pace is a necessary restorative.

A key factor for workplace counsellors to consider is how to manage their time in ways that accommodate appointment times for clients working shifts or more regular hours, part-time or full-time. While employees are allowed to use the service during their working hours (requiring their manager's permission and therefore sometimes subject to work demands), some choose to come in their own time so that they do not need to tell their manager where they are or that they are attending counselling. For example, an 8 am appointment is useful for someone who wants to come before the work day starts or at the end of a night shift.

Just occasionally I may have to offer counselling support at short notice in the event of a trauma. This is a key requirement in this setting, knowing how best to support individuals or groups after a trauma. Traumas occur in all workplaces; some are work-related when violence or accidents occur due to the nature of the work, while others may result from a sudden death or other non-work-related tragedy affecting employees.

To complete the picture of my typical day, a brief description of the setting is appropriate. Birmingham Social Services department employs a wide range of staff including field social workers, residential social workers (children's homes), care staff in residential homes for adults, home care (day and night care) and administrative staff. During 2001–2 the workforce profile was 79 per cent women, 21 per cent men, with ethnic origins 57.7 per cent white, 19.4 per cent black African-Caribbean, 7.7 per cent Asian and 15.2 per cent other. By definition, a workplace counselling service works with people of working age. Clients bring the usual range of problems to counselling including loss and bereavement, divorce, domestic problems including debt and domestic violence, work-related stress issues including harassment and bullying, redundancy and work insecurity, personal stress such as childhood sexual abuse, role pressures such as combining single parenthood with a demanding job, and so on. In addition, the nature of their work is often stressful, including:

- adult and child protection work (social workers)
- sectioning people, under the Mental Health Act (approved social workers)
- working alone at night in someone's home (night carers)
- walking to a number of clients to do breakfasts or tuck-ins, as well as collecting pensions and shopping during the day (home carers)
- daytime and waking night duty in residential homes for children, elders, people with learning difficulties or mental health problems.

Issues such as loss and bereavement often arise in the work setting. The stresses of working with dysfunctional and struggling families and the statutory responsibilities that arise in this area of work can be particularly distressing. Violence in some residential settings can be a regular element of an employee's working day, an additional stressor for this cohort of employees to be added to the normal stresses of shift work.

My route in

I left university with a degree (in Russian language and literature) and without a clear idea of what kind of work or career I wanted. A number of jobs followed until, a couple of years later, I joined the civil service in Wales. I became active in my trade union, over the years holding most key posts in the branch. This work allowed me to develop skills in negotiating on behalf of members both locally and departmentally, plus opportunities to travel, to meet people, to attend conferences, to speak in public. The day-to-day administrative work was also rewarding. It seemed like I had found my niche. Then I passed a promotion board and I was asked if I would be interested in a new post that was being created at the department's head office in Edinburgh as a welfare officer, the civil service title for workplace counsellor. I accepted. Of course, I had some idea what counselling involved, I thought I would enjoy it, and my partner was prepared to relocate so I could take up this opportunity. After four very rewarding years, I knew I wanted to continue a career as a counsellor (requiring me to seek a post outside the civil service) and was able to obtain this post as Employee Counsellor with Birmingham City Council Social Services department. The advertisement stressed that it was looking for someone who knew how to set up and run the service, and the ideas I presented during the interview were accepted.

I was trained initially, in the mid-1980s, in the Egan (1975) model: listening, reflecting, (counselling), challenging and ending. These skills, together with input on aspects of the work such as working with occupational health, recording case notes and report writing, and personal development group work, were designed to equip welfare officers to do a 'tour' of about five years in the post. The training was provided through residential courses at the civil service college, with trainers from academic and voluntary sector backgrounds and experience of counselling. I attended a third (optional) module, where the emphasis was on advancing counselling skills and further personal development through group work. Since then, I have gained a diploma in counselling and BACP accreditation.

I do not believe that any one approach can help every client, so I work eclectically. My theoretical approach is underpinned by a person-centred approach, in order to deliver the core conditions (Rogers, 1957) and make psychological contact with clients, together with solution-focused or other approaches, according to the personality, needs and presenting problems brought by clients. I consider that this way of working is particularly appropriate within a workplace setting where a wide range of problems can be presented and where the expectation is that counselling contracts will be short-term.

A client story

Ruth has come for counselling for work-related stress. She is on sick leave and is in discussion with the GP about medication. She feels that her caseload (volume, complexity and distressing nature) as a field social worker is wearing her down, and that her requests for help in supervision were not attended to.

Ruth is a white woman in her mid-forties. My first responsibility is to help Ruth lower her stress levels, and I explore the routes to this goal with her. Her reluctance about medication needs to be checked out, as it could be for a number of reasons. She might fear dependence on medication (and have possible fears of dependency on other forms of help), or she might have had a previously unhelpful experience of medication for stress, or she might be a person who likes to resolve health problems without medication if possible. Ruth decides that she could benefit both from counselling and a self-help approach. She accepts the offer of a reading list (bibliotherapy). This list is based on learning from clients about books they have found helpful, as well as drawing from other sources such as book reviews and my own learning from reading. While there may be personal reasons contributing to Ruth's stress, for the purposes of this vignette, the focus will be on the work-related stressors.

At the first session Ruth is given a copy of my personal information sheet. This contains additional (to the service publicity leaflet) information about the way I work, my policy on case notes, report writing, and that when writing for publication, I use 'composite' or 'fictional' vignettes or case studies, with material heavily disguised so that no one individual can be identified. When contracting with me, Ruth is particularly anxious about confidentiality, and confidentiality in this setting is discussed in depth. The service is advertised as 'working to BACP standards', and the department also has its own statement drawn up and printed both on the service publicity leaflet and my personal information sheet.

> Each Counsellor operates to a code of confidentiality, which is designed to protect your privacy and your autonomy. Matters discussed are treated as highly confidential and will not be disclosed unless the Counsellor is required to do so by law or if, in their opinion, the matters are likely to affect the work of the Department or the welfare of other employees or service users. In such an instance, the Counsellor will suspend the meeting until the client has been made aware that any further debate cannot be held under the protection of confidentiality. Information will only be passed on to those who need to know when the Counsellor has first discussed with you the necessity for disclosure.
>
> (Birmingham Social Services Department, 2000)

Counselling can enable Ruth to discuss her feelings about her caseload and explore how to check out whether the volume and complexity are typical or whether she has been unfairly overloaded. Ruth needs to contact her trade union for this information and talk to colleagues in comparable posts. If the workload is reasonable, she can look at how to enhance her resilience, and there may be time-management issues to explore. Ruth needs more confidence to challenge her white, male line manager about some aspects of her job in ways that ensure she is heard and attended to. Regarding the distressing nature of Ruth's work, this is certainly a stressor and may also have more personal roots in Ruth's own past or present, touching on other issues that she may also wish to address in counselling. Usually, there is no conflict of interest in client work of this kind: the employer wants the employee back at work and functioning well, and the client wants to be back at work and enjoying her normal routine. While there may be problems here for the senior line management structure to address, my role is to offer Ruth the opportunity to work out her own way of resolving the difficulties she is experiencing by providing the core conditions (Rogers, 1957) and by drawing upon my repertoire of skills (Berne, 1968; O'Connell, 1998, 2001; Burns, 1999).

During our sessions, I have noted that Ruth has been careful not to name her manager. I have wondered about a connection between this and her concern about confidentiality. It occurs to me to ask Ruth whether she has worked with him previously, and she confirms this. At this point she talks about a 'fling' they had ten years ago, when both worked in a residential unit. Ruth's shame about this is explored as she identifies that this is a hurdle to her ability to confront him about the current situation. She would not have applied for the post in her current team had he been manager at that time, but he joined the team some time after she did. Ruth now speaks openly about other important information – that her manager has been disciplined in the past for bullying and sexual harassment. Ruth does not want to make trouble for him, and respecting her autonomy, we focus on how she can resolve her problems directly with him.

This is a typical case that I would bring to supervision. Working with clients who feel bullied evokes strong feelings in me, and I need to discuss these within supervision in order to stay impartial, work competently and maintain my own resilience.

Note: this is a fictitious case study, drawing upon my casework experience.

Evaluation

In this setting, statistics serve a number of purposes for both the counsellors and the employers. Both parties want efficient and effective services and statistics demonstrate, for example, demand for first appointments (gathered by reception staff), waiting times, presenting problems (client's assessment), take-up (by gender, age, background and so on) and the average number of sessions held. This service provides a user self-assessment (US-A) form to gather most of this information. Statistics show, therefore, if additional publicity is needed in particular areas of the organization. Statistics on presenting problems and underlying problems addressed in counselling are useful in determining trends in issues such as work-related stress, alcohol issues, bullying and harassment and post-trauma stress, redundancy and loss.

Attending to feedback, informally and formally, is an important element of workplace counselling. Informally, clients give feedback during sessions to their counsellors, who attend to this as part of their commitment to helping that particular client and as part of their ongoing learning. More formal feedback is possible in a workplace setting. Our service provides user evaluation (UE) forms – together with the US-A form and a stamped addressed envelope – to clients at their first session. Clients are asked to complete these at the end of the counselling contract. The forms provide anonymous feedback, without necessarily identifying the counsellor involved. These are posted to our line manager and stored where the counsellors can access these for an overall picture. In addition I also like to offer my own evaluation form, when appropriate, to clients (Jones et al., 2000, p. 130). Again, clients are invited to complete this anonymously and keep their own copy as the form is designed to be a helpful record for them, too. With any method of evaluation, however, it is not possible to be sure how representative the feedback is when the response rate is low (approximately 10 per cent). To try to increase the rate of response we give clients the US-A and UE forms at their first session as well as again at the end of the counselling contract.

Continuing professional development

Birmingham Social Services department has always recognized the importance of continuing professional development (CPD) and has supported its counsellors in gaining qualifications and attending short courses, seminars and conferences, and other activities that are integral to CPD. This commitment has, in recent years, become a more formalized aspect of the work, with the efforts towards and achievement of Investors in People (IiP) status. IiP status is awarded to employers that demonstrate commitment to the professional development of employees. Eligibility for support for CPD depends on the relevance of the activity to one's job. I have had additional training in post-trauma stress, for example.

Funding CPD is often an issue as there is never enough in the budget to provide for all employees. My CPD is usually self-funded, although I am allowed work time to attend some events. Not all CPD activities need cost money. During the 1990s I requested and was granted three days a year towards my BAC(P) activities. At that time I was a member of the BAC Standards and Ethics Committee, and required up to ten days a year for attending meetings and related work. The choices made by counsellors about their CPD are very personal. Where these have a direct bearing in their paid work, there is an overlap between what benefits them and the organization that pays them. Other areas of development may be for more personal satisfaction, or in areas clearly outside the job description, such as training as a trainer or supervisor, or personal growth, where it seems reasonable for individuals to find the time and costs themselves.

Conditions of work

There is no standard job description for a workplace counsellor and there are a number of 'models' of workplace counselling provision. In addition to offering counselling, some services have a broader remit, with proactive initiatives such as training managers in counselling skills, stress management training, mediation and advocacy, running support groups, health promotion work and critical incident debriefing. Within counselling services, the staff may have similar or differing job descriptions, and similar or different qualifications, allowing for greater versatility. Useful information relevant to workplace counselling can be obtained from BACP (Gabriel, 2002).

A factor to note, in this setting, is the place of workplace counselling in relation to claims against employers for damages for stress-related injury. The Health and Safety at Work Act (1974) states that employers have a duty of care, so far as is reasonably practicable, for an employee's health, safety and welfare. Dyer (2002), reporting on recent Court of Appeal judgements, states that an employer should make reasonable efforts to minimize the stress in their workplace and that where appropriate counselling help is available to an employee suffering stress, an employer is unlikely to be deemed negligent, unless totally unreasonable demands have been placed on that employee. Similarly, employers have responsibilities under law to employees with alcohol or drug problems (Misuse of Drugs Act 1971 and Transport and Works Act 1992).

Employment in this setting has many positives. For local authority employees this includes a regular salary, PAYE, sickness benefits, pension, paid leave, flexible working hours, funded counselling supervision and accommodation. I enjoy the benefits of flexitime and work longer days, both to avoid the rush hour, an aspect of modern life I find very stressful, and also to enjoy additional time off. The support of a professional association is helpful if there are any difficulties to resolve relating to counselling work. For example, the BACP (www.bacp.co.uk) has drawn up information sheets about the requirements of counselling supervision, about workloads and other issues if there are any problems in these areas. For example, working full-time with a busy and demanding caseload requires more counselling supervision than the BACP minimum for accreditation (one and a half hours per month). Three to four hours' supervision a month would be reasonable for a full-time workplace counsellor. I now have one and a half hours' counselling supervision every three or four weeks.

Earning potentials vary according to experience and qualifications, with BACP accreditation or equivalent often required at recruitment.

In-house training is also available, according to the kind of work undertaken. I have benefited from departmental training on how to be safe when working away from base, offering common-sense advice on safety on foot, using public transport and using one's own car.

A particular advantage of workplace counselling is that there is no need to invoice clients for sessions (whether held or missed), and this means less paperwork and the opportunity to work with clients who might not have been able to access counselling, as not everyone can afford to pay for private counselling. This is a satisfying element of counselling in this setting, and it fits with the principle of justice (BACP, 2002) which states 'practitioners have a duty to strive to ensure a fair provision of counselling and psychotherapy services, accessible and appropriate to the needs of potential clients'. The investment by employers in workplace or employee assistance counselling provision has greatly contributed to the achievement of justice. There is an argument, however, that there can sometimes be less commitment by the client to counselling when this is free at point of contact.

This service advertises itself as short-term, up to six sessions. This establishes realistic expectations in service users, and there is sufficient flexibility to allow longer-term work if this is appropriate. Here, the statistical work benefits both the counsellors and the employers by demonstrating that the average number of sessions is around six or fewer.

I enjoy the challenge of new clients each week coming with any of the range of presenting problems. I am prepared to account for my caseload management and other use of resources. For counsellors who prefer to work longer-term with clients, or do not like a regular turnover of clients and the challenges every week of starting new contracts, this setting is less likely to be comfortable.

Another benefit of counselling embedded in a workplace is that in the event of a complaint clients can use the organization's own complaints procedures, which are accessible and probably less daunting to use than the formal complaints procedures of the professional associations. Clients are, of course, free to lodge complaints with the appropriate professional association as well.

A problem that can arise in this setting, however, particularly when there is only one counsellor in post, is the ethical dilemma that occurs when two employees in conflict with each other both seek counselling. Going back to Ruth, I might be approached by her line manager seeking counselling while I am working with her. In the past, before the second counsellor was in post and without the telephone reception staff to handle his initial enquiry, I might not have had as much warning and time to think about how to handle this.

We have less autonomy about office settings. For example, our current building comprises well-sized rooms, reasonable natural light and accessibility for those with mobility difficulties. The location, however, is not particularly convenient for public transport users. In contrast, my first office was tiny and gloomy but in the city centre, therefore very convenient for public transport users.

At the time I was recruited, I was the first person in post. The plan had been to recruit two counsellors to provide a service to a staff group of over 8000 at that time. Nearly two years later another full-time counsellor was appointed and more recently, a second part-timer. Until 1999, we were managed by a succession of personnel managers until the employee counselling service was positioned within the health, safety and welfare team. This is fairly typical within local authorities.

There are occasional opportunities for career progression, although most of the workplace services of which I am aware have one or two counsellors in post. This kind of structure (again fairly typical in a local authority setting) does not offer 'career prospects' in terms of promotion, but does offer opportunities to diversify into counselling-related areas of work. I have always been interested in the issues of work-related stress and work/alcohol issues. My colleagues have developed their own counselling-related areas of work, such as links with black workers and initiatives that progress race equalities within the department, and developing a group work approach to stress management.

Workplaces are subject to reorganizations. At the time of writing this chapter, we were informed that our service was to be moved away from the social services department into a new corporate counselling service under the city council's occupational health service. One result of this change has been the creation of a counselling manager post. The person specification for this post included:

- at least 5 years' experience of providing workplace counselling within or to a large UK employer
- substantial experience of people management
- ability to initiate projects and see them through
- membership of a professional association
- minimum qualification of a degree in counselling
- professional indemnity insurance.

Future developments

Workplace counselling is on the map and it serves the needs of organizations and their staff. I cannot predict how such services will develop, but look forward to participating in discussions and implementing changes that fit with the nature and purpose of counselling and psychotherapy.

Ten top tips

Generic tips:

- Enjoy a constant turnover of clients bringing any kind of problem.
- Hold a philosophy, theory and practice that accommodate short and longer-term work.
- Enjoy responding to the unexpected.
- Look after your own health and well-being in order to maintain the stamina for a high volume of work.

Context-specific tips:

- Gain experience of working for a large organization in another role to prepare you for the typical problems and tensions employees usually face.
- Have the ability to meet deadlines for paperwork such as statistics and reports.
- Be in sympathy with the aims and objectives of the employer and to the needs of the organization.
- Have or gain the skills to publicize the service to groups of staff.
- Volunteer for projects that offer the opportunity to demonstrate additional skills.
- Undertake training in management skills in addition to counselling-related CPD.

 Overlapping worlds can occur in workplace counselling: how would you manage these boundaries?

Bibliography

BACP (2000) *Guidelines for the Employment of Counsellors, BACP Information Sheet 9*. Rugby: BAC.

BACP (2002). *Ethical Framework for Good Practice in Counselling and Psychotherapy*, Rugby: BACP.

Berne, E. (1968) *Games People Play*. London: Penguin.

Birmingham City Council Social Services Department. (2000) *Employee Counselling Service*. Birmingham: Health and Safety Unit.

Burns, D.D. (1999) *Feeling Good*. New York: Avon Books.

Dyer, C. (2002) Considering counselling. *Health and Safety Bulletin* Jul., 11–20.

Egan, G. (1975) *The Skilled Helper: Model, Skills and Methods for Effective Helping* (2nd edn). Monterey: Brooks/Cole.

Franklin, L. (2003) *An Introduction to Workplace Counselling: A Practitioner's Guide*. Basingstoke: Palgrave Macmillan.

Gabriel, L. (2002) Working in a multi-task job. *BACP Information Sheet P5*. Rugby: BACP.

Jones, C. et al. (2000) *Questions of Ethics in Counselling and Therapy*. Buckingham: Open University Press.

O'Connell, B. (1998) *Solution-Focused Therapy*. London: Sage.

O'Connell, B. (2001) *Solution-Focused Stress Counselling*. London: Continuum.

Rogers, C. (1957) 'The necessary and sufficient conditions of therapeutic personality change', *Journal of Consulting Psychology*, **21**(2), 95–103.

13

Independent Counselling in the Workplace

Elspeth May Schwenk

Workplace counselling is a relatively young but rapidly evolving arena within counselling. While its roots began in the United States, it has taken hold in the UK, emerging as a most exciting and challenging area within which to work. Workplace counselling involves both in-house and externally based counselling services. The latter can be resourced through employee assistance programmes (EAPs) and independent workplace practitioners. In this chapter I describe my work as an independent workplace counsellor, working for several EAPs, staff support contracts and in private practice. As a self-employed practitioner my overall work also includes teaching, coaching and mentoring.

A typical day

As I am a portfolio counsellor, supervisor and trainer my typical day is a varied menu of different delights. There is a 'combination feel' to each day with a particular main focus of activity and secondary aspects alongside.

Today begins at 9.00 am with supervision, which I find a creative way to start any day. Diane is a competent secondary school counsellor, and brings both clinical issues and questions of theoretical/philosophical discussion as we consider her workplace context. By 10.15 I change roles, ready for Jeremy, a client from the local further education college where I provide staff support. Stress has been the major issue here due to a recent merger. In his fifth session, Jeremy has made significant changes in his work–life balance and general ways of working. We plan to conclude at the next session. The next client at 11.15 am is Peter, a new employee assistance programme (EAP) referral. I have minimal information and must complete considerable paperwork during the one-hour session. Peter is worried about possible redundancy from his telecommunication company. He complains of loss of appetite, poor sleep and being 'edgy' with his wife and family. This particular EAP provider will pay for four more sessions after assessment.

I now have to complete the paperwork and call the EAP to book a time when I can review this first session with my case manager. Being independent requires staying alert to the ongoing aspects of invoicing, administration, report writing and case management, for example, and this requires precious time.

The afternoon begins today at 1.00 pm with a supervision meeting for a team of occupational health nurses at a nearby hospital. Our focus is to review the systemic issues of the various workplaces they visit and how they manage the relationship between management and staff. On the way out, I confirm a supervision meeting with the manager of the hospital's EAP service for the following week and then leave for a 3.00 pm counselling session with Emma, a long-term client who has been exploring personal development issues and possible career change.

The last client of the day is at 4.00 pm. Susan was referred by another EAP provider with issues of bullying in the workplace, having felt unable to say 'no' to her demanding line manager. This is the third of four sessions, focusing on self-confidence when

meeting the manager. I must now snatch some time to catch up on
e-mails, phone calls and so on, and prepare for the evening's
schedule and review the following day. Tonight, I am out teaching
on a counselling course nearby from 7.00–9.30 pm. Tomorrow is a
different day.

As an independent EAP affiliate workplace counsellor, I manage
my own diary of appointments, liaise with various providers and
work to their individual specifications, complete paperwork and
conduct any client follow-up necessary. I am currently associated
with four EAPs, occasionally receiving referrals from other EAPs that
need a counsellor in the area and check the United Kingdom Register of Counsellors (UKRC) for local accredited counsellors. Some
EAP providers require counselling to be delivered in a formal setting,
and I have suitable arrangements with a local health clinic. It is
important, where possible, to set aside a clinic morning to minimize
travel time and rental costs (which are not recovered by the EAP).

Other 'typical' days might include team meetings with a local
consultancy of workplace counsellors, which requires travel (and
loss of earning), but provides support and professional development. Every three weeks I have my own supervision, which also
involves travel, expense and loss of earning, and bi-monthly I
attend a supervisors' forum to monitor my supervision practice and
provide support, challenge and development.

I am very much the sculptor of my 'typical day' and must
manage the various contracts that give it shape and focus. With this
level of independence comes control and freedom alongside responsibility. It can feel lonely and requires a high degree of organization
and autonomy. A good example can be seen in managing EAP referrals. From an affiliate's perspective, EAP referrals are not
predictable: I am unable to anticipate either frequency or number.
However, in accepting a referral, I must be able to see the client
within five working days. It is important therefore, to confirm my
availability before I take the case, looking ahead to scheduling subsequent appointments alongside other aspects of my portfolio.

My route in

My practice today reflects both careful planning and the integration of past experiences: I completed my core training with

an M.Sc. in counselling-psychology in Boston, USA, and this laid the cornerstone of my family systems theoretical approach. I also experienced a style of counselling supervision while on my second placement that has guided my own supervision practice in recent years. A graduate internship in career guidance demonstrated the need to plan a career path and be aware of professional trends and developments. This has been an invaluable insight.

Upon relocating to the UK and beginning a family, I decided to establish my own practice, thereby balancing both home and career needs. Joining the British Association for Counselling and Psychotherapy (BACP) provided an introduction to counselling in the UK and awareness of current issues. This insight influenced my decision when considering updating my qualifications. Staying with my systemic theoretical worldview, I saw a new area emerging: workplace stress and workplace counselling. I enrolled on the BACP-accredited postgraduate diploma in counselling at work (CAW) at Bristol University, to develop a workplace orientation alongside my systemic approach.

In addition to private practice, I joined a local consultancy of systemic workplace counsellors. I also began teaching counselling at a college of further education (FE) and have since extended my portfolio by providing a range of bespoke workshops. I find teaching informs my practice and vice versa, generating the impetus to keep up to date on counselling development.

The CAW diploma contributed toward a successful application for counsellor accreditation with the BACP. This fulfilled my intention to achieve the necessary qualification and thereby gain entry into the world of affiliate employee assistance work. BACP accreditation endorsed my private practice and laid the next foundation toward becoming a workplace counselling supervisor.

To strengthen these links with workplace counselling I joined the Association for Counselling at Work (ACW), a sub-division of the BACP. While initially unable to finance and attend the ACW conference, I recognized the value it offered. My first conference was a significant milestone: meeting others expanded my horizons. I enjoyed the workshops and explored new and exciting developments. I was energized by the experience and was co-opted onto the executive committee and subsequently voted on at the next conference. I am honoured by this opportunity to reflect and represent the needs of independent practitioners like myself, and contribute to the development of the profession.

As an accredited counsellor I have gained experience as an affiliate workplace counsellor working for several EAPs and have the appropriate credentials to develop independent contracts for workplace counselling with local organizations. My supervision practice has expanded and I am now a BACP accredited supervisor. I have also begun doctoral research, focusing on workplace counselling issues.

Client stories

Susan

Susan was referred through her EAP for brief solution-focused therapy regarding bullying by her line manager. She was tentative on the phone and hesitant during our first session. It was important to outline the structure of EAP counselling, case management and supervision, to assure her of confidentiality. During initial assessment, Susan disclosed a history of disempowerment. Feeling bullied had become the hallmark of relationships.

With four sessions, it is vital to clarify the focus of work and strategies to address it, and decide what cannot be resolved and how that can be managed. Susan's immediate choice of focus was the issue with her line manager. She felt overwhelmed by the current volume of work and daunted by the suggestion of another project, stretching her beyond her capacity. This highlighted an underlying issue regarding her lack of confidence. The outcome Susan identified was to be able to go into work, request a meeting and express her concerns about her workload.

Using the EAP pro forma and the material that emerged from the 'miracle question' (how will the client know, observably, that the problem is improving?) we identified a solution planning agreement. The purpose of this agreement was to plan the focus of counselling, that is, target problem, specific goal, strategies to achieve the goal and homework for the next session, and map out a similar route for those areas unable to be addressed by EAP counselling.

Susan identified the target problem: 'managing my work overload' with the specific goal: 'being able to speak to my line manager about this'. In exploring strategies, Susan decided that preparing a clear and detailed schedule of her work plan would equip her with firm data to support her statement, and enable her to focus on facts rather than emotions during the meeting. She thought a role-play interview would be of benefit. Her initial homework was to prepare the detailed work plan.

Susan's low self-esteem and lack of confidence were evident, and she wanted to focus on this as her second target problem. Her specific goal was to 'begin to value myself and my work'. The initial strategy and homework was linked to the previous strategy, in that alongside this very detailed account of her work schedule, she was to reflect on the skills and attributes she brought to the range of tasks she undertook. This was to be explored during counselling. We discussed the possibility of long-term work regarding relationship issues, and decided on referral at the conclusion of our work and possibly an assertiveness course.

By the third session, Susan had made significant progress. She had booked a meeting with her line manager, drawn up an extensive schedule of her work, and begun to explore and appreciate the skills and attributes that enabled her to complete her work. We had completed several role-play interviews and worked on deep breathing exercises and visualization to see herself speaking confidently, from a position of value and intrinsic worth. Although still nervous, Susan felt better prepared for the forthcoming meeting and how she wanted to conduct herself. Her focus was shifting to our final session to confirm follow-up plans for additional work elsewhere.

As an EAP affiliate, I work with the client and bring this to my supervisor (which I finance) and EAP case manager. At the conclusion, I call to close the case, complete and return the paperwork to the EAP provider. The client completes an anonymous satisfaction feedback form for the EAP.

Steve

My work as an independent and systemic practitioner can be seen as a complete contrast, particularly when addressing reintegration after long-term stress. Steve, age 41 and married with two children, is an engineer who had been off work for over three months, having tried unsuccessfully to return to work. Referred with 'long-term absence due to workplace stress', both company and client were keen to develop more effective strategies to enable him to return to work. His doctor prescribed anti-depressants and suggested counselling.

Steve had an open relationship with both human resources (HR) and his line manager who were willing participants in facilitating his reintegration. Because of that commitment, no immediate limitation was placed on counselling. In my first session I outlined the possibility of working systemically, using that open relationship to create a more structured and cohesive approach to reducing his workplace stress and facilitating return. We contracted that the sessions would remain confidential but some work-related issues could, with his permission, be brought to 'the team'. Steve selected the team: an HR representative, his line manager and myself. He chose to liaise with his doctor regarding medication and sick notes separately. This multi-communication contract kept Steve at the heart of the work and empowered him to 'direct' the team, since he controlled what material was brought. It required a reshaping of boundaries and clarity regarding confidentiality, to enable Steve and me to work from an individual perspective regarding his stress, whilst also exploring the wider, systemic perspective of the company.

The initial focus remained with Steve's stress. Still off work, he was experiencing loss of sleep, appetite, concentration and stamina. He had developed a stammer and his family found his irrational mood swings upsetting and unpredictable. Steve was concerned he would lose his family and his job. My first task was to 'normalize' these stress reactions and encourage Steve to give himself permission to be unwell.

I introduced a range of helping strategies in response to his stress, from meditation and relaxation to gentle physical exercise and keeping a journal. In therapy we explored the relationship between his thoughts and feelings, the agitation behind his stammer, and his core values and internal 'drivers' that influenced his 'ways of being' at work especially. In his previous attempt to return to work Steve had been ill prepared, with little self-awareness. However, in becoming more self-aware he found new concerns emerged: what was happening at work, how would he catch up, and what role, if any, was there for him?

Six sessions later, with the multi-communication contract in place, Steve was ready to meet with the 'team'. 'Jittery' about meeting on site, he requested somewhere neutral. Steve wanted to touch base with his line manager and hear from the company that his job was still open. During that initial meeting, Steve's agitation returned by way of the stammer but he was more self-aware and able to calm down. Both managers noted a significant improvement and affirmed their interest in his return to work, allowing Steve to be the orchestrator of that return.

Our sessions continued and Steve indicated a readiness to begin to prepare for a slow re-entry into the workplace. Working closely with both managers we devised a plan. Initially, the line manager visited Steve to bring him up to date on the current project. Steve had been coached in how to handle that meeting, and the line manager was briefed not to bring too much information. A second meeting occurred during which Steve was introduced to more of the project. This was in tandem with our sessions exploring what attributes and particular skills he brought to his unique role at work.

Steve's stress symptoms had reduced greatly by now. His mood swings lessened and he understood them better. His appetite improved, he slept more consistently, and stamina and concentration were strengthened. Steve had begun to review the project through regular meetings with his line manager, and felt ready for a site visit, asking for a 'team meeting' at work. We mapped out a plan of return, with checkpoints and support built in, and therapy remaining in place as a point of reflection and feedback. It proved a most helpful strategy as Steve began a schedule of half and full days. He developed insight into his irrational thoughts and behaviours, and could identify issues that were not generated from within but from the work system around him. We had already modelled systemic feedback, and Steve felt more able to discuss issues with his line manager. Since his HR manager had a welfare approach, she became the anchor point during any work day, while the gap between therapy sessions began to lengthen.

It took four and a half months for this client to reintegrate back into the workplace. During this time Steve experienced the support of his GP, HR and line manager, in addition to myself. His company had been appropriately informed throughout and had therefore been able to endorse this steady progress, act upon feedback and take an effective part in facilitating his return. It was a successful endeavour, enabling the client to take responsibility for his health and return to work, and the company to be informed and take responsibility to make and sustain constructive changes that would maintain the client's return (Schwenk, 2003, pp. 2–4).

As an independent practitioner, I field my own calls and determine the appropriateness of counselling and my suitability to respond. It is important to know the source of referral and the nature of the contract and discuss the possibility and process of systemic work at the outset. It is imperative when working with an employee on behalf of the employer that everyone is clear about the contractual relationship. Trust is a crucial ingredient to effective counselling and it is essential to honour all the relationships when committing to workplace counselling.

Evaluation

For an independent workplace counselling practitioner the 'tools of evaluation' may vary, so it is important to clarify these with each contract. I manage a range of feedback and evaluation measures, and this requires close attention to detail.

With EAP clients, once I have been sent client details and completed the initial session, I contact my case manager and using the pro forma assessment procedures, present this material for a brief case conference and decision regarding suitability for brief counselling or referral, and the number of sessions allocated to the client. Generally the accompanying paperwork is returned at the conclusion of counselling, together with brief records of subsequent sessions and a telephone debrief. Most EAP providers ask clients to complete an anonymous user self-assessment form, which is returned separately and provides feedback regarding the provision of service.

My independent workplace counselling contracts have a more systemic form of feedback and evaluation. One example is a contract whereby I meet twice a year with the company director to discuss general issues and themes relating to the company that have emerged during counselling. Clients are made aware of this facility, and can use it anonymously to convey upstream feedback they may otherwise not have the opportunity to voice. I also provide general statistics regarding the counselling service, for example, range of presenting problems, average number of sessions, gender, age and ethnic origin.

My ethical accountability and best practice are also maintained through personal supervision, a bi-monthly supervisors' forum and annual BACP re-accreditation. In my one-to-one supervision I present and discuss my work and receive feedback, and explore developmental issues. My contract is one to one and a half hours per three weeks to accommodate my workload, and this is self-financed and reviewed annually. The supervisors' forum is a shared opportunity to exchange ideas, discuss themes and receive both challenge and support for my supervision practice.

In establishing workplace supervision, I keep English's (1975, pp. 222–39) 'three-cornered contract' and Micholt's (1992, pp. 228–33) thoughts on 'psychological distance' in mind when I explore the system of feedback required. Towler (2002, pp. 10–11) highlights the importance of the context within which supervision takes place in order to remain clear regarding ethical and contractual responsibilities.

Continuing professional development

Since continuing professional development is another key aspect of my counselling and supervision practice, I may be away on a course for a day or longer. This is self-financed and must be logged into my portfolio of evidence for annual re-accreditation purposes. A major part of my personal and professional development has been BACP supervisor accreditation and embarking upon a doctoral programme, both requiring significant commitment. This involves balanced diary planning and budgeting of time. As I am an executive member of the ACW, there are monthly meetings to attend and these may also generate additional work.

Workplace counselling is a young 'industry', and I sense its emerging evolution in my own work. My practice has developed into offering mentoring, mediation, bespoke training, team development and contracting new counselling relationships between company and client that facilitate a systemic approach. I have also begun to write, reflecting upon these exciting new developments within workplace counselling. Managing this variety and being open to such transitions is not only a key aspect of my work setting but also an essential aspect of my professional development.

As an independent, BACP-accredited counsellor and supervisor, I am also mindful of CPD for my training and supervisor roles. While delighted by unexpected opportunities, I believe my professional development should have some underpinning focus and function. It is important to budget time and money wisely, developing an overall plan of direction to maximize best value. This requires continual refinement. Supervision offers that reflective space to review personal and professional development and, used in conjunction with the BACP's re-accreditation pro forma, to develop a sense of clarity.

Having established my CPD 'wish list' I weave the various elements and ideas into a framework. Opportunity is the next challenge. On a simple level, I take what comes my way in terms of cost, availability and accessibility, assessing opportunities to see if they match my needs or provide an unexpected adjunct. There is not a wealth of workplace counselling CPD opportunities, and I must remain clear regarding those key areas that will maintain and expand my practice. Contributing agents can be discussions with colleagues, the filtration and synthesis of books and professional journals, networking, workshops, conferences: all of which become pointers for ongoing professional development.

A potential pitfall of independent work is isolation, and CPD can be a tool to avoid this hazard in addition to the professional development. Active membership in the ACW contributes towards my CPD and generates a network of colleagues and ideas for the following year. It also provides a wider perspective on the workplace counselling industry, and informs and regenerates my enthusiasm.

Independent practitioners have total responsibility and personal freedom regarding CPD. This is both daunting and liberating, requiring proactive planning wherever possible. It may be a drawback for those who shun autonomy or are new to the profession. For those more confident and experienced, here lies an area of enormous scope.

I usually pay for all training and take a loss of earning for the day, paying associated costs. Budgeting is therefore important. While planning a whole year's CPD is difficult, elements such as fixed committee involvement can be anticipated in the year's framework.

Conditions of work

These are portfolio-driven and require complex management. This is a continuous balancing act, to fulfil personal and professional development. Areas to maintain are supervision, CPD, counselling and supervision practice, and training development. I also manage workflow and provision for vacation and illness.

My office is my home, and this brings not only the general factors to be considered when working from home, but confirmation with each EAP, since some prefer affiliates to use more official premises, for example, a room in a GP surgery or health clinic.

I am currently an affiliate with four EAPs. It is my decision to take a referral, judging overall caseload and availability and suitability, and combining EAP with private practice. Since there is no guarantee of referral or indication of rate of referral, scheduling is a possible limitation. In accepting a referral, I must see the client within five working days; otherwise I should decline the case. With freedom to plan my schedule comes responsibility, for example, when planning a two or three-week vacation. I alert the EAPs and temporarily stop accepting referrals. If I am unable to meet with a new client more than once before the vacation, I do not accept the case. When going away, I discuss with my EAP case manager and supervisor any clients I am concerned about, and arrange 'temporary cover' with a local colleague if necessary. Clients are forewarned of any prolonged absence and given emergency counselling alternatives. Should any illness occur, I must be able to access my records with sufficient ease to enable either myself, or a colleague, to make alternative arrangements, through a network of local counsellors.

For an EAP affiliate, BACP accreditation or equivalent is the base line qualification. The route toward this is varied. While it helps to have qualifications in workplace counselling, since there are so few BACP accredited courses (Bristol, Roehampton and Belfast), this is desirable but not a requirement. I can become an affiliate to as many EAP providers as I can manage realistically. Since much of the work is short-term, it is advisable to take relevant post-qualification courses, for example, in brief solution-focused therapy. My background lies in systems theory and this provides an invaluable perspective, especially as a workplace counselling supervisor. Career progression within the EAP field might be the transition from an independent affiliate to case manager. Some EAPs employ supervisors, generally part-time.

For an independent practitioner, there is no career pathway other than of one's own devising. A natural progression is becoming a supervisor through establishing a supervision practice, sufficient experience and qualifications toward accreditation.

Qualities contributing to success include a significant degree of independence and autonomy, the ability to be organized and multi-task, a broad range of therapeutic knowledge and depth of professional experience, an inclination toward administration and the ability and confidence to network, develop and negotiate contracts and gain new work. Carroll's (1997) research of employee counsellors in the private sector found other attributes included flexibility, a pioneering spirit and assertiveness.

It is important to know that the work is suitable and to turn it down if it does not fit within my skill set or portfolio. This must be balanced alongside the need to keep up to date and take on new challenges. I return to the fundamental root of independent working, that is, keeping in mind clear goals and objectives. Understand and be in control of how you want your career to progress and evaluate your work accordingly.

Future developments

Workplace counselling is a developing profession. This presents an opportunity to contribute toward ongoing changes. Although it is perhaps a daunting challenge, I am convinced that more practitioners could engage with the development of their particular niche in the profession – that we all have a contribution to make.

I believe we are entering an exciting stage. EAP providers have helped put counselling 'on the map' and given it sustainable viability. However, they also shape and dictate how that provision is delivered and, for some, this can be a narrow and uncreative expression of workplace counselling. There are new 'ways of working' to be explored and developed. Employee support can be delivered both internally and externally, through EAPs, welfare or occupational health departments, or tendered to local providers.

My own consultancy has been developing systemic ways of working (Schwenk, 2003) establishing a broader relationship with the company and employees, facilitating two-way feedback and fuller communication. This illustrates the possibility of bespoke counselling contracts, for example, for reintegration after long-term stress, team building, mediation and mentoring programmes: all of which require training and regular supervision. Many practitioners in counsellor management roles are themselves now seeking an additional aspect to their regular supervision beyond clinical review, to include mentoring and coaching with regard to the organizational perspective of their work.

How does this impact on current and future prospects for counsellor employment? I see possibilities for independent practitioners to take the initiative, working in tandem with colleagues, to establish workplace focused consultancies delivering a range of helping skills including training in people management, listening skills, assertiveness, stress management. We could also harness and develop our particular skills towards areas such as mediation, mentoring, coaching and team building.

Ten top tips

Generic tips:

- Keep up to date with your BACP accreditation and use CPD effectively through careful planning.
- Manage your own work–life balance, being aware of new areas of development and opportunity and marketing yourself accordingly.

Context-specific tips:

- Independent practice is isolating – locate a network of peers for general support – and provision of mutual 'back-up' for holiday cover and referrals.
- Budget wisely: plan for professional costs, for example, BACP membership, insurance, office requirements, CPD and for vacation time.
- Develop a back-up for any particular contracted work requiring a designated non-home location.
- Schedule weekly administration to ensure tracking of appointments, invoicing, the secure and confidential storage of documentation, deadlines.

- Develop a philosophy of counselling practice that accommodates the nature of workplace counselling (for example, systemic, short term, solution focused).
- Locate a supervisor familiar with workplace counselling and EAP work if possible, but general private practice in particular.
- Join ACW and attend the conference to establish further networking support and get ideas about future trends and developments.
- If you are thinking of using your own home, explore this option extensively with your family and other independent colleagues first.

 In considering workplace counselling, as an independent and/or affiliate counsellor, how do I see myself contributing to this exciting and developing field and what do I already have in place that would enable me to get started?

Bibliography

BACP (2002) *Ethical Framework for Good Practice in Counselling and Psychotherapy*. Rugby: BACP.

Carroll, C. (1997) 'Building bridges: a study of employee counsellors in the private sector', in M. Carroll and M. Walton (eds), *Handbook of Counselling in Organisations*. London: Sage, pp. 222–39.

Carroll, M. (1996) *Workplace Counselling*. London: Sage.

Carroll, M. and Holloway, E. (eds) (1999) *Counselling Supervision in Context*. London: Sage.

English, F. (1975) 'The three-cornered contract', *Transactional Analysis Journal*, 5(4), 383–4.

Macwhinnie, L. (ed.) (1998) *An Anthology of Counselling at Work*. Nottingham: Russell Press.

McLeod, J. (2001) *Counselling in the Workplace: The Facts. A Systematic Study of the Research Evidence*. Rugby: BACP.

Mearns, D. (2001) *How Much Supervision Should You Have? BACP Information Sheet S1*. Rugby: BACP.

Micholt, N. (1992) 'Psychological distance and group interventions', *Transactional Analysis Journal*, 22(4), 228–33.

Oshry, B. (1996) *Seeing Systems. Unlocking the Mysteries of Organisational Life.* San Francisco: Berrett-Koehler.

Parkinson, F. (1995) *Listening and Helping in the Workplace. A Guide for Managers, Supervisors, and Colleagues Who Need to Use Counselling Skills.* Guernsey: Guernsey Press.

Schwenk, E. (2003) 'Re-integration or exit with dignity', *Counselling at Work*, **40**, 2–4. Rugby: BACP.

Shea, G. (1992) *Mentoring. A Guide to the Basics.* London: Kogan Page.

Towler, J. (2002) 'Supervision + organisation = ?', *Counselling at Work*, **37**, 10–11. Rugby: BACP.

Section V

FREELANCE AND INDEPENDENT SECTOR

14

Pastoral Counselling

Alistair Ross

Wandering around the supermarket I stumbled across the section I required in order to buy some rice. I was overwhelmed by the variety of choice. To some people rice is simply rice, to others it is an expression of fair trade, an organic commitment, a desire to try something different, a vital aspect of a healthy diet, a boil-in-the-bag convenience; and so the aisle stretches on and on. The term 'pastoral counselling' has just as many variations, and such counsellors can be found working in NHS trusts (often as part of a chaplain's role), prisons, churches and other faith communities, Christian and secular counselling contexts, schools (though the term pastoral care means something different in this context), in private practice and in charitable or voluntary agencies. As a group there is no one body that coordinates, controls, authorizes or speaks on behalf of pastoral counsellors, though the Association of Pastoral, Spiritual, Care and Counselling (APSCC) exists as a subdivision of the British Association for Counselling and Psychotherapy (BACP). The Association of Christian Counselling (ACC) attracts counsellors from a predominately evangelical theological tradition but also has interests in developing pastoral care. Their theological stance, especially in areas of sexuality, puts them in tension with the respect for difference enshrined in the *Ethical Framework for Good Practice in Counselling and Psychotherapy* (2002) adopted by BACP. Lynch, an acute and incisive commentator in the area of counselling and culture writes:

> This lack of voice and lack of a core identity are perhaps the greatest threat to Christian pastoral counsellors being able in the future to deliver a useful service to their clients that is valued both by their peers in the wider counselling profession and by society more generally.
>
> (Lynch, 1999: 3)

Anyone using the term pastoral counsellor is choosing a self-constructed identity shaped by 'the cultural context in which the pastoral counselling takes place, the religious tradition that informs the work of the pastoral counsellor, and contemporary understanding of the therapeutic process and of the appropriate structure of the counselling relationship' (Lynch 1999:3). This chapter therefore describes my own development and practice in the area of pastoral counselling and provides general pointers for those identifying themselves as pastoral counsellors. I also recognize that others who wish to identify themselves as pastoral counsellors may well have travelled a quite different route.

A typical day

A typical day for a pastoral counsellor will depend entirely on the context in which he or she works. It is unusual for pastoral counsellors to be in full-time employment, so it may be more accurate to describe a typical week. Take three common scenarios. The first is being part of a pastoral team in a church or faith community context. The second is a chaplaincy role in a university, hospital or prison context, and the third is in church-based care and counselling centres that exist in many parts of the country.

In a church context Monday often consists of a team meeting where priorities are decided and others in the team are updated about wider developments. This meeting takes place during the day for salaried staff, although if there are lay leaders it is more likely to be in the evening. Inevitably the shape of the pastoral counselling that takes place will be influenced by the beliefs and values enshrined within the particular faith tradition. This more contextual pastoral role will often mean that the pastoral counsellor has a wider role that includes training: running listening skills courses, offering workshops on specific areas such as developing relationships, marriage preparation, managing depression, stress matters and so on. Depending on the exact contract pastoral counsellors will often be deemed to be 'experts' and become involved in the more complex issues of pastoral care, where their counselling skills can best be used. This is likely to involve: dealing with marriage/partnership breakdown; debt; and issues of sexuality including adultery, same sex relationships, helping parents whose children 'come out', transsexual and transgender issues, and physical and sexual abuse.

These subjects raise a fundamental issue for pastoral counsellors, namely, how much does their work reflect the orthodox beliefs of the faith community they are part of? The commonest response I have encountered in working with pastoral counsellors is that they hold the tension between a split over public and private belief. What they do and how they are in the counselling session may well be very different from the stated beliefs and values of the community they are part of. This exposes an underlying paradigm in pastoral counselling that is rarely articulated, and brings it into conflict with the nature of counselling as contemporarily understood. In pastoral counselling attention is given to the wider contexts of family, faith and community, rather than just the one-to-one individual encounter enshrined as a fundamental part of counselling relationships. A consequence can be the inner conflict between the pastoral counsellor feeling for an individual client and being caught in the vice of the faith communities' beliefs held by some representative religious figure such as a minister, priest or rabbi.

In a chaplaincy context, the nature and scope of the pastoral counselling that can be offered is to a great degree determined by the individual context. In a prison, can there ever be total confidentiality if a prisoner confesses to a crime? In a hospital, can chaplains establish clear enough boundaries between their public role, their personal role in offering pastoral care and their specialist role as pastoral counsellors? This area of dual relationships is a crucial area to be addressed. Boyd and Lynch focus on the issue of the therapeutic frame and conclude:

> Difficulties in establishing an appropriate therapeutic frame for counselling in pastoral settings have been identified, and it has been suggested that the pastoral practitioners' attempts to be 'all things to all people' can hinder the process of setting clear boundaries in their therapeutic work.
>
> (Boyd and Lynch, 1999, p. 77)

My experience as a minister and as a counsellor suggests that while in some team working contexts good practice can be developed with clear and negotiated boundaries, this is much more difficult to do in a sole ministerial role, and it is not something I would recommend. Bearing the burden of unboundaried transference and projection is more than the minister and the church-based client can endure. Another issue for those in a chaplaincy context relates to supervision, which is often provided by a member of the pastoral team.

> When counsellors are supervised by colleagues who have little understanding of the nature and process of counselling, let alone the nature and process of counselling supervision, this can leave the counsellor in a situation where their work is not being properly monitored or understood.
>
> (Boyd and Lynch, 1999, p. 75)

Partly because of this issue of boundaries the chaplaincy role is becoming more focused, and the opportunity for pastoral counselling as part of that role is diminishing.

In a church or faith-community-based care and counselling centre, the day by day pattern is similar to most other professional counselling agencies. A team meeting once a week provides group contact and cohesion, while the centre manager determines individual workloads. Most such centres adopt a more open stance in terms of accepting areas of difference, even if they are challenging for the faith community they represent. The greatest difference might be that the pastoral context gives implicit permission for its clients to raise issues of faith, belief or spirituality. Clinical discernment is required to decide if such issues are the core reason for the client seeking counselling, or if they are a defence that needs to be eased down gently to explore inner anxieties, such as self-acceptance. Whilst there is a growing recognition of the place of spirituality in counselling, it is often still thought of as a form of pathology or simply not relevant to counselling. Rose (2001) found a huge diversity of response when she researched the place of prayer in counselling, and enabled some counsellors to see that this was a vital part of a client's experience to which they had been culturally blind.

My route in

My route into pastoral counselling was influenced by four particular factors, a much more detailed account being found in *Evangelicals in Exile: Wrestling with Theology and the Unconscious* (Ross, 1997). First, there was my own need for counselling while training to be a minister. I was part of an evangelical theological tradition that generally eschewed the need for counselling, especially if it was secular. As one theological tutor stated, 'What the church needs is not more counselling but better preaching.' I felt that it needed both, and did not see the issue in such a polemic way. There was a huge level of guilt and failure I experienced in needing help that was not 'Christian', but I did find it through a counsellor at the Westminster Pastoral Foundation in London. After ten sessions some issues were resolved and at that stage I began to explore this experience further.

Second, there was a natural listening ability I had always had, which I found was being used more and more in my ministerial work. As time went by I began to see that this ability needed further development to listen to people at a depth that they obviously required and often expected.

Third, I did a placement at Claybury Psychiatric Hospital, Essex (now an executive housing estate) where group work and other forms of therapeutic interactions were encouraged. Through working with Peter, Judith and Deirdre I was introduced to psychodynamic group therapy, psychodrama, gestalt exercises and supervision. This heady mix in the early 1980s fuelled a desire to work as a pastoral counsellor whilst also being a minister.

Finally, I did a thesis on a 'Christian evaluation of Freud', which opened up the world of psychoanalysis and eventually led to my doing a research degree evaluating clinical theology (Ross, 1994). During this period I undertook various courses that reinforced my intuitive and experiential learning of counselling, which I worked out in a pastoral context. I received referrals from GPs, psychiatrists, other church leaders and the people from the local community who were attached to the fringes of the church. Most people wanted someone who would listen to their faith questions as well as their problems. Often their faith questions were noted, given space or permission to be voiced but not explored, and by the end of the counselling they were not deemed to be significant. However in some cases the use of religion as a defence became all too clear, and this is an issue dealt with in more detail elsewhere (Ross, 1999 and 2003).

By the mid-1990s, after a move to another part of the country where I had no contacts, and with the increased requirement for professionalism in the counselling profession, I decided to do a proper counselling training and chose the course at Leicester University run by Michael Jacobs and Moira Walker. I had always found Jacobs' book on pastoral counselling, *Still Small Voice* (1982) immensely helpful in linking faith experience to a psychodynamic perspective. At the same time I became a tutor on the pastoral counselling diploma at St John's College, Nottingham, and a little later spent valuable time as a student counsellor at Coventry University. In due course I gained my accreditation with BACP. I also made an important decision to leave the employment of the church, and the biggest indicator of this change in perception of my counselling role was to regularly charge clients for the counselling, pastoral or not.

A client story

Jill, a 21-year-old student, arranged to see Yvonne, the pastoral counsellor who was employed as part of the church staff team. This counsellor worked two days a week, and people from within the church community and the local community were able to access her services. While the counsellor attended staff meetings, she was not directly supervised by the team leader, who was also the senior minister of the church. Yvonne was in supervision with me on a twice-monthly basis. She felt supported by the team, and they were pleased to have a colleague to whom they could refer people requiring a greater degree of help than they felt able to provide. Yvonne had a psychodynamic counselling training and was an accredited member of BACP.

Jill contacted Yvonne by telephone, wanting an urgent meeting. Yvonne had a cancellation and so was able to see Jill the next morning. During this first session (which Yvonne treated as an informal assessment) Jill revealed that she had become suicidal and the thought had shocked her. 'I always thought I was a good Christian and would never do anything like that,' Jill said.

Yvonne did an informal risk assessment and clarified that Jill was not suffering from any form of psychiatric condition, was not on any medication and was not engaging in forms of behaviour that put her at risk. Yvonne suggested that if this happened again Jill needed to visit her GP, but that she would work with her for an initial phase of eight sessions, with a review at session six.

Over the next few sessions Yvonne helped Jill to explore what she meant by the term 'good Christian'. At the Monday team meeting the senior minister asked Yvonne if Jill was okay, as she had stormed out of the service the day before. When he had called, Jill had told him it was none of his business and that she was okay as she was seeing Yvonne. Yvonne replied that she was seeing Jill but felt unable to discuss any material.

Jill arrived late for the next session (often an important indicator in psychodynamic counselling) and said that she was going to give up this 'church lark'. As Yvonne explored Jill's anger, some of which she was turning on herself, Jill wept for the first time in the session. She talked about her feelings for another young woman in the congregation, who had rejected her several weeks earlier, just before she had come to counselling. Jill felt confused about her feelings, what she believed, what she wanted, and overwhelmed by waves of shame and depression. Yvonne asked if Jill had felt like this before. Jill sobbed and a muffled 'yes' was heard. 'My father used to come in my room and say, "Just give me a special cuddle" but I hated it, touching him down there. He made me promise to never tell anyone but I'm telling you. I feel so alone, as if I have been spoiled in some way. I don't like men, I don't trust them, but then I think "Am I gay?". I don't want to be gay either, I just want someone to love me.' Yvonne knew that Jill's father was a well-known legal and prominent social figure.

The following week at the team meeting the senior minister announced that their plans to develop their outreach into the community had taken a huge step forward. This included a purpose-built centre with space for the counselling service for which Yvonne had been actively campaigning. A donation from 'a well-known legal and prominent social figure' had enabled the target to be reached and work to begin. At the subsequent counselling session, Jill informed Yvonne that it was her father who had made this donation and that she was sick of his hypocrisy. She said she would not be attending beyond the next session (number eight), despite having agreed that she would come on an open-ended basis at session six. The next week, the senior minister informed Yvonne that Jill had stormed out of the service again shouting that the church was full of hypocrites. He wanted to know what she was going to do about it.

The following issues emerge from this clinical vignette:

- What pressures does the context create for the pastoral counsellor in terms of confidentiality? Is there a difference in understanding about individual counselling confidentiality and team pastoral care confidentiality?
- What is recorded on the notes held by Yvonne, given that others may read them if legal action is taken?
- How does a pastoral counsellor manage the tensions of short-term contracts with clients who often need long-term work?
- What boundary issues emerge? How might Jill feel about encountering Yvonne at some church function? In this case Yvonne was a member of another church, however there were times when she was present and might encounter Jill. What would Yvonne do if this major benefactor asked to meet the counselling team for which he had raised a large sum?
- What are the responsibilities on the counsellor for issues of disclosure of sexual abuse?
- What burden does the pastoral counsellor bear in a voluntary funded context, with continual pressures on finance? How might this inhibit the work?

- To whom is the pastoral counsellor responsible? The faith community? The senior minister? The supervisor? The professional body, BACP? The client?
- How are matters of risk assessment and self-harm dealt with in a voluntary context? Is there a standard procedure?
- How are matters of sexual orientation dealt with in a faith community context? What dynamics might be set in motion if a pastoral counsellor adopts a view different from the beliefs or values of the faith community?
- What support do pastoral counsellors have to unravel the complexity of some pastoral contexts outside of supervision?

Evaluation

There are few tools currently available in the UK that evaluate the role and effectiveness of pastoral counselling, though pastoral counselling is one of the core subjects explored in *CONTACT: The Interdisciplinary Journal of Pastoral Studies*. The United States has a longer tradition of pastoral counselling linked to the development in the 1940s of the clinical pastoral education (CPE) movement (Hurding, 2003, pp. 222f.). A key contribution made by CPE is the development of the concept of the reflective practitioner and over time there has emerged a wide-ranging body of evidence advocating the value of pastoral counselling (Stone, 2001, and more generally see the *Journal of Pastoral Care*). Being a reflective practitioner is a form of qualitative research methodology that has gained greater academic significance in relation to counselling in the last 15 years (Lynch, 1999, p. 89) and it is still very much in its infancy. One encouraging sign has been the publication of the recent BACP journal, *Counselling and Psychotherapy Research* (CPR). With the aim of cultivating the relationship between research and practice, CPR provides an important vehicle for ongoing publication for research concerning pastoral counselling.

Of greater concern for contemporary pastoral counselling are the forthcoming demands for registration and membership of a professional body, namely BACP. As BACP sets high standards for its membership and accreditation, the result could be catastrophic for counselling, where a large number of those involved do not have formal counselling training or at the level required by BACP.

A great deal of pastoral counselling training has been experiential in nature, such as the seminars offered by the Clinical Theology Association since the 1960s, now known as the Bridge Pastoral Foundation (Hurding, 2003, 9, pp. 369f.). Over the years many very good counsellors have been trained this way, through seminars that were designed before validation was seen as a crucial aspect of training. This aspect of pastoral counselling training will be changed forever. It presents therefore a huge challenge to pastoral counselling centres that rely on volunteer counsellors. However the benefit might be that such centres move to a new standard of professionalism and employ counsellors who are accredited with BACP.

Employment as a pastoral counsellor is best enabled by three qualities. The first is to be professionally accredited. The second is to have some experience of, or understanding about, what a faith community is and does. This is essential if the counsellor is going to be able to manage the contextual side of the client base and the employer. A third is to be a reflective practitioner. This is sometimes expected by the work context. For example, an innovative counselling service offered as part of the city centre community role of St Martin in the Bull Ring, Birmingham recently required the counselling team leader to be both professionally qualified and able to reflect theologically on the place of counselling within a centre for health and healing. Yet for most pastoral counsellors the ability to develop as a reflective practitioner needs to come through a personal desire and commitment to achieve this. There are various groups of professional counsellors who want to reflect on issues of faith or spirituality, and one such group meet at a biennial 'Continuing the journey' conference. Others attend conferences arranged by the APSCC, or follow up local contacts to provide a network of people with whom they can explore vital issues. Such meetings can profitably be built into the ongoing continuing professional development (CPD) requirement for BACP.

Continuing professional development

As employment as a pastoral counsellor is so varied, it is often either the precedent set by a predecessor or the personal negotiating skills of the employee that determine how and what is provided in the way of ongoing professional development. There are several examples of good practice in this area, although as with other voluntary funded agencies some areas of pastoral counselling find it difficult to fund CPD.

My former employer, the Bridge Pastoral Foundation (formerly the Clinical Theology Association), gave me time and paid fees for me to see someone on a monthly basis. It was not personal counselling or supervision (though the person was able to offer both) but it did give me space to reflect critically and creatively on my own processes and those of the organization that employed me. One significant conclusion of this arrangement was that I felt that I was being given something that was not a measurable, work-related outcome. It felt as if the organization was interested in me. This is a desirable goal of all CPD, above and beyond the specific activity engaged in and the ongoing demands for continuing counsellor accreditation.

Conditions of work

The context in which pastoral counselling takes place is of vital importance for the client and the counsellor. If you work in private practice, careful attention needs to be given to how this is set up and whether you practise in or outside your own home. In many church or faith community settings, good or adequate rooms can be found. However in working in a chaplaincy context, what an unsympathetic manager would deem as suitable for counselling may be very different from what is required.

Every pastoral counsellor should be supervised in the same way as other counsellors. Some church or faith-community-based centres do not pay their counsellors but offer supervision for the work that is done on their behalf. The difficulty about this arrangement is that the counsellor has little choice and the supervisor might not have any training other than having been a counsellor and experienced supervision themselves. One pastoral counsellor approached me to be her supervisor as she had negotiated that she should have supervision external to the centre where she was based. I later discovered that the centre manager nearly had a heart attack when he discovered my fees. It is not that these were exorbitant; they were the 'going rate' for supervision at that time. The problem was that the centre was run on a shoestring basis and it had never paid appropriate fees before.

Future developments

The future for pastoral counselling is complex. In Lynch's opinion:

> the fragmented nature of the British pastoral counselling scene involves a loss of opportunity for sharing expertise, a wasting of resources and an inability to develop a clear image of pastoral counselling... . The fundamental rationale for the existence of pastoral counselling is to meet the needs of clients in appropriate and constructive ways as an expression of greater truths about our existence. Continued reflection, collaboration and communication are important means to fulfilling this task.
>
> (Lynch, 2000, p. 342)

As people's desire for meaning is no less now than it ever has been before, pastoral counselling has an important place in holding to truths, traditions, symbols and narratives enshrined in religious structures or contexts. The challenge for the future is to become inclusive of a more generic spirituality and avoid a retreat into fundamentalism.

Ten top tips

Generic tips:

- Be clear about the nature of the context that you are in, including any tensions, perhaps in the areas of confidentiality, professional ethics or difference.
- Resource personal growth through reading and reflecting on practice with the aim of becoming a reflective practitioner.

Context-specific tips:

- Explore how you understand your own faith, spirituality or search for meaning.

- Examine the points of contact between your understanding of counselling and your faith or spiritual perspective.
- Evaluate the areas of diversity between your understanding of counselling and your faith or spiritual perspective.
- Decide how you will be supervised and supported in a way that adds to your pastoral counselling experience.
- Clarify the nature of your contract, determining precisely what you are able to do and not do.
- Find a way of exploring your own faith or spirituality issues, as they are touched on in counselling and supervision.
- Attend conferences that allow these aspects of your work to be addressed as part of your continuing professional development.
- Enjoy being able to help clients explore spirituality, a comparatively neglected area of counselling until recent times.

? How much do I, as a trainee counsellor, need my work to be paid for as recognition of the training I have undertaken, and how much can I contribute for little or no fee as an expression of a personal faith commitment and a desire to support the work of pastoral counselling?

Further reading

The most helpful book available is *Clinical Counselling in Pastoral Settings* edited by Gordon Lynch (1999). While this does not detail how one works as a pastoral counsellor, it explores a wide range of issues that need to be understood and owned if someone wishes to be a professional in this field. An example of how counselling skills can be used in faith contexts is to be found in my own book, Ross (2003) *Counselling Skills for Church and Faith Community Workers*. A broader exploration of the themes of spirituality and counselling can be found in West's (2000) *Psychotherapy and Spirituality*.

Bibliography

BACP, (2002) *Ethical Framework for Good Practice in Counselling and Psychotherapy*. Rugby: BACP.

Boyd, A. and Lynch, G. (1999) 'Establishing the therapeutic frame in pastoral settings', in G. Lynch (ed.), *Clinical Counselling in Pastoral Settings*. London: Routledge.

Hurding, R. (2003) *Roots and Shoots* (2nd edn). London: Hodder and Stoughton.

Jacobs, M. (1982) *Still Small Voice*. London: SPCK.

Lynch, G. (ed.) (1999) *Clinical Counselling in Pastoral Settings*. London: Routledge.

Lynch, G. (2000) 'Pastoral counselling in the new millennium', *Counselling*, 11(6), 340–2.

Rose, J. (2001) *Sharing Spaces*. London: DLT.

Ross, A. (1994) *An Evaluation of the Significance of Clinical Theology 1958–1969*. Oxford: CTA.

Ross, A. (1997) *Evangelicals in Exile: Wrestling with Theology and the Unconscious*. London: DLT.

Ross, A. (1999) 'The place of religious tradition in pastoral counselling', in G. Lynch (ed.), *Clinical Counselling in Pastoral Settings*. London: Routledge.

Ross, A. (2003) *Counselling Skills for Church and Faith Community Workers*. Buckingham: McGraw Hill.

Stone, H. (2001) 'The congregational setting of pastoral counselling: a study of pastoral counselling theories from 1949 thru 1999', *Journal of Pastoral Care*, 25(2), 181–96.

West, W. (2000) *Psychotherapy and Spirituality*. London: Sage.

15

Freelance Counselling in a Residential Rehabilitation Centre

Joyce Evans

The achievement of counselling is not that it makes us stop smoking or takes our depression away or makes us more confident... . If we gain the courage to face up to our conflicts and fears rather than avoid them and push them away into symptoms then we have made good use of [it].

(McLoughlin, 1990, p. 65)

The rehabilitation programme at Phoenix House aims to 'rebuild the lives' of between 30 and 40 adult residents who are funded for six to nine months. They are usually asked to leave if they are using drugs or drinking, or if they use threatening behaviour or language. Schedule one offenders (who have convictions of serious offences against children), arsonists, people with a long history of self-harm or suicide and those with ongoing mental health problems are not accepted. All the full-time staff have basic counselling training, several have diplomas or degrees, and some are also past drug users. They work as a team, counselling but also sharing information about the residents, giving advice, offering support throughout the day and enforcing house rules. These roles can compromise one another, hence the need for the 'outside counsellors' who guarantee confidentiality and who are completely separate. Yet paradoxically there is always a sense of working with the staff. Our parallel tracks enable the clients to proceed on their journeys.

A typical day

Due to a shortage of suitable rooms the other independent counsellor, a cognitive behaviour therapist (CBT), and I work on different days. Over the years we have provided mutual support but rarely see each other unless the project manager meets us to provide general information and an opportunity for discussion. We work autonomously but not in isolation: the atmosphere within this community is warm and valuing.

Residents who think they would benefit from counselling are referred when they have been at the rehab for several weeks. By this time they are completely drug free. The only information I am given is the client's first name, which is all I need to know: the full-time staff liaise with all other agencies. In this setting an additional clause is added to the basic counselling contract: I must inform the staff of anyone bringing drugs into the house or using drugs or drinking. These offences mean that the resident is usually asked to leave the programme.

Today, as usual, I enter the glass-fronted office to check the diary with the staff; clients rarely fail to attend counselling. The door is usually left ajar, thus I am visible and potentially audible to any passing residents. Long ago one who had been sexually abused remarked, 'If I see the staff laughing and joking I imagine they are talking about me.'

This would never be the case but it made me realize that not only am I separate from the house but that I must be seen to be separate in order to allay any doubts about my confidentiality.

The day begins on a low; a client has left the rehab unexpectedly between sessions. My new client, Paul, carefully checks the confidentiality then immediately begins unburdening racking guilt by graphically describing violent drug-related behaviour and crime. In this situation I am very aware that the police have powers to seize confidential files if they have obtained a warrant from a circuit judge. My records are minimal; sometimes I make no notes at all after hearing particularly incriminating material. This is a difficult choice because while I am protecting my clients and myself, I am also vulnerable if a client has reason to complain of professional negligence or misconduct.

The next client, Alison, who was sexually abused as a child, became a prostitute and has just returned from her first home leave. Her pimp has threatened to disfigure her if she doesn't return to work and she is desperately missing her children. In tears she tells me she is considering leaving the programme. As I empathize with her fear and loss I am also conscious of my own temptation to try to rescue her by talking to the staff.

Hassan felt that he could never live up to his strict parents' expectations. His father died suddenly one evening while Hassan, at 15, was out drinking with his friends. I spend much of the session in silence as he weeps, silently too. At the end of the hour he leaves, composed but still grieving. On one hand I know that support is available if he seeks it, on the other hand he is free to walk out of the rehab, immediately find solace in the maximum amount of heroin he used in the past – and death. In these cases it is essential but not always easy to stick to the established boundaries.

Later in the day I see Ben who was in care from the age of eight and has recently been focusing on his homosexuality, torn between concealment and openness. He enters smiling broadly. I share his joy; he has revealed his secret of over 20 years to the staff. In this setting empowerment comes from the client being his own communication channel.

My last client's habit escalated from soft drugs to heroin after witnessing terrorist atrocities in Northern Ireland. I feel a certain sadness as Darren says goodbye but optimism and great pleasure in knowing that he will complete his programme next week. This is the high at the end of the day when I fill in the diary and leave.

My route in

Drugs, as we know the term today, were virtually unknown in rural Shropshire where I lived over 30 years ago, and counselling would certainly have been scorned. Teaching was a respectable career for a young woman; so I taught – neither enthusiastically nor well – in mainstream schools and eventually in a special school, which I loved. However my need for some basic counselling training became glaringly apparent when parents expressed their sorrow or anger at the loss of the perfect child they had anticipated. More courses and more certificates followed when I joined the educational psychology department to provide a pre-school service for families with special needs children. At last, in 1989, I began a three-year person-centred counselling diploma course.

The placements I chose were a national bereavement centre and, because I live in an area with a bad reputation for drugs and one of my own children was then a cannabis dabbling student, the residential drug rehabilitation centre which is organized as a therapeutic community. At the end of the course I continued to work there on a voluntary basis. Six years ago I gave up the education employment, took on some private counselling and, together with the CBT counsellor, negotiated a basic rate of pay at the rehab and gradually increased the number of counselling hours. We were pleased the counselling was perceived as sufficiently beneficial to be extended and recompensed.

My belief is that when 'the counsellor offers ... congruence, unconditional positive regard and empathy, therapeutic movement takes place' (Mearns and Thorne, 1988, p. 18). When working with people whose addiction has, as so often, stemmed from the very lack of these conditions in childhood and who have been condemned and despised during many years of drug use, the relationship with the counsellor is crucial and constitutes the essential therapy. To be able to have faith in the potential of those who have lost hope for themselves, and to value and accept them in a non-judgemental way, is of paramount importance in this setting. Within this frame I use person-centred art therapy and elements of transactional analysis. In the later sessions solution-focused brief therapy (SFBT) has proved a fast, effective way to review progress and facilitate clients in setting their own goals; in the following case I explain that this is a different form of counselling.

A client story

> The causes of addiction ... always lay hidden in childhood.
> (Miller, 1987, p. 18)

Fred was 33 and had done nearly three months of his nine-month programme. This was his third rehab; he was asked to leave the first after seven weeks for threatening behaviour. In the second, he formed a relationship with another resident. They voluntarily left together but both resorted to drugs when she had a miscarriage. His increasing jealousy and possessiveness culminated in his physical abuse to his partner.

Fred and his sister, five years younger, had grown up with their parents who had a greengrocer's business. They were always well fed and clothed. The mother was quiet, the father popular with his mates down at the pub. Occasionally he would drink a bit too much and then they all had to watch out. That's just how it was. Fred used to spend Saturday morning with nan. She died when he was ten but she was getting on by then anyway. He'd always clowned around at school, began drinking and stealing at 11, then smoking cannabis at 12. At 18 he was addicted to heroin. The basic facts suggested a painful past but, more significantly, Fred spoke of himself emotionlessly, as if describing someone he had never met. Even in this way the reality appeared too difficult to contemplate: he minimized and rationalized.

During the first session he expressed his anger at two residents who were 'taking the piss'; he felt lonely and isolated. The staff had suggested that he was avoiding his issues, which he had identified as his father, his mother and nan. Gradually Fred went into more detail of his life as a child. He saw his father as a hard working, hard drinking man, who physically abused his wife and began using a belt to his six-year-old son. On many occasions Fred had been kept away from school because of bruising, and he had twice been to accident and emergency after his father had effectively flung him across the room.

Fred had soon learned that crying resulted in further assaults and anyway he 'wouldn't give the f… bastard that satisfaction'. He had virtually no recollection of his sister until he was about 12 when, powerlessly, he first watched his father punch and kick her, too. From the time he attended junior school he went home to clean and tidy an empty house before his parents came in. If his mother was satisfied he would be allowed out to play after tea, otherwise his father punished him. At secondary school he rebelled, climbing out of his bedroom window and running away. Father's drinking increased. The beatings increased. At 16 he left home to live with his girlfriend's family. Her brother injected heroin.

Initially Fred dismissed his mother as weak and unable to stick up for herself, but then he recalled resignedly that 'she'd had the guts' to leave briefly for another man. He considered his father 'Not worth bothering about.' He showed little feeling when he spoke about them but continued to feel angry with some of his peers.

At the beginning of the fifth session he recounted his earliest memory, at about four, of lying in bed listening to his mother scream and furniture being overturned. He'd gone to the top of the stairs to see what was happening but, not daring to go down, he had sat there 'freezing' for what seemed like hours, until his mother found him when she went to bed. She told him sharply that he had better get back in his room before his dad came, and then she went into his parents' room, turning her back and closing the door on the child outside. Again this was described emotionlessly; he met my eyes and shrugged dismissively, perhaps trying to dismiss me too, another woman whom he didn't know if he could trust. Yet there was a sense of unbearable pain and loneliness in both the child and the man. I asked if he could draw how it was. He drew in silence; without speaking we regarded his picture together for several minutes. Then he wept. Afterwards it seemed that it was with my physical acts of offering paper and crayons and moving fractionally towards him – maybe towards his unacknowledged suffering in a way his mother had been unable to do – that trust first emerged. It grew as he risked showing his pain and found it safe to do so.

Over the next few weeks he was able to empathize increasingly with the terrified, powerless child and express his anger towards his father. Finding this accepted, he allowed his absolute fury with his mother, whom he saw as coldly allowing brutality to her children in order to deflect it from herself, to be released in a torrent of verbal abuse. Between sessions he wrote letters to both, saying everything he would have liked to have been able to say as a child and wanted to say now. He brought them to counselling where he tore them into tiny fragments, opened the window and let them disappear in the wind. The adult wrote a letter to the child, and treasured it. Fred felt he was making progress in his programme: getting on better with other people and feeling less isolated. He looked at his abusive relationships with women and eventually spontaneously began to talk about his nan. Perhaps there was some transference at this point. 'You're a bit ...' he began but stopped and moved away rapidly, choosing not to say any more.

His grief was intense for the one person he felt had loved and understood him; his greatest sorrow that she would have been so ashamed of the way he had lived. He faced the loss with new-found courage and finally drew her garden, in summer, filled with flowers, as he remembered it.

Fred blossomed too. He prided himself on not seeking comfort in a relationship in the rehab and began to make preparations for the future. He spent a weekend with his sister and met his parents for the first time in four years. Part of him was still hoping for the love and attention he had never had. He returned disappointed and told me, 'It was hard to take. I went out on Friday night and didn't feel too good on Saturday.' Then he added, 'I wasn't using drugs.'

Tentatively I asked what it was about. He shrugged and smiled ruefully. Thus I was aware that he had been drinking but could not tell me openly because he knew I had to disclose the fact. For the rest of the session we worked on a hypothetical basis, looking at the feelings that might lead to drink, how it could be avoided. I was colluding with him. I discussed this with my supervisor and continued to collude.

Fred's fragilely built self-esteem wobbled at this point but the SFBT technique of scaling enabled him to see how far he had progressed and what potential he had. A month later, after meeting his parents again, he felt hopeful that an amicable relationship might eventually be established but that, as an adult, he 'could manage very well without them'. They didn't travel to his completion ceremony but did send their congratulations. Fred's success was applauded loudly by members of the community and by his delighted sister.

After Fred had left I clarified the alcohol situation with the project manager. As long as I am not specifically told that a client is drinking I do not have to reveal what, in fact, I do know. Ethically this is difficult. I know I am compromising.

Evaluation

Success of rehabilitation is notoriously difficult to quantify. Nor can it, perhaps, be measured purely in abstinence from drugs. Approximately a third of the residents complete the programme. However, some of those are likely to return to drugs and some who left without completing might well remain drug free. Separate statistics are not kept for completion numbers of clients seen by the outside counsellors who constitute but one part of a wide programme. Throughout the week there are large and small group counsels run by the staff as well as their individual sessions with residents, so the effectiveness of one person is difficult to assess. But the 'sophistication of the Therapeutic Community is evident in the fact that Therapeutic Communities of America has established criteria and procedures for evaluating counsellors and certifying their competency' (De Leon, 2000, p. 6). Such procedures will probably operate here in due course. Unlike the private counsellor, for instance, who might be tempted to take any credit for a client's growth, a counsellor within a therapeutic community is part of a team, even when working independently.

So how is my work evaluated? Openness is valued highly. This means that everything I say or do is likely to be discussed by the client with staff as highly qualified as I am. Some counselling has probably been unintentionally (or possibly intentionally) misrepresented but this has not yet caused difficulties. Throughout the programme residents have five focused care plan meetings with senior staff, in addition to key work sessions, when their therapeutic work is discussed in detail. My work is therefore being constantly monitored through clients' verbal reports, by staff and ultimately by the project manager who is in charge of resources and employment. There could be a danger of worrying about other people's opinions or needing to be seen as an effective counsellor in order to ensure continuing employment. I constantly question my work: but only in relation to my clients. We review the counselling process together every six weeks, or immediately if there is a difficulty. I ask what has proved helpful – or unhelpful – what the client wants from counselling and is gaining from it. Residents also monitor their own counselling carefully too, saying for instance, 'I had a care plan and realize I need to do more work on ...' The more complex task for any counsellor lies in being self-aware during times of personal change, which can affect the counselling in indefinable ways.

Continuing professional development

As an independent counsellor I am responsible for my own professional development and usually anticipate paying for it myself, although recently there has been an indication that there could be money available from the rehab for additional training. The SFBT training was funded by the educational psychology service during my last year there. Four years ago I paid for the art therapy course myself as it is a medium that interests me. One constraint of the setting is lack of time for working with residents who might have suffered a lifetime of abuse but have only a six-month programme. Imagery or a picture drawn with the non-dominant hand sometimes produces as much insight and self-awareness in one session as several purely verbal ones. 'When trust begins to develop, talking about abuse may yet be difficult because it relies upon verbalisation that the client may not be able to engage' (Glover, 1999). This medium seems particularly helpful with residents unable to get in touch with their feelings and the 'art' can afterwards provide a tangible point of discussion with the key worker. But proper training is essential: partly to ensure that the counsellor does not analyze or interpret but rather, facilitates the client to make sense of what is often on the edge of their awareness.

Two years ago I completed an MA in English literature. My dissertation was on the manipulation of conscience, which has undoubtedly given me a greater skill in sensing what lies behind defences and more empathy with clients who justify, minimize and rationalize. Any practical experience, such as work with alcoholics or the homeless, which brings the counsellor into contact with the realities of drug life would be regarded very favourably by potential employers as a basis for understanding the residents.

Conditions of work

Models of rehabilitation treatment vary but counselling trainees should be warned that they are unlikely to find luxury or grow rich if they choose to work in this area. I counsel in a small portacabin – perfect in size but also very shabby – and occasionally residents disrupt the session by talking nearby.

For tax purposes I am registered as self-employed and am paid monthly from the Phoenix House central office. The rate of pay was originally £6.40 a session. Over the years we have negotiated increases and I now earn £25: still not a lot for a qualified and experienced counsellor. However, there are compensating advantages; this is a counselling culture, confidentiality and boundaries are understood and not questioned. I fund my own individual monthly supervision with a supervisor of my choice who is highly experienced and supervises counsellors from a wide range of agencies, including the prison service. She is also a tutor for a counselling degree course and has taught ex-addicts; but for me her essential attribute is her acceptance and valuing of my clients.

Working with another counsellor who has a different approach means that I do not have to try to be everything to everybody. To work independently in itself affords freedom of choice, and within this setting there is also flexibility. My methods of counselling are unquestioned and there is no restriction on the number of sessions offered to clients apart from the ultimate limit of their funding. In the wider field, opportunities for working with groups and for training staff have been proposed. There seems to be a need for counselling to facilitate better relationships between some residents and their families who are allowed to visit at weekends. It is noticeable that staff who change jobs choose to remain in this field, often moving to similar work in prison or the youth service.

A therapeutic community might not appeal to every counsellor however, and there are attributes that are particularly important in this setting. The work here is with deep-rooted issues rather than problems. Lack of confidence and low self-esteem are endemic. Many residents have lived for 20 or 30 years with the secret of having been abused without recognizing the root of anger, which they have sometimes found terrifyingly uncontrollable. The first release of such accumulated emotion can be accompanied by violent swearing and the desire for graphically described physical revenge. The counsellor needs to have the skill to facilitate the release of such anger, be able to accept this way of expressing it and to stay unwaveringly with all strong emotions. As a senior member of staff aptly commented, 'Counselling here is not about drugs, it's about blood and guts and horror.'

Some clients experience crippling guilt; conversely others initially feel no guilt for actions that have left people permanently scarred. The ability to remain non-judgemental, valuing and empathic in these situations is essential. Whereas it might be easy to offer these qualities to a victim, counsellors considering work-ing with ex-drug users must consider with absolute honesty if they could consistently offer them to clients who have, perhaps, tortured or raped innocent people. A counsellor is sometimes not told until much later, that the perpetrator was first a victim, as was the case with Paul, my new client mentioned in the typical day section. Counsellors should be unshockable, confident of their safety in the rehab setting and not rendered fearful in the wider community. Because of the nature of the setting there is a greater than average loss of clients and yet change can be dramatic in those who remain. The independent counsellor needs to have the ability to work without reassurance and to resist the temptation to be proactive. It is not so much that specific attrib-utes are needed but rather that, because the issues are invariably huge, then huge reserves of the generic attributes required of most counsellors are essential.

A diploma or degree would be required for my particular job and some additional counselling training or practical experience would be an advantage. Knowledge of the effects of drugs and drug-related illnesses is helpful but above all employers are looking for people who can quickly form good counselling relationships and who can accept the realities of the residents and their drug world.

Future developments

The government proposes a 'stronger focus on the 250,000 Class A drug users ... , new improved treatment for crack and cocaine users, expansion of treatment services tailored to meet individual need, including residential treatment where appropriate ... and funding for treatment services to be increased to £589 million by 2005' (Blunkett, December 2002). Nationally the use of crack is rising faster than heroin. Twenty specialized crack projects in high crack areas should be in place by April 2004. Structured counselling is widely used in non-residential programmes and has proved effective for many users, but the National Treatment Agency for Substance Misuse found that: 'Cocaine-dependent users with extensive complicating factors such as criminality, multiple dependency and low social support, do best in intensive rehabilitation services .... Traditionally these take the form of residential communities' (National Treatment Agency, 8/2002).

Drug abuse treatment outcome studies concluded that:

> Once in treatment the quality of the counsellor relationship is highly influential. Empathy, a non-judgemental style, flexibility, an ability to be welcoming and relate respectfully to antiauthority, deprived, troubled and vulnerable people and to misusers from Black and Ethnic Minority populations are important. For heavier crack misusers CBT approaches have a relatively large and positive US evidence base. Group Therapy has been found to be as effective as individual therapy.... Psychodynamic therapies which analyse the clients' emotions and thoughts have been found to add nothing.
>
> (NTA, 8/2002)

The overwhelming evidence is that drug and alcohol abuse continues to escalate. There is a rapidly increasing demand for 'drugs counsellors', who use both counselling skills and counselling with users and their families, and there is a severe shortage of male counsellors from ethnic minorities. Non-residential rehabilitation programmes that incorporate counselling are expanding throughout Britain. Residential treatment, such as is provided by Phoenix House where every member of staff has a counselling qualification, will be primarily for users with 'extensive complicating factors' regardless of their drug of choice. The future of the independent counsellor in this setting is likely to depend upon the ideas and resources of the project managers, but there will always be a need for staff with good counselling qualifications for full-time employment here.

Finally I want to say how enormously privileged I feel in being trusted to see behind the defences of a lifetime, to be told the unsanitized truth by those who have often had to lie and manipulate in order to survive, and to be present for the growth of residents who all have the potential to refute society's perception of drug users as beyond hope. In this setting you, as a counsellor, will find clients who are immensely rewarding to work with, living in an environment which is positive and supportive for them, and for yourself.

The clients mentioned do not exist but the situations are typical of my everyday work.

Ten top tips

Generic tips:

- Talk to counsellors in similar settings to build up a network of contacts.
- Choose a supervisor who will accept and value these particular clients.
- Be prepared to counsel on a voluntary basis, even in a shoebox at first.
- Then be prepared to negotiate better conditions.
- Make your boundaries absolutely clear and stick to them. But be flexible within them.

Context-specific tips:

- Try to do one placement in a rehab and one in a different setting for contrasting perspectives.
- Work voluntarily with the homeless or in any situation where people are likely to use drugs.
- Arrange to visit prostitutes with an outreach worker. They will describe drug life. Read *Trainspotting* or *Nil by Mouth* or watch the videos. Think carefully if you can work with this reality.
- If you have you been a victim of crime or abuse consider whether this could affect your relationship with perpetrators.
- In rehab terms: if you're up for it and you've got what it takes, then go for it!

Being an independent counsellor allows freedom and flexibility but it could be financially precarious and lonely. Furthermore, it is possible to be isolated by your beliefs when working with ex-drug users. Look at yourself and your personal circumstances carefully and then consider with absolute honesty your ability to be consistently accepting, non-judgemental, empathic and hopeful with this group of clients.

Bibliography

Ashurst, P. (1989) *Understanding Women in Distress*. London: Routledge.

Blunkett, D. (2002) *Educate, Prevent and Treat – Key to Success in Tackling Drug Problems*. Press release, December. London.

De Leon, G. (2000) *The Therapeutic Community*. New York: Springer.

Glover, N.M. (1999) 'Play therapy and art therapy for persons who are in treatment for substance abuse', in N. M. Graf (2002) 'Photography as a therapeutic tool for substance abuse clients who have a history of sexual abuse', *Counselling and Psychotherapy Research*, **2**, September, 202.

McLoughlin, B. (1990) 'The client becomes a counsellor', in D. Mearnes and W. Dryden (eds), *Experiences of Counselling in Action*. London: Sage.

Mearns, D. and Thorne, B. (1988) *Person Centred Counselling in Action*. London: Sage.

Merry, T. (ed.) (2000) *Person-Centred Practice: The BAPCA Reader*. Ross-on-Wye: PCCS Books.

Miller, A. (1987) *The Drama of Being a Child*. London: Virago.

National Health Report (2002) *Research into Practice*, *1b*. August. National Treatment Agency for Substance Misuse.

Oldman, G. (1997) *Nil By Mouth*. Southwold: ScreenPress Books.

Rawlings, B. and Yates, R. (eds) (2001) *Therapeutic Communities for the Treatment of Drug Users*. London: Jessica Kingsley.

Tyler, A. (1986) *Street Drugs*. London: Hodder and Stoughton.

Welsh, I. (1994) *Trainspotting*. Reading: Minerva.

16

Independent Counselling

Sally Wilson

I am a self-employed independent counsellor working from a dedicated room in my home.

A typical day

The morning post brings flyers for counselling workshops and seminars. Over breakfast, I ponder their relevance to my current work, and to the annual renewal of accreditation; also their affordability. My first client is due at 9 am. I check that all is in order in the counselling room, place a glass and a jug of fresh water, together with a box of tissues, at hand for the client, put the 'Do not disturb' notice on the door and set the answerphone.

Reading through the last session's notes for my first clients of the day, I consider any ways forward. My first client arrives promptly. A 50-minute session just gives me time to rearrange the sofa cushions, replace the water glass if necessary and scribble a few key words relevant to the session before the next client arrives. The earlier client shows signs of progress: she has begun quietly but firmly to assert herself against a domineering husband. The second client, whom I had seen only once before, is still hesitant; I need time and patience to build up his trust.

At 11 o'clock I am off for fortnightly supervision. I leave the session with renewed confidence, having discussed at length two clients with whom I have been feeling stuck, and another who is being exceptionally resistant. Afterwards I do the day's shopping.

Lunch is at one. My usual practice is afterwards to have half an hour's feet-up with a book, but the telephone interrupts: a call from a prospective client. We make an appointment, after I have made it clear that this will not necessarily commit her to making a contract. We discuss my fees and the fact that I will require 24 hours' notice if I am not to charge for a missed appointment. I also give her information regarding transport and/or parking facilities.

From two to three o'clock I write up my notes, then lock them away in my cabinet.

This is quite a hard day: I now face having three clients in succession, something I normally try to avoid. At four, I have the final session with a long-term client, who expresses her satisfaction and shakes my hand warmly before departing: I shall miss her.

Next comes a trainee counsellor, who wants to talk about a placement he has undertaken as part of the course. There is an issue of boundaries here: I make it clear that I cannot act as his supervisor, but as his counsellor I am properly concerned with details of the counter-transference he has been experiencing, in terms of its relevance to his past life.

At 6 pm I sigh inwardly, as I admit a client seriously addicted to self-pity. Today, following the discussion with my supervisor, I am quite tough with her and it seems to pay off. Maybe there is real progress in sight!

At seven, after completing my notes, I have a glass of wine, and unwind by cooking the dinner. The evenings are for entertainment and replenishment of a somewhat depleted counsellor: a time for books, television, theatre, music, conversation.

My route in

A qualified teacher, I returned to London after two years in Hong Kong. Working with refugees in rooftop schools there had strengthened my interest in the pastoral side of education. In London, I obtained a post as welfare tutor in a mixed comprehensive school on a council estate. I was engaged to help the year heads with truancy, difficult pupils and young people with a multiplicity of problems. The demands of the job led me to seek training as a counsellor.

I qualified after three years of part-time study, for some of which I was released by the school, and after a further two years moved to a young persons' drop-in centre. Here the age range of my clients extended to 25. I undertook extra training (workshops and reading) in dealing with post-abortion reactions and housing problems. I worked part-time for the next five years (I had two young children). My private practice began when a woman who knew of my work at the drop-in asked whether I would see her privately.

Later I worked solely from home, advertising in a local magazine and at the library, gradually obtaining clients through personal contacts and recommendations. Eventually I was asked to help out at the Royal College of Nursing, where I worked one day weekly for the next two years, gaining valuable experience in short-term work. Later still, contacted by an agency, for two years I provided fortnightly clinical supervision – a form of group support involving counselling skills – for the nurses in charge of the stoma department at a local hospital. I spent a year as a member of the British Association for Counselling (BAC) accreditation team, and for some years have been on the register of the British Association for Counselling and Psychotherapy (BACP) media representatives.

I first achieved accreditation in 1991 and by 1996 had become a UK registered independent counsellor. I am now entitled to call myself a senior practitioner. I originally qualified as a person-centred counsellor, but have undertaken short courses on various approaches, and have worked with both person-centred and psychodynamic supervisors. (I try to suit my approach to the client, and their circumstances.) These days I work exclusively from home, in a room set aside for the purpose. I occasionally accept referrals from agencies and local doctors' surgeries.

A client story

David first approached me by telephone, having obtained my number from the BACP website. At the first appointment, I opened the door to a man who was plainly very nervous and who chose the corner of the client's sofa furthest away. To give him time to settle, I took him gently through the preliminary questions I ask of every new client. His father and mother were alive, and still together. He had two brothers, aged 12 and 26. He himself was 30, a primary schoolteacher. He had never had psychological or psychiatric treatment, or any serious illness. He smoked 20 cigarettes a day, having tried several times to give up, but drank only at weekends.

He had come, he said, because lately he had been very depressed, was sleeping badly and finding his job – which he loved – exhausting. He was also having constant rows with his girlfriend, Pauletta, who lived with him.

Asked whether he had seen his doctor, he denied there was anything wrong with him physically and said the doctor would only give him pills, which he would not wish to take. I assured him that I, too, did not believe in taking pills without careful thought, but said I thought it might be wise to consult a doctor if his condition was seriously interfering with his life, as seemed to be the case. He looked doubtful and I said no more. Instead, I asked him to tell me about his girlfriend and their relationship.

Pauletta, a nursery nurse, was, he said, a wonderful woman. They had been together for four years, having lived together for the past two. Normally they never quarrelled, but lately they had become irritable with each other. The main area of disagreement was David's desire to marry and start a family. Pauletta, 25, wasn't ready to settle down.

As the session continued, David visibly relaxed. By the end of the assessment hour, I knew that Pauletta was of West Indian descent and that David's parents were unhappy at the prospect of mixed race grandchildren. David was anxious they should not know of the rift between him and Pauletta, as he felt they might use it to urge him to break off the relationship. In other respects his parents were supportive, as were his brothers, who got on well with Pauletta and had no racist feelings. I asked whether David worried that, unless they married, Pauletta would one day leave him for another man, but he replied that there was no question of others:

she was the only one for him, and he for her, if only they could return to their former harmonious relationship. He felt that he was usually the one to blame. From his description, Pauletta emerged as an energetic woman of strong opinions and emotions, with a nurturing side which obviously meant a great deal to him.

David himself seemed a serious, even solemn, young man. For the most part he spoke hesitantly and his depression was obvious, but he suddenly became animated in talking about Archie, his young brother, to whom he seemed to relate in an almost fatherly way. They were keen football supporters, sometimes went fishing together and occasionally camped at weekends. The other brother, Kim, was uninterested in outdoor pursuits. 'He's the family egghead, into computers and all that,' said David, smiling for the first time.

By the end of that first session David felt able to make a four-week contract.

By the third session, he seemed much more confident in his decision to come to counselling. He admitted that he was afraid his mates might think him a wimp if they knew. I pointed out that, on the contrary, it showed both courage and good sense to seek help in dealing with his problems, particularly in the face of this worry.

Meanwhile, he had persuaded Pauletta to talk in detail for the first time about her views on marriage and children. Previously she had thrown off such attempts on his part, not, apparently, realizing how much it meant to David to see fatherhood on the near horizon. Now she impressed him with a realistic estimate of the amount of hard cash – and hard work – involved in bringing up a family. She wanted, she said, a few more years of fun and light-heartedness. Things between them were improving, though not yet as much as he would wish.

It was only in the fourth session that David revealed a fact he had been at pains to hide: he was adopted, and his siblings were no blood relation to him. He spoke with obvious pain of his circumstances: his mother had died in childbirth and he knew nothing of his father. The first five years of his life had been spent in care, in an establishment that he described as 'cold, not cruel; nobody ill-treated us, but nobody showed much interest, either'.

Beneath his longing for children was a yearning, hitherto unacknowledged, for flesh and blood of his own. He now recognized for the first time that his early years in the care home had given him a particular rapport with children and a deep desire to help them realise their potential. It was, in effect, the need to come to terms with his feelings about his adoption and his bleak start in life that had unconsciously fuelled his coming to counselling.

David's counselling continued well beyond the four sessions of our initial contract. His need to work through his feelings about his adoption gave an intense focus to our work, and as he began to release the pain and tensions buried deep within him he became much less desperate in his need for fatherhood, much more able to talk to Pauletta about his early life, more able to see things from her point of view. In the end they reached a compromise: she agreed to marry him in three years' time, with a view to starting a family a couple of years later. With regard to his parents' evident shrinking from the prospect of mixed race grandchildren, he said (by this time his depression had dissipated), that his parents were basically good people, who might, in the end, see children as individuals, not as people of a particular skin colour.

This client brought up several ethical issues for me. First, I had to persist in gently persuading my client to see his doctor: sleeplessness and acute depression must be taken seriously. Secondly came the boundary issues and possible need for self-disclosure. I had discovered at an early stage I had a passing acquaintance with the headmistress of the school where David worked, though it seemed obvious that neither need ever discover the fact. Perhaps more germane was the fact that I am the adoptive mother of (now adult) mixed-race children, with personal experience of a reluctant grandparent who quickly came to love his brown-skinned grandchildren. Self-disclosure is always a risky option, and in this case I thought it would serve no purpose. But such decisions can be a lonely matter for the independent counsellor, and underline the need for consultation with a really good supervisor.

Evaluation

What I look for, as important pointers in evaluation, are the presence, or absence, of significant life changes in the client. A person may overcome depression; come to terms with bereavement; begin actually to like him or herself; resolve a difficulty in a relationship, or find the courage to break it off; may be able to express the rage, shame or bitterness that has been poisoning life for years. Such things as these, and the general mien of the client, may speak for themselves. There is however no room for complacency and I make every effort to obtain objective feedback from the client, concerning both the ongoing counselling process and any significant effects, good or bad.

In terms of the therapeutic process, the steps taken towards an ending can be revealing. Periodic reviews, in the form of discussions of the client's current situation, how far they have come and where they may yet need to travel, are useful. A final review, going over the initial problems and the ground covered, will often make plain the degree of achievement and the path ahead. In terms of the service, a personal recommendation is a good indicator of satisfaction. On the other hand, you need to think carefully about the possible causes of less successful outcomes: the client who decides not to return after the initial assessment, or who breaks off after two or three sessions with what is obviously a long-term problem.

A client referred by an agency such as an employee assistance programme (EAP) is given a client satisfaction questionnaire and a freepost envelope in which to return it at the end of the counselling. The contents are not usually passed on to the counsellor, but clearly you are unlikely to be employed again if the client's judgement is unfavourable.

Some counsellors devise their own questionnaire. I make a point during the assessment session of stressing that I welcome any negative, as well as any positive, feedback about me or the counselling, as soon as it comes up during the work, however difficult revealing it might seem. I explain this as being part of the work: counselling is not a normal social situation, where negative feelings or thoughts must often be suppressed. Honesty is, in this respect, much the best policy. The quarterly journal *Counselling and Psychotherapy Research* (*CPR*), distributed to members by the BACP, is helpful in promoting information about various aspects of evidence-based practice, including evaluation.

Continuing professional development

Continuing professional development is vital for counsellors in any setting, but particularly so for the independent counsellor, denied the daily stimulus of working with colleagues. The last thing you need is an ivory tower.

Workshops, seminars and conferences are advertised in the BACP's *Counselling and Psychotherapy Journal* (*CPJ*) and once your name is in the BACP directory and on its website, some providers will communicate by post. Beware! Some, but not all, commercial firms offer experienced lecturers on useful topics such as dealing with anxiety, depression, low self-esteem, and so on. You will need to balance helpfulness against cost. Check whether an opportunity for discussion or workshops is included, as I find a whole or even a half-day of simply being talked at can be stultifying.

It is important to work towards accreditation, now renewable annually, and to UK registration as an independent counsellor. The cost of workshops and so on, relevant to accreditation, is tax deductible. Well worth investigating are any local branches of BACP, which often organize training workshops at relatively low cost. Other training may be found via the list of counselling organizations given in the BACP directory at the beginning of each geographical area. In London, for example, the Westminster Pastoral Foundation runs workshops and seminars open to counsellors at reasonable cost, as does the South London Psychotherapy Group. If you can afford to do unpaid work, voluntary counselling may broaden your experience of particular areas, such as bereavement (Cruse), or Victim Support.

Finally, the importance of networking cannot be over-emphasized. The more circles you mix in, the more opportunities for personal development are likely to appear, not just in counselling as such, but in myriad ways which will contribute to your experience and understanding of human beings and their problems.

Conditions of work

Anyone contemplating private practice must have suitable premises. If there is nothing available in your home, a room may be rented: advertisements appear in the BACP journal. This will entail extra expense and travel. Check that the surroundings are congenial, have a waiting area and that the client cannot be overheard during counselling. Working from home can have its problems. It is essential that anyone else living in the house is willing to cooperate.

The comings and goings of other members of the family, including children, the visits of domestic or window cleaners, the ringing of telephones and the smell of cooking are all distracting. The route to the counselling room should not entail a trek through other parts of the house, yet it is important to provide a toilet and hand washing facilities. The client must be comfortably accommodated, but not distracted by evidence of the counsellor's private life. The counselling room, a quiet one that suffers minimum possible disturbance from the neighbourhood, should be arranged so that the client is not easily visible from the street. There should be parking facilities nearby.

Having settled on a base, the next hurdle is to acquire enough clients to provide a reasonable living. Many counsellors combine private practice with part-time work in an institutional setting or a doctor's surgery. This has advantages: regular pay tides you over lean patches and also keeps you in touch with the outside world. On the other hand, it limits the number of hours available for private clients.

Another consideration is the provision of insurance. (For agency work, the minimum is £1–2 million.) BACP have the names of recommended insurers. On private premises, you should insure against physical injury as well as professional liability. Then there is the matter of personal safety. Keep a personal alarm to hand and, with newly acquired clients, try to make sure there is someone else in the vicinity.

Light, heating and wear and tear are tax deductible, together with the expense of a supervisor. Finding a good supervisor, who ideally should be both challenging and supportive, may be a matter of trial and error. Again, advertisements in the BACP journal are helpful or try contacting local counselling associations. Supervision fees, along with insurance, personal development costs and charges arising from the use of premises should be taken into consideration in calculating net income. In trying to establish a private practice, you might consider offering reduced fees to students, or a sliding scale according to income. To generate referrals, you may find it worthwhile to send a leaflet indicating your qualifications, fees and any special areas of expertise to local surgeries, hospitals and voluntary agencies.

The BACP recognizes 20 client hours weekly as full-time: this is quite a heavy load and does not include note making and administrative matters. At, say, £30 an hour this comes to £600 a week, from which holiday weeks must be deducted, along with all expenses, including tax and pension contributions. This estimate is assuming that you have a full roster of clients, which, even in well-established practices, may not always be the case. There is no doubt, then, that the independent counsellor must be prepared to work hard and, above all, to be businesslike. The ability to manage your finances is of prime importance. Equally vital are organizing skills, including time management, networking, record keeping (you should be familiar with the implications of the Data Protection Act) and credit control: how to ensure that your clients pay you on time, that you have money in reserve to tide you over lean periods and to pay for further training and professional subscription fees. If taking referrals from an agency, you will be expected to contact new clients within a day or two, to set up appointments promptly, to communicate with the case manager, and to submit completed forms relevant to the case, along with your invoice, by a certain date. Failure will result in lack of re-employment. It is important to note that a counsellor working for such an agency is not permitted, by the terms of the contract, to continue to work privately with the client referred by the agency once the scheduled number of sessions is completed.

Since agency work is short-term and clients often cannot afford, though they may need, to continue long-term within a private practice, the independent counsellor must accumulate knowledge of reputable local voluntary agencies, to which such clients may eventually be referred. You may also need psychiatric or medical advice. I have an arrangement with a GP whom I can consult in confidence occasionally.

I would discourage any newly qualified counsellor from attempting to set up as an independent too soon, unless he or she had a part-time post in addition. I write this from a financial point of view and because working alone makes it desirable to have as wide an experience of any problems that may crop up as possible. You need also to have had personal therapy to deal with your own material. You need, moreover, to be able to recognize the limit of your own competency and to know when, where and how to refer elsewhere.

For the established independent counsellor wishing to move back into an institutional setting, a combination of having worked in private practice and at least one other setting would prove a stronger recommendation. Working towards expertise in a particular field, for example, bereavement, group or couple counselling, health education or student counselling, is a way of widening chances of future employment as well as continuing personal development. If you wish to move on, remember that speculative letters can be used to probe possibilities.

Future developments

The Times recently quoted figures of 30,000 counsellors working full-time in Britain plus over 200,000 volunteers. Individual membership of the BACP stood at 20,500 in 2003, compared with 1300 in 1977. There is no doubt that there is steadily increasing competition for available counselling posts.

Counselling agencies in the form of EAPs have proliferated in recent years, many of them international corporations based on profit, and having extensive contracts with large employers to provide counselling for their employees. Such counselling is invariably short-term, though counsellors are encouraged to refer clients on where they deem it necessary: either to voluntary agencies, or, if the client can afford it, to another counsellor.

As larger organizations such as commercial firms and local councils provide in-house or EAP counselling they further increase competition for the independent counsellor. With this in mind, I would advise widening your experience or acquiring a degree of specialization, advertising, and the cultivation of any talent for writing or speaking about counselling.

For advertising, consider using the *Yellow Pages*, a local magazine and even shop windows. These will require fees, but the local library may display a leaflet about your service free of charge, particularly if you join with others to set up a small local counselling association. Writing articles is costly in terms of time and there may be no guarantee of publication; it must be something you do for love as much as money.

If independent counselling is what you have set your mind on, time will be your greatest help, in the form of personal recommendation. You are unlikely to grow rich, but the satisfactions can be immense.

Ten top tips

Generic tips:

- Find a really good supervisor.
- Continue personal development.
- Make careful and systematic notes, and keep them secure.

Context-specific tips:

- Choose premises carefully.
- Work out finances in advance.
- Combine with a part-time post.
- Get adequate insurance.
- Network!
- Cultivate a specialization.
- Be businesslike in all ways.

? How will I be happy, businesslike and competent working on my own?

Bibliography

BACP Publications. *Data Protection Act*. Rugby: BACP.

BACP *Psychotherapy Resources Directory* (published twice annually: February and August). Rugby: BACP.

Burridge, C. (2000) 'Counselling in your own home', *Counselling*, **11**(6), July, 364–5. Rugby: BACP.

Clark, J. (ed.) (2002) *Freelance Counselling and Psychotherapy, Competition and Collaboration*. London: Brunner-Routledge.

Jones, C. (2001) 'Access to case notes', *Counselling and Psychotherapy Journal*, **12**(5) (June), 10–12.

McMahon, G. (2000) 'Do you mean business?', *Counselling*, **11**(7) (Aug.), 404–5.

McMahon, G. and Litton R. (2001, 2002) 'Are you covered?', *Counselling and Psychotherapy Journal*, **12**(10) (Dec.), 36–7 and **13**(1) (Feb.), 32–3.

McMahon, G. and Palmer, S. (eds) (1997) *Handbook of Counselling*. London: Routledge.

Milner, P. and Palmer, S. (eds) (2000) *The BACP Counselling Reader*. 2 vols. London: Sage.

Taylor, D. and McMahon, G. (2000) 'Credit control', *Counselling*, **11**(9) (Nov.),. 566–7.

Yalom, I. D. (1989) *Love's Executioner*. London: Bloomsbury.

17

Final Reflections

Maggie Reid

The book contributors have discussed how to gain entry to paid counselling work and once in it, what is needed to build a portfolio of practice or fully commit to one setting. The day-to-day reality and survival skills have been described alongside realistic appraisal of progression possibilities. Having glimpsed the realities of counselling practice in the selected different settings in the book, you may be left with certain questions in mind. Indeed after writing their contributing chapters the authors met for a round table discussion about professional practice issues. The following points are some of my own and others' reflections.

Flexibility versus rigidity

How far does the setting impinge on core theoretical counselling principles and practices? You may need to be open to adapting these. For example, you have read in the preceding chapters of education settings affecting core practice ideals, like length of session and contract. In fact many contributors think 'working agreement' might be a better descriptor than 'contract', which has tightly worded legalistic implications. Contributors seem unanimous in valuing the need to respond, in an ethical manner, to the individual client rather than being hidebound by theoretical 'rules'. Sometimes it seems positively beneficial to a client who might be described as having a 'personality disorder' for example, to extend the confidentiality of the therapy beyond the one-to-one of the counselling room. This might help the client by avoiding counsellor collusion and consequent exacerbation of the problem. The whole issue of confidentiality – its bounds, obligations and limits – needs careful consideration in practice.

The replacement of the BACP *Codes of Ethics* with the *Ethical Framework for Good Practice* in 2002 is an example of professional endorsement of the need for counsellor training and ongoing practice to be less about 'ground rules' and definitive practices, and more about reflection on the 'maybes' and 'grey' areas. It encourages us to stay with these, think through issues and situations, discuss them with colleagues or supervisors and be more prepared to use our judgement backed up by good reasoning, rather than blindly follow a rule.

Often the counsellor is 'multilingual' in his or her counselling approach and able to draw on a variety of intervention tools and styles so that the needs of a particular client in that particular setting are better met. You need to be willing to learn new approaches and integrate them, at the same time as having the professional integrity to root you sufficiently to withstand the counter-influences of your setting. As the book shows, over time the setting experience seems to influence the evolvement of your counselling style.

Generic versus setting-specific skills

Do different settings require particular counselling skills? I asked contributors which they considered were the most important skills they needed to do their job. Answers included patience, tolerance, empathy and establishing rapport. Can you guess the settings concerned? This is more difficult. Undoubtedly some generic skills are common to practice in all settings. In some settings a generic skill may need to be especially honed. We all need to establish rapport but work with young people, for example, requires you to do this especially quickly or the client is lost to you. The skills are sometimes already part of the overall repertoire of the counsellor and the setting brings them out, or there is an aptitude to picking them up. This is what makes the person particularly valuable to that place at that time. Eventually I think these specific skills fuse with their professional therapeutic counselling mode. These then become the setting specific skills.

Nearly all the book chapters exemplify the way particular skills are sharpened in particular settings. For example the short-term therapeutic skill of tuning into the peaks in the overall client therapeutic landscape and keeping very focused on these as they relate to current client needs, has been likened to the difference in skill in tennis between playing at the net and at the baseline. It is an essential skill in workplace settings as well as in HE. The skill of dealing sensitively yet potently with a particular set of clients with possible similar traits like women in a refuge or addicts in a drug rehab unit and the skill of counselling through an interpreter in some settings where foreign clients are unable to speak English, or with the aid of a signer in the case of deaf clients. Transcultural counselling skills and awareness may also be particularly heightened in these circumstances and others where those who feel 'outsiders' or 'different' are suddenly thrust into the unfamiliar western or middle class mores of the counselling room in British settings like HE, voluntary centres and the NHS. In secondary NHS mental health settings counsellors need the skills to deal with complex enduring cases and longer-term work. Some respond to the more pre-packaged, evidence-based 'treat and discharge' approach but not everyone. Many are looking for a less structured, relationship-based intervention, with goals like optimal emotional survival and self-empowerment: for example, people who have problems with emotional development, survivors of abuse and trauma, and people who have lost their way in terms of their identity within a complicated and often disadvantaging system.

Everyone has emphasized the support of a good supervisor. Defining 'good' is on the one hand a very personal thing, but on the other, it seems to be about getting a supervisor with direct personal experience of, or familiarity with, the setting, type of clientele and referrer. Lawton and Feltham (2000) support this idea saying supervision needs to be increasingly appropriate to context. Supervisors may need knowledge of organizational thinking, for example.

Institution versus freelance

What are the advantages and disadvantages of being embedded within an institution versus practicing freelance? Here factors favourable to an institution might include financial security and the feeling of being part of a wider enterprise, which can be outside your direct control. This can be positive when it brings a ready-made social structure, support, unexpected stimulation and contacts, but perhaps negative when more oppressive cultural forces impinge on your practice. Against this needs to be balanced the value of autonomy and freedom. In both there are varying rights and responsibilities to consider as various chapters highlight. In both again, some abilities are needed above others. For example, in independent practice you need to be highly organized, financially literate, confident and assertive. In institutions it helps to be a good communicator, a team player and perhaps familiar with and adept at IT.

Conditions of work vary with differing settings. Some practitioners have been looking into the possibility of a union for counsellors. This would represent, support and assist them should they be the subject of a complaint, for example. At present the most practical suggestion has been to join a larger union as a specialist section.

Contributors indicate in their chapters what factors affect how you are regarded and placed within a setting hierarchy. You might also draw your own conclusions about who benefits most from counselling in a particular setting: the client as an individual, the institution or the counsellor? It is these kinds of questions that affect whether counselling should be fully integrated into organizations or remain on the periphery.

The setting can cloud or clear counsellors' minds when they attempt to help clients. It can provide a containing safe background for both to freely engage. On the other hand, through demands like the need to get maximum efficiency out of a workforce or retain students within an educational institution, could the setting subtly restrict the scope of counselling?

In what ways does your initial discipline, vocational training or life experience influence your choice of setting and ways of working within it? It seems clear that you can trace a definite link in most contributors' cases. Your total background, which has brought you to counselling in the first place, needs to play an important part in how and where you later choose to practice. And preferably this is not by accident but through self-awareness. All your experience, knowledge, attributes, skills and predisposition can enhance your contribution to a well-chosen setting for practice. In my view this could go on to contribute to the overall standing and regard of the profession as a whole, if it is well used.

Does setting affect counselling effectiveness?

Clearly, in assessing the therapeutic encounter the setting is one aspect that should be borne firmly in mind. It can affect all those issues you think of when the term 'professional practice' is under scrutiny: boundaries, confidentiality, contract, focus, outcome, evaluation, records, ethical standards, theoretical frame, supervision, even counsellor confidence and respect. Clinical effectiveness undoubtedly rests on a good grasp of, and respect for, the realities of functioning within the setting concerned. In my view counsellor training and CPD ignores this at its peril.

The effect of the setting on what happens in the counselling room is profound. It needs exploration and further attention. This would fit us better for the task of counselling including how to ensure it matches what consumers need. Carroll and Walton talk of the context giving meaning to the behaviour. They also discuss the significance of the counselling room being filled (consciously and unconsciously) not just with the counsellor and client, but also with all the individuals, systems, groups and organizations that are part of their lives (Carroll and Walton, 1997, pp. 1–4). The systemic dynamics which tend to accompany clients with complex needs can be distinctly disturbing to the unprepared counsellor. For example you need to perhaps deal with calls from anxious support workers or angry relatives. Being seen as having relatively less 'clout' than colleagues, for example, in a secondary NHS setting, can lead to unpleasant effects such as being implicitly blamed for a client's lack of 'progress' or having one's professional judgement overruled by a colleague with a different case formulation.

Greater consideration of 'setting' in counselling training and research would help lead to the avoidance of dangers, pitfalls and blind ignorance. As well as this, it would help us justify our employment and argue our case for the proper use of counselling, within the psychological therapies. Even in 1995 in their book *Issues in Professional Counsellor Training* Dryden, Horton and Mearns encouraged training to include not so much learning about particular institutions themselves, but about issues involved in relating to managers and other colleagues, and issues concerning responsibilities. Has this been taken up by trainers? The chapters in this book also illustrate the range of questions this angle of initial counsellor training and CPD could touch on. The 14 suggestions for discussion issues could be used as a way in to this whole arena. The 'personal fit' box in the Appendix also offers a practical way to engage in personal thinking about using and applying initial training.

Counselling is emotionally intense. You are your most important 'tool'. Many practitioners in our discussion felt it more efficacious to work part time rather than full time. Others stated it is most important to watch out for signs of 'burn out' and take good care of your needs for the sake of all concerned. Some believe there is a natural 'life' for them as counsellors and after a period of 10 to 15 years it is time to move on to something else.

If you are a counsellor with experience, take time to appraise yourself and evolve a career action plan. I believe the setting we work in impinges on our practice. After a certain number of years you probably attain a sufficient degree of proficiency to be described as an able practitioner in the setting. To stay where you are could then mean remaining relatively static as a professional counsellor. This is because, to some degree, once adjusted to the setting, you create your own work world within the boundaries of the counselling room. Unlike other professionals perhaps you can remain so closely contained by this that it can, in effect, insulate you from the external world and its stresses. If there is no obvious career ladder or way of expanding your horizons or taking on new challenges within the current environment, choosing to move to a new setting, enlarging your practice portfolio or moving to a new supervisor prevents this potential 'cosiness' setting in and helps keep you fresh and growing. There is no growth without a degree of fear and risk. But this is surely the stuff of life. A compromise is to hold on to what you currently do but reduce the commitment, freeing up time to dip your counsellor's toe into new waters.

Diversity

As we move further into the twenty-first century it would be good to see the practitioner face of therapeutic counselling reflecting the diversity in our society as a whole in terms of ethnicity, cultural background, class, sexual orientation, disability, gender and age. To do a good job I feel this is an essential ingredient of our future direction as a profession and the contributors all wish to add their voice to encouraging this healthy change.

The contributors to this book were chosen using as democratic a process of selection as I could devise. I placed a notice in the *CPJ* asking for those who liked writing and were experienced practitioners to respond if they wanted to write a chapter. I received well over 30 responses. I also contacted chairs of the BACP divisions for their suggestions to a similar request and received some responses from this too. I sorted through the responses, looking for appropriate accreditation, qualifications and experience within a particular setting, bearing in mind the five sections of the book. I then set everyone a relevant writing task and those who did not keep to the wordage and deadline were rejected. After this, I looked at quality of writing and diversity of representation of situations, routes in and clientele. It was a balancing act of many criteria for such a broad-stroke book. The contributors are the result of this selection procedure. We are diverse in some ways and not in others. What emerged from the process I adopted may well reflect the situation as it is out there at present in the counselling world, among current experienced practitioners, who like writing. The book therefore does not set out to be a role model in terms of diversity of personal identities of contributors.

Gaining a paid position

The current reality is that finding and obtaining a paid counselling position is challenging. Our training is geared to using our 'selves' to assist others to achieve self-fulfilment and to lead as fully functional an existence as possible. It is not geared to competing successfully for the few jobs out there. I know many counsellors who would be great at encouraging and listening to an interviewer talk rather than the reverse. We need to be proactive in engaging our worldly acumen to harness and create a potent portfolio of evidence to persuade an employer to pay us to do our work. Not only this, but to be able to back it up with personal presence which suitably impresses and fits the bill. We need at the most a well thought-through career strategy and at the very least some realistic personal appraisal. These words may not be the soft fuzzies some may want to hear, but do you want a job or not?

Trainees turning to the voluntary sector for their first placement need to assess how they can be helped to develop a portfolio of skills and competencies, develop contacts and build networks, and use their experience of voluntary work to move on to gain paid work if this is their ultimate aim. They need to be strategic in their choice of placement perhaps initially visiting a career advisor for expert guidance so they are better equipped to target and 'sell' themselves. Trainers, in planning their course curriculum, might consider how placements are introduced bearing this important issue in mind. I have been told a reality factor might need injecting into the mindset of some students. Perhaps extracts from, or an exercise based on, chapters in this book might help.

Once employed, the book chapters illustrate the importance of communication with others, like colleagues and other mental health professionals. Counsellors can add value to the whole enterprise of a setting by recognizing their own special skills and knowledge and then being prepared to pass these on, in a structured way, to others with a different but contributory role. This requires not only self-confidence but also knowledge of the whole setting and how it fits into the larger community. The value of educating colleagues about counselling is in part to sort the myths from the realities. In turn contributors have been prepared to be educated about the realities of other colleagues' roles. A vital highway of respectful two-way traffic is forged this way. The essence of success seems to be a mix of communication alongside curiosity, honesty and openness without prejudice. Defensiveness plays no part.

Motivation

The book has shown how professional aspects of counselling practice occupy and unite us, bind us and free us, protect us and expose us. Different settings have different professional demands and different rewards. Why do we do it? Why do we offer to counsel in any setting in the face of huge initial anxiety, the possibility of deep isolation, hearing horrific stories, anticipating empathy with deep pain, stuckness, loss, stress, existential angst? The preceding chapters may have some answers. The struggle of being human, of never really knowing, the sense of contact and shared questioning of purpose, intent, reason and beyond: all this is scary; it's also exhilarating. It's about touching a common humanness. In between, you can be lost or anxious. This is where your developing professionalism, proficiency and setting knowledge steps in to help.

How far is counselling a political activity and where does the setting fit in here? Some contributors discuss this issue head on, and for them it is central to their motivation to work in that setting. Others imply its significance. I think you need to work out your own philosophical position and be aware of what values underlie your work and then whether the setting is likely to support these or undermine them.

At present career structures are rarely laid down but ways forward can be found by an intelligent appraisal and creative response to the prevailing conditions. The point is – there are no 'givens' – you create your own work pathway.

The message then, is clear. You need to harness and develop your strengths at the same time as recognizing your weaknesses and working on them perhaps through appropriate CPD activities. Above all you need to be self-aware and look after yourself and your needs albeit within a mutually negotiated social context. I believe the way forward is to develop our professionalism alongside nurturance of our human soul and creativity. This makes a powerful combination. I wish you luck in your search for a suitable professional outlet for your counselling ability. There are not only paths out there to follow, but there is room for forging new 'flyovers' of your own.

Bibliography

BACP (2002) *Ethical Framework for Good Practice in Counselling and Psychotherapy*. Rugby: BACP.

Carroll, M. and Walton, M. (eds) (1997) *Handbook of Counselling in Organisations*. London: Sage.

Dryden, W., Horton, I. and Mearns, D. (1995) *Issues in Professional Counsellor Training*. London: Cassell.

Dryden, W. and Thorne, B. (eds) (1993) *Counselling: Interdisciplinary Perspectives*. Buckingham: Open University Press.

Lawton, B. and Feltham, C. (eds) (2000) *Taking Supervision Forward*. London: Sage.

Patrick, E. (2003) 'Values? Now where did I put them?', *Counselling and Psychotherapy Journal*, **14**(7), 30–1.

Appendix

PERSONAL FIT BOX

What attracts you about this setting?

....
....
....
....

What puts you off this setting?

....
....
....
....

Fill in your personal grid with this particular setting in mind:

Abilities	Skills	Experience
Aptitudes	Knowledge	Qualifications

What further training or experience would help? Who provides this training? Contact details.

....

....

....

....

....

....

....

....

....

The personal fit box is intended for self-guidance. You can fill it in after reading a chapter. Then at the end take time to reflect on all the completed boxes and discuss the implications with a colleague, friend, fellow trainee, counsellor or career coach. Questions posed in the 'Overall introduction' may be used to guide discussions.

Index